MW01672547

Dorothea M. Schlickmann

Joseph Kentenich

Father Joseph Kentenich on the train, Stuttgart Train Station, 1966.

Dorothea M. Schlickmann

Joseph Kentenich

A Life on the Edge of the Volcano

SCHOENSTATT
EDITIONS • USA

Original title: *Josef Kentenich: Ein Leben am Rande des Vulkans*
by Dorothea M. Schlickmann
© 2019 Verlag Herder GmbH, Freiburg im Breisgau
All rights reserved.
www.herder.de
ISBN 978-3-451-38388-5

Joseph Kentenich: A Life on the Edge of the Volcano
by Dorothea M. Schlickmann
Translation: Schoenstatt Sisters of Mary, Waukesha, WI, USA, 2020
© 2020 Schoenstatt Editions USA
All rights reserved.
Cover design: Finken and Bumiller, Stuttgart, Germany
Cover photo: © Jaeger (see photo credits, p. 327)
Format: Schoenstatt Sisters of Mary, Waukesha, WI, USA
Printed by Citypress, Inc., Waukesha, WI, USA
ISBN 978-1-59438-080-8

To prepare the way for a yet higher age ...
For that end many brave pioneers are now needed,
who, however, cannot originate out of nothing—
and just as little out of the sand
and slime of present-day civilization ...
men silent, solitary, and resolute,
who know how
to be content and persistent in invisible activity:
men who with innate disposition seek in all things
that which is to be overcome in them:
men to whom cheerfulness, patience, simplicity,
and contempt of the great vanities belong
just as much as do magnanimity in victory
and indulgence to the trivial vanities of all the vanquished:
men with an acute and independent judgment ...
accustomed to command with perfect assurance,
and equally ready, if need be, to obey,
... men more imperilled, more productive,
more happy! For believe me!
The secret of realizing the largest productivity
and the greatest enjoyment of existence
is to live in danger!
Build your cities on the edge of Vesuvius!

Friedrich Wilhelm Nietzsche, *The Gay Science*, Book 4

Translation: Thomas Common, 2020
S. L. Rattiner, J. B. Kopito, Eds.
Dover Publications: New York

Contents

Foreword

He really could've been broken by the family suffering of his childhood, or fallen into the abyss of insanity during his years as a student on account of existential struggles of faith, or died of his life-threatening illness, or gone crazy in the darkness of the Gestapo prison. How easily could he have been done away with for good in the Dachau concentration camp or through the many years of exile imposed upon him by the Church. But none of this happened.

During the First World War, while seriously ill with tuberculosis, he founded a vibrant movement of renewal that possessed a far-reaching influence yet was not sufficiently understood by official Church representatives in the time before the Second Vatican Council. Because of his resistance during the National Socialist dictatorship, he was taken prisoner by the Nazis. After a four-week imprisonment in darkness and solitary confinement, he spent several months in the Gestapo prison, followed by three years in the Dachau concentration camp.

Hardly had he regained his freedom and returned to his far-reaching apostolic work when he got caught in the crosshairs of Church accusations. He was separated from his foundation and sent to the USA. "You will only return in your coffin," was the prophecy spoken to him. But after fourteen years of exile—as the Second Vatican Council was taking place—he was allowed to return to his movement's place of origin, where he was able to work for another three years before his death at age eighty-two.

It was a suspenseful living and working over the course of two world wars and in a century of tremendous change and radical upheaval.

Why didn't he break down under all the harsh blows? Why didn't he stand up against a Church that didn't want to listen to him? What gave him the strength to endure?

Father Joseph Kentenich (1885-1968), founder of the International Schoenstatt Movement, overcame these many challenges. His life was literally a life "on the edge of Vesuvius," with all the dangers that lie hidden in an active, unpredictable volcano. It was a dramatic and adventurous life inseparably bound up with the mission he undoubtedly had for a new time in the Church and society. It was a mission he didn't seek out; it was destined for him, and he sought to open the way for it—not in order to be honored, and certainly not in order to have it easy, but because he knew he had been commissioned by God. Such people are not always welcome, but they are interesting. And we need them.

There is something fascinating about his life, also for those who don't have faith. It could be a sign of hope with the encouraging message that a person's life can succeed and have a broad influence even under unfortunate circumstances, if ...

The following narrative biography is based on many years of extensive historical and biographical research, but foregoes a system of footnotes. Narrative parts as well as fictitious dialogues and letters are closely based on historical documents and authentic testimonies that also appear verbatim throughout the biography. *Original quotes* by Joseph Kentenich can be distinguished by quotation marks and *italics*.

My thanks goes out to all those who have accompanied this biography. Above all, I thank Dr. Elisabeth Braunbeck and Dr. Eva-Maria Amrhein, who offered their critiques, advice, and helpful support. Furthermore, I would like to thank the following persons for doing a book review: Rev. Bernd Biberger, Ph.D.; Prof. Joachim Soeder, Ph.D.; Martina Bernhard; Rev. Heinrich Hug; Theresia Strunk; and Benedikt Matt. For text corrections I thank Beate Altmeyer and Monika Fleitmann. I give special thanks to the Herder Publishing Company [in Germany] and its editor Dr. Bruno Steimer for their cooperative and amiable assistance.

Vallendar, Germany, November 16, 2018
Dorothea Maria Schlickmann

1. Childhood in Light and Shadows

"Someday, when I'm all grown up, I'll become a priest, and then I'll do it like this: 'Devout listeners ... Amen!' I don't know what I'll say in between. I still have to learn that!" Holding on to the banister, the almost six-year-old Joseph stood three steps higher than his playmates, who were a good head taller than he was. Back then, no one would have thought that his childlike desire would one day be fulfilled and that Joseph—as Father Kentenich—would begin his sermons right up until old age with the words, *"Devout listeners."*

A Little German Village with an Onion Dome: Gymnich, His Birthplace

Joseph felt happy in Gymnich, his rural hometown of 1,901 inhabitants where everyone knew each other. He lived with his mother in his grandparents' home. He had been born there on November 16, 1885, just as the village was celebrating its parish festival in the cheerful way typical of the Rhineland region. Throughout his whole life he kept his Rhineland sense of humor; it belonged to the charm of his personality. Joseph loved living in the country. At the age of eighteen he wrote to his future teacher Father Mayer that *"you can lead a pleasant life"* among the farmers and that his health had immediately improved: *"No sooner had I breathed in the air of home—and everything was fine."*

The landscape and its broad volcanic craters, fields, and forests, corresponded to his innate love of freedom and a child's natural need for development. He romped around the village with his buddies, played hide-and-seek with the big kids, or jumped freely with his cousins on the long stove bench in the house where his great uncle and unmarried great aunts lived. The children were always welcome there. They were given good, substantial cheese sandwiches and enjoyed their childlike freedom.

One time, when Joseph was a little older, he secretly climbed up into the church tower with his friend and cousin Peter Hessler. It was a quaint Bavarian-style onion dome, uncommon for the Rhineland. "Let's see what it looks like from up there ..." The church sexton was not especially pleased about this and locked the door of the tower behind the two boys. With that he had them trapped! But the two found another way out. Through a hatch in the rafters they lowered themselves down along the high altar pillars and escaped from the sexton through the back door of the church.

Joseph was no goody-goody. When the idea came up to secretly steal apples from the neighbor's property, he was up for it, "since stolen apples taste better," as he claimed. In the winter, the frozen moat of the Gymnich castle belonging to the "Count of Metternich" was an enticing spot for ice skating. But you couldn't afford to get caught, and if you stepped onto the frozen moat too early, the ice sometimes broke. Joseph, too, experienced this with his friend Peter on an icy winter day. Dripping wet and freezing cold from this unintentional bath, they ran to Joseph's great aunt's house, where they squatted in front of the open stove while their clothes dried out.

Joseph's worried mother would have been shocked to death if she had found out about this incident. She had already had to endure many shocks of this kind—for example, when a mad cow took the baby basket in which her infant was lying and hurled it into the air. Or when the two-and-a-half-year-old fell into the well at the neighbor's house while playing hide and seek. Joseph's grandfather quickly ran over and fished him out of the water. The fall had left the child unable to speak due to a kind of lockjaw. Joseph seemed to be unconscious. With great anxiety his mother sent for the children's nurse at the abbey, who also ran to the scene and tried to get Joseph to speak again. "And if Joseph is a good boy, he'll get a holy card, and soon he'll be able to go to nursery school."

At that, the little guy opened his eyes and resolutely responded, "I don't want a holy card and I don't want to go to nursery school!" He knew what he wanted and especially what he didn't want.

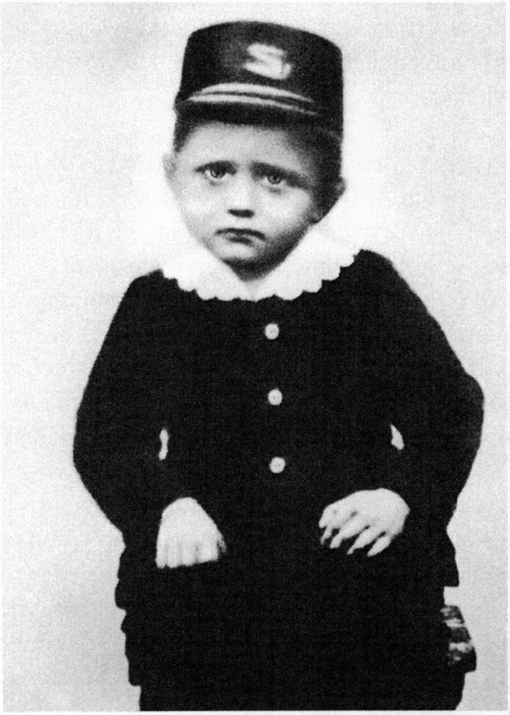

Photo 1: Joseph Kentenich at age two-and-a-half

Yes, Joseph possessed a good deal of self-assurance already early on. Those who didn't know him were tempted to interpret this as pride or arrogance, as was the case later, for example, on one of his report cards: "Now and then, the pupil displayed a haughty and conceited character." Joseph was highly gifted and had manifold talents. He possessed leadership abilities and felt personally loved. He was respected by his playmates, but later he was also envied by classmates and confreres.

Books fascinated him. Whenever his pious grandmother sat in her armchair and prayed the rosary while peeling potatoes, putting the removed "eyes" on the back of the chair as her rosary beads, five-year-old Joseph would climb onto her lap and reach for the bookshelf. He learned to read at an early age. Later, his mother would sometimes scold him for being a bookworm, as he himself once acknowledged.

In the baptismal register of St. Kunibert's parish, Peter Joseph Kentenich's birthdate is listed as November 18, 1885. But this is an incorrect entry. The parish festival in Gymnich had been celebrated so extensively in the preceding days that no horse and carriage could get through to the registry office in the neighboring town of Lechenich. Festival booths blocked off the entrance and closed the main street all the way up to the church. But since the Prussian government enforced compulsory registration, the officials at the Lechenich town hall quickly entered the registration date as the date of birth. This happened more often.

So far, everything seemed to be quite normal and uneventful during these first years of Joseph's life. And yet from the outset, his life began to take on the features of a life "on the edge of Vesuvius." His life had hung by a thread already from the first moment after his birth. The infant was so weak that it wasn't certain he would live to see the next day. The children's nurse quickly administered an emergency baptism. They had to wait anxiously to see what would happen.

Once the child's condition had stabilized, a solemn baptism took place in the parish church. November 19 was entered into the baptismal register as the date of baptism. Besides the names of the godparents—his grandmother Anna Maria Kentenich and his mother's brother-in-law Peter Joseph Peters—a special note was made on the official parish document: "illeg.," illegitimate. It was an entry that appeared in the baptismal register in Gymnich more often at that time, but it still cast its own shadows on the child's life. Joseph was born as a child of unwed parents.

Joseph's father was Mattias Koep, an estate manager. On account of social class differences, he did not marry the 22-years-younger Katharina Kentenich. Koep's sister, in whose home he lived, adamantly opposed their marriage and made every effort to influence her brother because she relied on his financial support. Moreover, according to comments by relatives, Mattias Koep was a confirmed bachelor who didn't want to settle down. Apart from that, he had a pretty good reputation in his hometown of Eggersheim. He was elected multiple times to the city council, went to church every day, and led an orderly life. He died at age ninety-one. His closest relatives aren't aware of any contact he might have had with his son or Katharina Kentenich. After he refused to marry Katharina, she no longer sought any contact with him. She had her pride, which Joseph also inherited. In any case she also never spoke negatively about the father of her child.

The social stigma that burdened Joseph's mother was hard. Joseph's life, too, was marked by it. Nevertheless, the Kentenich Family continued to be well respected in the village. Much of the gossip abated over time. When Joseph began his studies with the Pallottines, his pastor wrote in his official statement, "The family is good and honorable. The mother seems to have been seduced into sin. Therefore the irregularity (referring to the illegitimate birth) can be lifted by a dispensation. Petrus Josephus has been in Cologne most of the time and was brought up there. He has been staying here now for a few weeks and shows good moral values, giving him a good reputation here."

Such family problems were kept far from the children. No one ever spoke about the topic in Joseph's presence "in order not to hurt him." His cousin Henriette Esser, five years his senior, was like a big sister to him as they grew up. Her mother Margarethe, one of Katharina Kentenich's sisters, died just one day after Henriette's birth. Her father couldn't care for all three of the small children. So, Henriette was brought to her grandparents already as an infant. Because of their Christian social disposition, they took in and raised a total of three children who weren't their own.

Joseph had just turned five years old when he asked Henriette one day, “Why do you actually call your ‘aunt’ the woman I call my ‘mother’?”

The ten-year-old merely shrugged her shoulders and responded, “Well, Joseph, I actually don’t know that either!”

Henriette was able to recount many things from Joseph’s childhood and from the life of his mother, especially since she stayed in close contact with her aunt her whole life long. Henriette learned a number of things from Katharina that she didn’t confide to many people. One night during her pregnancy, Katharina had to suffer through a hard crisis. And it was precisely this night that gave her a powerful personal experience that would lead to a turn in her young life. Dark thoughts overcame her heart. Her whole situation had changed so much from what she had dreamed of for herself. Couldn’t she get out of this misery if she would just take her life? Suddenly the door opened and her mother stood in the attic room. What could she want in the middle of the night? “There is something strange in the house,” she tried to explain to her daughter, “something not good!” She took a palm branch and sprinkled holy water around the small room. She pensively looked at her daughter and then turned around and left the room. Katharina was stunned. This encounter with her mother had touched her deeply. How was it possible that her mother ...? No, she didn’t want to give free rein anymore to those dark thoughts ... That same night she entrusted her life to God. Her still unborn child was to belong to him and to Mary, the Mother of God. From then on, as she later told Henriette, she was carried by the firm conviction that God would not abandon her, that he would remain at her side. And from that night on, the young woman said yes not only to her unfortunate situation, but also to the child she bore. The boy became the very content and meaning of her entire life. She was not ashamed of him. She had him photographed as a two-year-old, which at that time was quite a costly and laborious affair. She herself dressed and undressed the little one personally; she didn’t want to let anyone else do it. She did not tolerate anyone hitting him. When she later had a position as a cook for various families of noble lineage in Cologne, she made no secret of his existence and asked for permission for him to come during his school breaks. She also presented each employer with the condition that she be allowed to take vacation whenever her son had a break from school. A set of letters from mother to son, diary notes, and poems from Joseph's school years—all of which are still intact—underline the loving relationship between them, which lasted her whole life long.

Although Joseph was very gifted intellectually and musically, he didn't like to go to the school in Gymnich. The teachers hit the students a lot and lacked the least bit of pedagogical skill. In order to be qualified as a teacher, it was probably enough—as is specifically mentioned in the documents—to have "served on the battlefield" in the imperial army. But the official documents also report serious excesses of corporal punishment as it was customary at that time. Joseph showed considerable courage before such teachers. In addition to his self-assured independence, a further feature of his character had become apparent already in his childhood: his pronounced love for the truth. This would later occasionally lead him to imprudence and a lack of diplomacy.

Henriette told of an occurrence that stayed in her mind for a long time. Joseph would always do his homework right after school and then run off to play. One time, she noticed that the frame of his slate was dirty. But as she tried to clean it, she accidentally erased his homework, too ... Oh no, when Joseph sees this! "Jettchen" accurately redid his homework. The next day, she was suddenly called into the boys' school. As she went into the classroom, she found Joseph standing straight and tall before his teacher, who was asking him strictly who had done his homework. He answered resolutely, "I did it!"

The teacher repeated his question in a threatening voice, "This is not your handwriting! Who wrote it?"

Joseph remained firm in his true statement and fearless before whatever consequences might come. But it was Henriette who finally clarified the matter. After school, when they were alone, Joseph asked her peacefully, "How did that happen?" Jettchen was still so upset that she cried into her apron and then told him everything.

She also keenly remembered another incident that had taken place years earlier. At that time Joseph was three years old. He had a poking stick and was poking around in the fire in the stove. Henriette warned him more than once that he'd better stop, but he kept at it. In order to stress her warning, she hit him on the back. At that he began to cry loudly. In order to quiet him, and because she was afraid he might tell his mother about it, she promised him a holy card, a very coveted item for children at that time. The tears stopped. But soon afterwards, as they sat down to eat, the little guy started to cry once more. *"You can have your holy card back! I'm going to tell that you hit me after all!"*

In the Midst of a World Trade City: Strasbourg

"Joseph's going to Strasbourg!" Henriette stood surrounded by her friends in the schoolyard. The news spread like wildfire through the whole village.

"But why? He's only been in school for half a year!" some people said.

"His aunt has died and now his uncle is alone with three small children!" Indeed, Peter Joseph Kentenich's wife had passed away on Christmas 1891, and his sister Katharina had made the spontaneous decision to help him. She took Joseph out of the school he had been attending only since Easter and traveled with him to Strasbourg. Even just the trip there must have been an exciting experience for him.

They had already changed trains four times since they got on in Cologne. Joseph stood in awe before the huge black steam engine and admired the conductor in his classy red and blue uniform. His alert eyes followed the porters, the elegant horse-drawn buggies, and the many, many people who passed through the train station. He closely studied the train compartment in which they were sitting, how the window could be pulled up and down with leather straps; he looked at the wooden benches and hat racks. So many travelers had a seat here! Then, his attention remained riveted on his mother. She looked elegant in her Sunday best, even if she also looked quite serious. From the window he could see forests and meadows and many little towns flying by until Strasbourg finally came into view—with its glorious cathedral rising high above everything else!

Together with his mother, Joseph now discovered a large garrison city with soldiers marching up and down in splendid parade uniforms, four- and five-story buildings lining all the streets, and many canals of the Ill River winding through the city, filled with innumerable small boats and fancy little ships. The streets and alleyways bustled with activity: carts, wagons, carriages, the ringing train tracks. The first honking automobiles that pushed their way between the market stalls and the walkway left Joseph practically speechless—coaches that could go traveling around the area by themselves, without a horse or oxen! For the first time, Joseph experienced an international trade city of more than 150,000 inhabitants, which at the same time could boast of one of the largest fortresses of the German Empire. How different all this was from the little rural town of Gymnich! Alert and eager for everything new, he soaked in life in the big city. It was the place where he would live from now on. It was here that he very quickly learned the French language, which was just as customary as German in the border region of Alsace-Lorraine.

Joseph's uncle, Peter Joseph, who had picked them up at the train station, worked as a blacksmith in the imperial army and made a good living. He lived in a large, spacious, second-floor apartment on the Sonnengasse, later known as the Rue de Marechal de Juin. It was directly across from the elongated barracks that stood at the front end of the large military property. Joseph's uncle walked to his forge there every day.

A few weeks after their arrival, Joseph's mother registered him at St. Mary Magdalene's School for Boys. Under the category "Parents," she and her brother filled in their information: Peter Joseph Kentenich, blacksmith, residing at Sonnengasse 7. St. Mary Magdalene's School was a large building with fourteen classrooms, many students, and committed teachers who had all completed studies in pedagogy. This school could not be compared with the one in Gymnich. Joseph really had fun at the school in Strasbourg. There they incorporated several pedagogical reform approaches in the school program and endeavored to give the boys good formation, particularly because a number of them came from well-to-do families. Every day, Joseph's walk to school led him through the narrow alleyways lined with tall buildings and past the splendid Strasbourg cathedral, its high church tower rising majestically above the city. The traditional glockenspiel was fascinating for the children. It sounded precisely at twelve noon each day as the time-honored wooden figures appeared on a rotating circular platform and slowly bowed left and right. But all this happiness didn't last long. After eight months, Joseph and his mother had to leave the beautiful city again. As they checked out of the school, his teacher expressed his regrets at "losing such a gifted student." But there was no choice. After his uncle remarried at the end of June 1892, mother and son said goodbye to Strasbourg and moved back to their hometown of Gymnich, where Joseph once again attended the country school there. However, a new question arose for his mother: How was she supposed to keep providing for her and her son's livelihood? Ever since the death of Joseph's grandfather, the family had come into a difficult financial situation. Yes, the little garden did yield some earnings, and she could help out in the castle, but in order to keep the family above water in the long run, she would need permanent employment.

Her confessor at Holy Apostles Church in Cologne, Father August Savels, was able to take care of this one day. He was a socially engaged priest oriented toward ideals, and he had good connections with a few aristocratic families. For example, the von Guilleaume

Family, who lived in a majestic city palace directly on the market place, had donated a side altar for Holy Apostles Church. They also gave funds for people in need whom the pastor had especially befriended. Joseph's mother experienced him as an understanding pastor who grasped the need of the poor population and made every effort to alleviate it. He had built an orphanage, Vincent's House, in his former parish in Oberhausen with the help of a citizen action committee. But not only there—in Cologne, too, he established an orphanage, a home for single mothers, and other social institutions. It was through this contact that Katharina got a position with the von Guilleaume Family. Von Wittgenstein, the district administrator for whom Joseph's mother later worked, also lived in a four-story house right next to Holy Apostles Church. At first Katharina went back and forth between Cologne and Gymnich. But as soon as the von Guilleaume Family recognized Katharina's culinary skills, they pressed her to work for them permanently as their chef. With this a new problem surfaced: Under these circumstances she always had to be in the house and available often until late in the evening.

From things Joseph's mother shared, Father Savels knew that her son had already expressed the wish to be a priest several times. They began to think it over. If the boy had wanted to be a farmer or a skilled craftsman like most of the children in his village, things would have been simple. He could have stayed with his grandmother in Gymnich. But in this case ...! The school in Gymnich was not suited to prepare him for high school; Father Savels recognized this, too. In 1894, school was canceled for a whole six months. The farmers were happy about this, as their children could then help in the fields and livestock barns. But what was Joseph supposed to do? There was no money for a boarding school or private tutoring.

During this time, Father Savels heard from the superior at the orphanage in Oberhausen that her efforts to establish an in-house school had finally met with success. Good teachers from the city were willing to give classes to the children in the orphanage starting on April 9, 1894. This would be Joseph's chance! The boy would be well taken care of by the sisters, and a better education would be secured. At their next conversation, Father Savels presented his suggestion to Joseph's mother. But it still took quite a few weeks until she could struggle her way through to a decision.

At the Orphanage in Oberhausen

April 12, 1894
Cologne

Reverend Father Savels!

It's done—and I can probably say that it has been the hardest day of my life. I know that the sisters are good. The house is clean and well cared for. Statues of saints stand in the hallways and stair corners, and religious pictures hang on the walls. A truly Christian house! The reverend mother superior showed us everything. There is a large dining hall with long tables and benches, and a dormitory with many beds. The beds are right next to and across from each other, without any little tables or dressers for the children to put their things. The mother superior explained that they are all 'children from poor families.' There is a high wall around the courtyard outside. You can't see the rest of the city from there. It's an industrial city with high smokestacks, factories, row houses, and a lot of soot and pollution in the air. Girls and boys are kept separate in two different schoolyards. They stood there in shabby clothing lined up in formation, well-disciplined, the boys with their heads shaved. It really did strike me—so many sad eyes and such serious, pale, skinny faces on those children!! It almost broke my heart. Certainly, Reverend Father, you were full of confidence that Joseph would be in good hands here, but I can't describe how hard this is on my heart. As we said goodbye, he clung to the cabinet in the visiting room and cried bitterly. Jettchen was with us. I didn't know what to do. So I simply went with him into the orphanage chapel. The mother superior had shown it to us on the tour through the house. We went to the statue of the Mother of God. There I simply entrusted Joseph to the Mother of God, consecrating him to Mary. I prayed out loud that from now on she should take care in a motherly way; she should be his mother because I can no longer do it. I asked her to educate him! So that she wouldn't forget that I was entrusting to her what I loved most, my most precious treasure, my only child, I hung the only piece of jewelry I had—my golden first Communion cross—around her neck. Joseph became very quiet, very prayerful. It seemed to me that he was somehow far away.

Reverend Father, please pray for him and a little bit also for me. I don't know when or how often I can visit him, or whether he will have vacation and can visit me. Please, Reverend Father, pray also for this!

But I also don't want to fail to give you heartfelt thanks for all your concern!

I know there is no other way. I know!

With gratitude and sincere greetings to you, Reverend Father,

Your penitent,
Katharina Kentenich

If Joseph's mother had written her confessor a letter on that day in 1894, it might have looked something like this. However, no direct records from her have been found concerning this happening in the orphanage. Everything that contributed to the conception of such a letter comes from archive documents and the things that Joseph Kentenich himself later shared about it. This happening in the orphanage chapel was so incisive for him that he came back to it his whole life long. Years later, when he took up his task as the spiritual director at the Vallendar boarding school, responsible for the formation of the boys there, he felt immediately urged to tell them something about this event of April 12, 1894—but without revealing that it was a story about himself. What stands out in every account is that Joseph Kentenich never said anything about his own pain at the farewell. He only talked about his mother's suffering, which he must have taken deeply into himself as a child. He illustrated *"her great concern," "her anxiety of heart," "her worries,"* and the *"adverse circumstances"* and *"unfortunate conditions"* that had forced her to take this step. There was no hidden blame, no bitterness, although he must have suffered much ... His suffering was evidently outshone by another experience that must have made an even deeper impression: his consecration to Mary. This became the central experience of his childhood and even the key moment of his whole life. Later, Joseph

Kentenich underlined that his entire life's work was based on this early consecration, in which he personally and deeply participated. He said that since then, Mary took on a key role in his life: *"She herself personally formed me and educated me from my ninth year of life on."* He shared that since his childhood he had always knelt to say a prayer he himself had composed, and that it almost seemed to him that Mary had educated him accordingly: *"Hail Mary, for the sake of your purity, keep me pure in body and soul. Open wide to me your heart and the heart of your Son. Implore for me deep self-knowledge and the grace to persevere and remain faithful until death. Give me souls; keep all else for yourself."* As he testified, this prayer grew sentence by sentence within him over the course of the years.

What was it about that consecration to Mary that touched him so deeply and was able to gain such power over his life? Without a doubt, the moment of Joseph's consecration was a personal experience of a mysterious reality that would determine the direction of his life even more than before: God. In the midst of the painful separation from his beloved mother, he experienced through Mary the marvelous nearness of God. "God is here. He loves me very personally, even when he permits suffering. In Mary's arms I am secure, as secure as the child on her lap." This experience was so strong that the impression of it never let go of him, even in times of crisis. Later references show that he had experienced through Mary what God is really like. It was an encounter with the *"mercifully loving Father God, who cannot do otherwise but love us inconceivably,"* as he later formulated it.

This central experience carried him through the following years in the orphanage—years that were not easy. His experiences there paved the way for him to develop a new pedagogy. *"From childhood on I always observed what education is and how it's generally done, and I told myself, 'No, that's not the way to educate; it must be done completely differently!'"* Already very early on, it was innate in him to observe life, to perceive the processes of the soul in human beings, and to ponder these things. Pedagogy was somehow in his blood. He believed God spoke through people and their *"disposition of soul."* He saw *"the voices of souls"* as a source of recognition for God's will, possibly also because he himself had to suffer a lot already early on and experienced the suffering of others at close range. The difficult experiences of his childhood and youth became a driving force that urged him toward the priesthood, as he himself revealed: He wanted to give a home to others *"even if one's own heart cries out for a home."*

Joseph experienced hard years. He was homesick and ran away from the orphanage twice. As he was picked up along the way, he asked where to find the Erft, the river that flows through Gymnich. One of the sisters from the orphanage stated that he was "not easy to educate." But another one said that one day she found him alone in the washroom where he had been ordered to go as a punishment. He was kneeling motionless on the floor; he was "far away" and didn't even notice her. But evidently it wasn't only the religious strength he sensed within himself that helped him to survive this time unharmed. Joseph grew in his love of learning, knowledge, and books. School became an intellectual refuge for him.

When the oldest ones were dismissed from the orphanage, he and his companions looked after them wistfully. One of them said, "Will we ever get as big as they are?"

Joseph responded, "That doesn't matter. What matters is"—and he tapped on his forehead—"what one has up here!"

His spiritual refuge was the inner certainty he possessed: "My mother is thinking of me. She is praying for me. She didn't just drop me off here; she *entrusted* me to Mary." In order to cope with his suffering and process it, he obtained a little rhyme book to learn how to compose poems. As far as Hermann Mueser—his companion in the orphanage and later journalist—can remember, his first poems were all about suffering. Joseph was forced at an early age to learn how to handle difficult circumstances and suffering without losing oneself or breaking down. One has to face the pain and suffer it through. It may not be suppressed. Writing helped him lift it from his soul.

On April 24, 1897, at age eleven, Joseph made his first Communion. It was the day on which he assured his mother anew that he wanted to be a priest. "My son, then we will have to pray very much." This was the only answer his mother gave. But this one sentence didn't give him much hope. At that time, a child of unwed parents couldn't become a priest. The situation painfully forced him to grapple with the fate of his family situation. But he remained firm in his decision.

The end of the school year in Oberhausen was approaching. Katharina Kentenich visited her son once more. He had noticeably changed since his first Communion. The thirteen-year-old had reached adolescence. Reiner Greiss, an uncle by marriage from Cologne who was especially close to them, accompanied his mother and now sat between the two on the bench in the garden of the orphanage. He talked and talked in an attempt to explain the situation to Joseph. "He's a fine person," thought Joseph. "He only wants to help." But still, Joseph stared ahead sadly and with disappointment. Why couldn't his mother help him? Suddenly his uncle pulled out his new camera and proudly showed it to them. Joseph thought, "You can only buy something like that in Cologne. Here, only real photographers have one of those!" His uncle stood up and wanted to take a picture. Mother and son were not used to this at all. Joseph's mother posed a little, as she had seen her employers do, but Joseph was very uncomfortable with the whole thing. After all, he didn't have shoes and socks on! It wasn't common to wear them in the late summer months. Only in winter did people wear their wooden clogs. His clothes looked so miserable, especially his childish medium-length pants that were so scuffed and worn out. And then his close-cropped haircut! The corners of his mouth betrayed a hint of pained seriousness. Everything looked so hopeless.

As Joseph's mother rode back to Cologne, she couldn't get his sad face out of her mind and she thought about everything over and over. The future her boy imagined seemed to be out of the question. But how could his heart's desire to be a priest ever be fulfilled? How could the obstacles possibly be overcome?

Photo 2: On his first Communion day, 1897

One day a possibility presented itself. Father Savels had heard from his sister, an Arenberg Dominican, that the Mission Society of the Pallottines in Ehrenbreitstein ran a boarding school for their vocations. It was possible to obtain a private high school diploma there. The Pallottines, she said, formed priests to be missionaries for Africa. They also accepted boys from families without financial means or other similar situations like Joseph's. But his mother hesitated. Yes, the joy was great at first that Joseph could become a priest—but she had hoped he would stay closer to her. But now she would have to part from her child again, and this time for a long time. Joseph would go to the missions in Cameroon and possibly never come back?! Wasn't there any other possibility? Or, as she had suggested to Father Savels, should she marry the child's father after all so that Joseph would be legitimized by canon law and be able to become a diocesan priest? Then he wouldn't need to specifically enter a mission society and could stay in Germany ... No! Her confessor had emphatically spoken against it. If that was the only reason for getting married, he would not advise it. What should she do? Joseph's mother found herself unable to get used to the idea that Joseph was meant to become a missionary priest. This can be seen from a poem composed by the fourteen-year-old on Easter 1900. In a certain ode to love (*"The Power of Love"*), Joseph expressed the plea: *"May you guide my mother's mind, for I do not want to hurt her feelings!"* A central theme of the poem even dealt once more with the question of a possible marriage of his parents. Joseph didn't feel drawn to the alternatives suggested to him. As of Easter 1900, the struggle still hadn't come to an end, even though by this point Joseph had lived in Ehrenbreitstein for half a year already. And it happened like this ...

The Boarding School near the Ehrenbreitstein Fortress

Joseph had received his graduation diploma in Oberhausen already on August 15, 1899. But the decision for Ehrenbreitstein had been delayed until far into September. At the last minute, his mother had finally agreed, with a heavy heart, to the suggestion of her confessor. Now everything had to move fast, since the school year in Ehrenbreitstein had already begun. While still in Oberhausen, they had to get an official physical examination and certification by a doctor, and Joseph had to fill out and sign the questionnaire for acceptance. All of this took place on September 22, 1899. Already the next day, Joseph sat in the train headed for Koblenz-

Ehrenbreitstein with a little suitcase his mother had prepared and brought along for him to the Cologne train station. Dressed in a new suit, finally with long pants as was proper, he enjoyed the ride along the Rhine River, full of expectation and joyful anticipation for what would now commence: high school, the first important step on the way to his long-awaited priestly vocation. Father Savels sat across from him and looked thoughtfully at the boy. How much Joseph—barely five feet tall and of slight build—had already experienced! And how much he had done to make the impossible possible! The boy was strong.

Having arrived at the Pallottine boarding school, Father Savels first took care of a few formalities and counted the 200 gold marks, the yearly advance payment for room and board. Katharina Kentenich had proudly declared to her confessor that she herself wanted to pay the costs of his studies, although of course she wasn't able to collect the money so quickly.

Now Joseph stood for the first time in the courtyard of the Pallottine property with its elongated main building, the two adjacent buildings opposite each other, and the former mill. Joseph looked around and contemplated his new home: the beautiful ivy-covered terrace up by the old quarry stone wall facing the mountain. He turned around and saw on the opposite side—at right angles to the main wing of the building—a handsome, stylish annex with a large study hall on the lower level. It had direct access to the courtyard and many windows on both sides, making the room bright and friendly. Joseph heard that the study hall even had a built-in stage because it also served as a recreation room and a festive hall for the four older classes. Beyond that was the house chapel with its colorful arch-shaped, stained-glass windows. To the right of this—parallel to the main building—were the two somewhat structurally neglected adjacent buildings containing the gymnasium and an additional space used as a classroom. At this point, Joseph had no idea that in the future he would give classes there as a German and Latin teacher.

Now he took a closer look at the elegant main building that bordered the main street on the other side. His glance wandered up to the windows, where the dormitories and the Fathers' rooms were probably located. Down below, the clanging of plates and cups could be heard from what had to be the dining room. All of this had such a different feeling in comparison to the dark brick building in Oberhausen. Here, everything was bright and airy, opening new horizons before him. The upper rooms offered a glorious view of the Rhine River and the surrounding wooded hills. Above the hillside bordering the Pallottine property there arose the mighty fortress from the time of Napoleon. His eyes became fixed on it. "Yes, the boarding school is really beautiful, friendly, inviting," he thought, "and yet built in the shadow of a military bastion, maybe the largest on the Rhine. With its many cannon holes and outposts, it is reminiscent of the battles and wars of times gone by." Actually, it fit. So far, his life had been like this, too ... Quiet seriousness covered his facial features. Yes, a battle, no child's play ...

The rector came out into the courtyard to greet the new arrival and took him directly to the classroom. Father Johann Mayer greeted him with a lively and friendly handshake. Father Mayer was young and extraordinarily loved by the boys. He was pedagogically talented; he loved his task and had a heart for the boys. Joseph very quickly gained confidence in him. How nice that he would be in his class!

Father Savels helped with the rest of the registration formalities. Joseph was told that he still had to write his biography; this was missing among the documents. But he refused. No one could demand that of him! He replied with determination that in that case he would rather be a brother and care for the sick. His family secrets were no one's business. That was something private! Such determination was astonishing, but in the end they gave in. Even today, no biography of Joseph Kentenich exists in the files of the Pallottines. After this brief discussion, Joseph stashed his few belongings in his half of the closet. He was really starting a new life!

When he sat down on Sunday to write to his mother, there were many things to share. They now had Latin every day, eight hours per week, and then German, math, geography, natural history with botany or zoology, and of course, religion. He wrote about how many classmates he had, about the total number of fifty students at the small school, about how nice the Fathers were, especially Father Mayer, and how they were all fairly young. Then of course he also wrote about the food and the daily schedule: the 5:40 a.m. rising time and the good deal of study time and class time, nine hours per day all together. Then there were the times of prayer such as morning and evening prayer, the rosary, and holy Mass. He hardly left out a single detail: when and where silence was to be practiced and how the two-and-a-half hours of free time and breaks were scattered throughout the day, even though they weren't always allowed to speak during such times. In the evenings, the lights were turned out in good time, just a little after 9:00 p.m., because the boys had to "climb out of their feather beds" early in the morning. His later letters weren't as long as this first one from Ehrenbreitstein. Most of them were about one-and-a-half small pages and actually never pious, as Henriette told. Soon he had hardly any time left to write. He studied diligently and indulged in his hobbies: reading and hiking. He made a note in his composition book of every extracurricular book he read in those years. It was a colorful collection of various types of literature.

The teachers noticed Joseph's intellectual gifts already after a few weeks. He had made considerable learning progress in a very short time. After some months, he was able to skip a grade, making it possible to finish high school in five years instead of six. That was definitely noteworthy, since the six regular years at the Pallottine boarding school were already tightly packed in comparison with the nine years of high school studies in the public schools. Joseph really enjoyed his "humanistic studies." He was also enthusiastic about classic literature. Inspired by Heine's travel writings, he himself began to write travel accounts after his long hikes. Until the end of his life he liked to quote classic works such as Schiller and Goethe's

Faust. Free time activities, too, had their attraction: extensive hikes in the splendid nature of the Westerwald; happy festivals and uplifting celebrations, including the emperor's birthday; the exciting eve of the feast of St. Nicholas; and not least of all, theatrical pieces. Joseph loved acting and even wrote his own drama that made it to the stage: "Conrad, the Last Heir of the House of Hohenstaufen." His interests and his gifts were manifold. Because of his musical talents, he was offered a chance to learn piano. But contrary to all expectations, he turned it down. If the others didn't get piano lessons, he didn't want them either.

Of course, everyday life was strenuous and boarding school life was very strict, as was customary everywhere at that time. But for the boys, this was hardly a reason to complain. Strictness, discipline, obedience, and order were attributes of the time that were seen positively in the Prussian Empire. But the boys did have a secret meeting place: the old mill, where the Fathers never went and which was therefore left unsupervised. Here they enjoyed many freedoms and many forbidden reading materials. The basement vault of the mill stored the literature left behind by the prior owners. There were books that particularly awakened their curiosity, for example, books about the "mysteries of developing life." An actual class on sexuality thus rendered itself superfluous.

After the intensive study program, Joseph especially looked forward to school breaks or a weekend with his mother. "*Saturday, Sunday, Saturday, Sunday,*" he scribbled dreamily into his composition notebook, lovingly decorating his mother's name, "*Catharina,*" with squiggles and little flowers, right next to the train departure schedule for "*Cöln*" and the various transfer stations. He also listed in a column what he wanted to bring back from home: "*Knife, winter slippers, notebook, journal, toothbrush + powder.*" On another side he recorded how he planned to spend his vacation. Getting up later (6:45 a.m.) was among the first of the vacation pleasures, but he didn't want to omit the next scheduled item, holy Mass. He intended to study French and Italian in the morning and even planned to take a nap after lunch. Already as a boy, his health was not the best. He had been suffering from frequent headaches ever since the hatch to the attic storeroom once fell on his head. Moreover, he fatigued quickly and also had to struggle with cold infections. Toward the end of his time at Ehrenbreitstein, even symptoms of pleurisy appeared.

Joseph planned to use his vacation afternoons after around 2:00 p.m. to study history and Greek; then after a break for coffee he scheduled a three-hour walk. He absolutely loved to walk and didn't generally care for "worldly" enjoyments. Once when he was sixteen years old he expressed to his mother that it was not so easy to be poor and that he would really like to drink a glass of beer or smoke a cigar sometimes. The extremely thrifty woman countered, "Sure, Joseph, you can choose—either one or the other! Your studies cost a lot of money! That means cutting back on beer and cigars." After this he decided to give up smoking entirely and declared to Henriette, *"It's easier to renounce it completely than only a little."* Even as he had to watch out for his physical health, his intellect worked all the better. He brought home outstanding grades. Not only his mother, but also his entire town was proud of him, because ultimately Joseph wanted to become a priest and later work for the conversion of heathens.

During these years, even amid all outward successes, a painful struggle took place within him as he tried to cope with his family situation. His outstanding talents and intellectual abilities, but also his reserved way of being, made him increasingly lonely. He was quickly misunderstood, and sometimes not understood at all. Many teachers had a hard time correctly assessing the character of this gifted, independent, and seemingly self-assured youth. There was only Father Mayer, to whom Joseph had confided his personal situation right at the beginning of his high school years and who had apparently accompanied and supported him during these years. Joseph gave him a number of autobiographical poems. Already for Christmas 1899, he composed a poem with a special dedication to his teacher, expressing his personal thanks *"for the goodness you have shown me in the short time I have been here, and especially for the consolation you gave me in my circumstances."* Father Mayer sensed that the boy was different and encouraged him wherever he could. He tucked a few of the letters and poems carefully into a drawer and kept them for decades. In 1901, this teacher became the rector of the boarding school. Joseph kept contact with him until 1904, when Father Mayer was sent to Freiburg to study pedagogy, and Joseph moved to Limburg.

Additional youthful poems from the Ehrenbreitstein years give a sense of his inner development: the search and longing for God, for childlikeness, for happiness and the fulfillment of life. Some of his own verses also reveal the growing loneliness he felt. A poem with the title *"Homeless"* is especially representative of these.

September 15, 1902. Joseph had returned to Ehrenbreitstein. The students and teachers, including Father Mayer, weren't all back yet. But there was already lots of lively activity in the house. Each of the newly arrived students was busy telling all kinds of stories from summer vacation. Joseph's vacation with his mother had been a short one this time because she was needed by her employers. He withdrew outside on the terrace and gazed upon the Upper Rhine River plain. Quiet pain slipped across his face. He began to write down what was moving him on the sheet of paper he had brought along. His inner sorrow flowed effortlessly into his feather pen:

Homeless

Abandoned and alone
I go through the world,
Rejected by my father
Without a tent to call home.

By iron hand torn away
From motherly love,
No one really knows me
In the jostling cold.

Photo 3: With teachers and students, Ehrenbreitstein (front row, second from left), 1902-1903

I see peace all around me,
A word of enthusement
Sings the praises of parents—
I weep and leave.

My heart consumes coldness,
Loved by no one
I hold on, in case someone
Might give me love.

Good thing he knew how to write. His family situation weighed heavily on him throughout the years at Ehrenbreitstein; again and again he tried to process the suffering. If he hadn't had Father Mayer and the possibility to write ...

However, a new danger loomed in the following years. It came from within and drove him to the edge of an intellectual and spiritual abyss that had been previously unimaginable to him. *"My struggles began,"* he later explained, *"with mathematical precision the moment I entered the novitiate. Such things weren't present before."*

Things started to brew and boil within him. It became noticeable once more—and this time in a very different way—how dangerously close "Vesuvius" was to his young life ... Joseph would have to overcome the years of "*dreadful inner and outer struggles*" that followed. The battles involved more than what the seemingly harmless words "*struggles of my youth*" implied. What were they about?

2. Standing before the Abyss

"Soon it will be the 15th, and if my mother hadn't reminded me, I almost would've forgotten that you will only be in Ehrenbreitstein until then.

"First, I want to pay a tribute of gratitude to you. If I have succeeded in reaching my goal so far, I owe it mostly to you. Hopefully the years to come will also pass by happily. My health is doing better again. No sooner had I breathed in the air of home—and everything was fine. I had been afraid the signs were indicating a recurrence of pleurisy. Now there's not a hint of it anymore. But I still have my daily plan: eat, drink, sleep, and go for walks, as Herodotus says, in the continuous cycle of eternal monotony. You can lead a pleasant life among the farmers, and truly, I'm getting to know and esteem Horace and his Epodes more and more: Beatus ille, qui procul negotiis [Happy the man who, far removed from work ...], etc.

"I happily recall these past years. An exceedingly melancholic feeling comes over me when I think to myself, 'Your humanistic studies have or must now come to an end.' It was such a nice time! Is it possible that the chance might come again some time? Maybe I'll like my higher studies just as much. At least I hope so. But for you, too, a new sphere of activity beckons. You'll be going to the university to become an expert in one or the other branch of the humanities. I congratulate you, for in that I see my own ideal. If you have students again, I wish you a blessed time of teaching and grateful subordinates. In any case you can be assured of the gratitude of

Your former student,
Joseph Kentenich

"P.S. Having thus far given you personal thanks, I hereby also wish to extend it to the whole congregation, my teachers, and my superiors."

Joseph wrote these words to his former teacher Father Mayer during his vacation in 1904, which he spent with his mother in Gymnich and enjoyed once more to the full. Many people in the village felt honored that he was a son of their hometown and they invited him to a meeting of the "Youth Association" at the parish. Even his mother couldn't hide her pride. Many years later, recalling those high school years, she wrote to him about how happy she was with him and how she could still see him standing before her in his "blue student's suit."

But soon, at his solemn "investiture," he would exchange the suit—with its stylish starched collar, tie, and fancy tiepin—for a religious cassock. The higher studies of theology and philosophy wouldn't start immediately, as Joseph had excitedly expected; the first year of the novitiate was to precede them. Only in the second year did the course of studies within the community begin. All together, the two-year "novitiate" was primarily meant to provide a preparation for community life and an introduction to the spiritual life.

Not all the Ehrenbreitstein high school graduates had chosen the life of a missionary priest or been admitted to it. Only a few of Joseph Kentenich's classmates moved with him into the recently built (1898) motherhouse of the German Pallottines in Limburg in September 1904. It was an enormous, four-story, square building with a large courtyard and a considerable number of high windows on both sides, allowing a lot of light to flood into the rooms. Only recently had the Pallottines completed all preparations for ensuring a complete six-year course of studies for their vocations. A few diocesan priests were engaged in the teaching program to cover the core subjects. Just this year, the new "statutes" of the Pallottine Society had also been issued, hot off the press. Among other things, these statutes regulated the structure and content of the novitiate. The Italian founder, Vincent Pallotti (1795-1850), had passed away before he could complete the founding of the community, and since the Pallottines hadn't been in Germany very long, hardly any translated texts of their founder existed—only a biography about his

Photo 4: At entrance into novitiate and academic studies, 1904

saintly life which was released at the turn of the century. For this reason a Jesuit had collaborated in questions regarding the formation of the young brothers and in the drafting of the statutes.

Vincent Pallotti had called the community into being not only with the intention to lead its members to a holy life; more precisely, they were to form a kind of mobile task force that would have a powerful apostolic impact in a restless and disoriented time. With the help of his confreres, popularly called "Pallottines" based on his name, Vincent Pallotti especially wanted to strengthen the lay apostolate and unite all positive forces in order to spread the Gospel and Christian values effectively and wherever possible. However, the *Kulturkampf* [conflict between Prussia, the German Empire, and the Catholic Church in the nineteenth century] had forced the Pallottines in Germany to turn almost exclusively to the "pagan missions." Only then—according to the stipulations of the state authorities—would they be allowed to establish themselves in the country. This was good for the German Empire. Their aim was to curb the influence of the Catholic Church in their own country, but if this led to ecclesial communities helping to "cultivate" the colonial areas in Africa, this was most welcome. During Joseph Kentenich's time as a student, there was a trend among some of the German Pallottines who wanted to take their founder's apostolic concerns more strongly into consideration. Despite government opposition, the superiors no longer sent their young Fathers only to Cameroon, as their missionary bishop Heinrich Vieter would have liked, but also into pastoral care in the surrounding German parishes. Because of this, they had to withstand all kinds of battles with state authorities.

Initially, Joseph knew nothing of all this. He was excited for what was to come now in Limburg. He couldn't foresee the treacherous path he would take in the years to come ...

Beginning of the Difficulties: Novitiate

The official opening of the novitiate was set to take place on September 24 with the solemn investiture. The novice master, Father Peter Girke, stood at the top of the entrance stairway to welcome the future novices. He was a gaunt figure who looked somewhat sickly and pale as he peered tensely into the circle of new arrivals.

The things that would mark the life of the novices from now on were not foreign to Joseph: times of prayer and silence, and community life with its strict adherence to superiors and to the daily schedule. None of this was a problem for him. On the contrary, he began his novitiate with ardent zeal as an important step on the way to the priesthood. Month by month, he filled his little notebook with shorthand notes of the novice master's "instructions" in all detail. These consisted of hairsplitting rules of conduct and very few spiritual impulses. The novitiate was not characterized by any specific pedagogical inspiration of the founder for the internal formation of the order, but was based on traditional ascetical ideas of "mortification," "self-denial," and a certain "hostility to the world." A strictly ascetical life of penance was meant to atone for the ever-increasing spread of atheism. In addition, a peculiar mentality had become the mainstream in ascetical tradition: Human attachments should not disrupt a complete focus on God. One should "love one's relatives," as the novices were instructed, "only for supernatural reasons." The "world" and the "spirit of the world" also led away from God. Toward the beginning of the novitiate, Father Johannes Bayer, the novice master's assistant, gave an introduction into writing a personal "order of life," a personal life's program for one's future path as a priest.

Joseph withdrew into his cell and pondered what he had just heard. He began systematically recording his concept of a holy priestly life in his little notebook, point by point, in the form of personal guidelines and a personal code of conduct. Yes, he wanted to be radically serious about it. He wanted to become holy. And so he wrote in the introduction, *"God is my origin, God is my goal—he must also be the guiding star of my life, the focal point of all ideals. Everything is transitory; we alone remain—he, my Creator, and I, his creature. Both remain in eternity, either united with one another or separated from one another. So my whole striving and struggling here on earth must aim toward unity with God, that is, toward conformity with the divine will."* He saw only one way to reach this *"conformity"*: *"Jesus Christ, who invites me, 'Whoever wants to come after me must deny himself, take up his cross, and follow me'"* (Matthew 16:24). Below, he then subdivided his program of following Christ into large sections strongly influenced by the old asceticism of *discipleship of the cross* through self-denial. Joseph wanted to follow Christ all the way. His list of resolutions got longer and longer. In the end there were 105 individual points. But interiorly he wasn't quite satisfied. One restless thought remained within him: It seemed that all these points in his code of conduct were somewhat too restricting. So as a heading over everything, he wrote in Latin on the cover page, "*So speak and so act as people who will be judged by the law of freedom*" (James 2:12). And even though Father Bayer had advised them to read their order of life every month, the new novice added the remark, "*Don't adhere slavishly to this, and only read one part of it for confession.*" As he drafted the text, he tried to give the whole thing an inner core, a soul, something that would interiorly connect the many points. Actually, love was "the band that holds everything together." After all, was it not the starting point and the force that moves everything?! Precisely this connection seemed to be missing in Father Bayer's explanations.

As time passed, Brother Kentenich increasingly sensed that this type of old asceticism somehow caused him headaches. On the one hand, he shared the conviction that if a person wants to become holy, then sacrifices and renunciation, cross and suffering are part of following Christ. On the other hand, he wasn't able to "*come to terms with the ascetical trains of thought*" his novice master offered them. In the midst of this tension he finally took "*refuge*" in reading *St. Francis de Sales*, whom he had already named his "*model*" in his order of life and who was increasingly becoming his "*favorite saint.*" What especially appealed to him was how human and natural St. Francis de Sales was. Francis de Sales saw *love* as the *fundamental law of the world* per se, of everything that existed, of God's entire creation. Francis de Sales became a lifeline for Joseph to cling to. He sought a modern way of holiness, natural and close to life, that would simply correspond better to the new times. In the later years of his studies, when he read St. Thomas Aquinas in great detail, he especially remembered the words, "Grace builds on nature!" It doesn't float somewhere in a spiritual vacuum, apart from everything human and natural. Grace doesn't destroy human nature;

it elevates it. God's working in the human person presupposes precisely what is genuinely natural. In 1909, when Joseph read in a textbook on religious pedagogy that practical piety for youth consisted "in the first place of making it a habit, out of love for Jesus ... to combat and eradicate disordered tendencies," he quickly crossed out the word "eradicate" and wrote *"ennoble"* in the margin. By this point he had conquered his own ascetical standpoint. But during his novitiate and the years that followed, he found no confirmation for his idea of holiness and no one with whom he could speak about it. He walked alone toward an asceticism for the modern time. Father Girke was particularly not suited for this type of conversation, as Joseph immediately sensed. But he wasn't the only one who had difficulties with his novice master. Hardly would Father Girke leave the room when the novices would gather around to gossip secretly or speak against this somewhat narrow, fearful, and interiorly unfree man. Joseph never joined in. That didn't fit to his structure. He tended either to say frankly what he thought or to stay quiet. He noted in his order of life with regard to relating to superiors: *"1. When there is a difference of opinion, be extremely sensitive and careful. Act as though you wanted to learn, not teach."* Two points further down, he wrote, *"3. As far as possible, adhere to the superior. If that is too hard for you, at least hold back your judgment outwardly, particularly when quarrels have broken out in a community."*

Joseph looked for a reasonable solution for himself and asked Father Girke if he could turn to Father Kolb, the rector of the house, with personal matters from time to time. Surprisingly, the novice master gave permission, even though this wasn't the normal way according to the statutes. From then on, Father Kolb became Joseph's confessor. In this way he got to know the young brother more closely and came to esteem him. Over time it became clear to Joseph that the narrowness and awkwardness of his novice master were due to a great fear of sin. He interpreted self-determination and self-esteem as pride and a lack of humility. Father Girke, like many people of his time, was of the conviction that following Jesus meant to view oneself as always unworthy and sinful and that this was the only way to please God.

It was December 8, 1904. The fiftieth anniversary of the proclamation of the dogma of the "Immaculate Conception of Mary" was being celebrated. Father Kolb still remembered it clearly. Brother Kentenich was set to present a self-composed poem for the occasion. Bishop Dominikus Willi had been invited and sat in the front row with the provincial superior and other dignitaries. But when the program indicated it was time for the poem, no one came to the podium. Joseph Kentenich didn't appear. Everyone became restless. Father Kolb immediately had someone search for the brother and found out that the novice master had hesitated to let such a "freshly baked novice" step on the stage because he feared for the humility of the young man. But with that, the rector had "really had enough," as he said, and he ordered the novice to appear immediately. Kentenich hurried over, went up to the podium, and—as Father Kolb clearly recalled—presented his poem "with an enthusiasm and a fire such as I never saw in him again afterwards. The incident showed me there was something special about this young man."

For many years, Joseph himself considered "pride" to be his "*predominant fault,*" and he noted in his order of life that the "*occasions for failure will be countless,*" and that therefore his "*whole striving must be directed toward attaining humility.*" But as much as he strove for it multiple times, he still sensed a certain resistance within himself. Whenever he knelt far in the back of the house chapel of the Limburg Mission House—the first ones were supposed to fill in the back pews first—his thoughts circled time and again around the same questions: "If you want to become holy, do you really have to renounce joy, human love, self-esteem, and all self-realization? How much had Vincent Pallotti suffered by imposing mortification, sleep deprivation, scourging, and other acts of penance upon himself, in order to follow Christ?! Then I guess a saint should not be happy and joyful in this world!" This way was hard for the native

Rhinelander, who often tried to suppress his *"joking"* and *"cheerful exuberance."* Was it even the right way at all?

In addition to his innate drive for freedom, his deep way of thinking also went against the rigid and one-sided concentration on purely formalistic rules and regulations. And his esteem for love resented an asceticism that was so strongly fixated on sin, seeing and fearing only sins everywhere. As Joseph Kentenich later summarized, it was the *"morality of sin"* prevalent at that time which in the long run *"makes a person sick."* He noticed that the instructions lacked a spiritual background and inner connections; one section of regulations followed the other, mechanically separated, without any meaningful connection, as if the world of God and the world of human beings were two utterly separated realms. He had faithfully and obediently noted in his order of life, *"Love your relatives only for supernatural reasons."* But was that even possible? Didn't people also love in an emotional, natural, human way, without a mere act of the will or purely supernatural motivations? Such *supernaturalism* preyed on his mind. Was human love really an obstacle to love of God? His model, Francis de Sales, already a priest, cried bitterly for days when he lost his mother! And furthermore, were autonomy, independent thinking, and natural ambition actually bad? Hadn't he been able to see from his extensive reading how precisely those who had really accomplished something great had preserved their independent thinking and their own opinion and had gone their own way instead of just running after the masses? Wasn't this the very mark of a true personality? Could God want us to forfeit ourselves entirely and relinquish all originality?

In the many lonely hours Joseph spent walking along the Lahn River or exploring the broad, rolling landscape, he couldn't stop *"brooding."* Could an education that followed a template and expected the same from everyone even do justice to the modern person and the individual? It went against his entire being to do something just because others do it, or to go in the same direction as everybody else without independently asking and thinking. The masses run after everything that moves. That was foreign to Joseph.

There was something in him that somehow didn't fit in, and he sought the reason for it in himself and in his faults and weaknesses. Through all this, he remained independent and went his way alone.

From time to time, Father Kolb invited the students to a discussion session in order to foster an intellectual exchange. At some point Joseph stopped going. His fellow student Karl asked him why he wasn't coming anymore. He responded honestly that it was because the meetings weren't fulfilling their purpose at all. "The only one who speaks is Father Kolb. That's not a discussion. That's a monologue."

Life-threatening Illness

These weren't the only questions that tormented him. Soon after the novitiate, Joseph Kentenich showed symptoms of an insidious illness that neither he nor those around him suspected. Its early signs hadn't been correctly interpreted. He had suffered from frequent tiredness, loss of appetite, and poor sleep. He still attributed the latent headaches to the attic hatch that had fallen on his head. He had increasingly lost weight and had a slight fever for a longer time. In addition to this, he now had a strange cough; it seemed like a cold that refused to go away. The rector sent him to various places to recuperate, but he didn't get better. In April 1907, his condition became so critical that the provincial council ordered him to suspend his studies entirely until the fall. In the summer of that same year, a more thorough examination by a Koblenz doctor resulted in the shocking diagnosis of tuberculosis. Still that same month, Joseph was sent to Bad Wörishofen for a treatment that seemed very promising. Father Sebastian Kneipp, the founder of the institution there, had cured his own tuberculosis as a young man by bathing in an ice-cold mountain lake, and so had rediscovered the healing powers of water. Kneipp treatments had already documented great successes, also for tuberculosis patients. Father Kneipp's original plans to build a house just for them were impeded by the inhabitants of the town for fear of contagion. Consumption, as tuberculosis was commonly called, often triggered reactions of panic.

The doctor treating him in Bad Wörishofen, too, had recorded the diagnosis in the upper right-hand corner of the medical chart, in small print and unfamiliar shorthand so that it couldn't be easily deciphered. Joseph Kentenich was terminally ill and had to be immediately isolated due to contagion. The shortness of breath that sometimes occurred caused panic attacks, especially at night. A lot of rest, frequent rest cures, water treatments, and light walks were prescribed, along with rich meals made with lots of butter and milk. Joseph stayed there for two months, and contrary to all expectations, his condition seemed to improve noticeably.

Meanwhile, a debate had arisen in the provincial council in Limburg as to whether the "predisposition toward his illness hadn't already" been present "before entry into the novitiate." That would have made his acceptance into novitiate invalid. Joseph's confrere, Brother Weiler, who was also ill with tuberculosis, had had to leave the community fairly quickly. But remarkably, Kentenich did not. Those months were full of suspense, as he didn't know what would happen to him. This uncertainty, together with a sense of helplessness in the face of his frightening illness, made him feel his limitedness quite profoundly.

During the half year in which Joseph was dispensed from his studies, he immersed himself into the Latin works of St. Thomas Aquinas. Several things especially appealed to him. He stopped to focus on one point in particular in the teachings of Thomas Aquinas—namely, the teaching on the independence and "autonomy of secondary causes," that is, of human beings and creation. It was self-evident that God, as the Creator and primary cause of everything, had granted this autonomy and even expressly willed it. Little by little, the meaning of these detailed expositions and their pedagogical consequences became clear to Joseph Kentenich. If God had granted such independence and ascribed such intrinsic value to the human person, wasn't it obvious, then, that one should see the greatness of the human person, acknowledge his or her individual significance, and highly value everything the human person has created on earth, provided it has remained in harmony with the primary cause, with God and the laws of his creation?! Wasn't autonomy something God-willed, then? Wasn't self-esteem not merely misguided "pride" but a part of the divine plan? Didn't all further modern developments also correspond to divine providence? Weren't the times themselves also *"a voice through which God was speaking"*? *"The voices of the times are the voice of God!"* These words kept going through Joseph's head over and over. "This wasn't only true of the 'good old days,' but is also true today and will be in the future!" But all these individual recognitions or flashes of inspiration were still like fragments he couldn't piece together. Even as his body was recovering little by little, his mind and soul agonized over many questions that piled up within him beyond measure. And he couldn't really talk with anyone about them.

Intellectual Struggles and the Conflict with Modern Thinking

In the course of his studies, very difficult philosophical themes accumulated within his soul in the form of searching questions. Actually, the intellectual struggle had begun in a completely harmless way and almost as an aside. It wasn't philosophical reflection in the first place that provided the occasion for one of the most weighty questions that ultimately led to the onset of great inner hardships—namely, the question about the existence and meaning of human life. Rather, it was an almost trivial experience, hidden in the seemingly harmless ordinariness of everyday life.

In the novitiate, Joseph had made friends with a confrere who was one or two courses ahead of him. Despite his reserved nature, he had finally found a comrade who was equal to him and seemed to understand him. Karl was extraordinarily gifted, outgoing, and a markedly stimulating conversationalist. Joseph attentively followed the speeches he gave to fellow students and his participation in disputations. These disputations were academic, all-day debates in

Latin held three times a year in front of the whole house. They were meant to stimulate scholarly eagerness to learn. Karl's talks were brilliant and applauded by all without exception. Fundamental dogmatic statements and their intellectual analysis flowed out of his mouth in a skillful, masterly way. Joseph followed each sentence with great excitement and admiration. But one day, he walked into the study hall by chance just as Karl was bragging in an exaggerated and dishonest way. Joseph left the room quietly and unnoticed, deeply heartstricken. The person he had looked up to, who had become a point of reference after all these years of loneliness, was actually someone not too particular about the truth. But truth was exactly what Joseph valued so much. Certainly, it was a little thing, a human weakness, but it triggered a whole avalanche within him. Joseph began to wonder, "If Karl is speaking falsehoods here, who can actually tell me that what he so brilliantly articulates about dogmatics is true beyond a doubt?"

During the following weeks, he put this small incident and his fellow student behind him and moved into other areas. As he grappled with modern philosophy, far deeper questions confronted him: *"Does truth exist at all, and how can it be recognized?"* Is truth not just something relative, something that varies according to the observer, as Kant presented it? Involuntarily but drastically, Joseph was confronted with the question of faith and of credibility as such. Who or what guaranteed what he had believed so securely up until now? The more intensively he plunged into the study of modern philosophy and tried to find a purely logical answer to the probing questions that plagued him, the more the newly raised doubts increased. This made him even more strange to those around him and increased his experience of isolation. To whom could he entrust these questions? He was unprepared for the intellectual storm and the spiritual distress that now overtook him. Actually, the students weren't permitted to read modern philosophers because these were listed in the Church's Index of Prohibited Books. But they were confronted with these philosophies in the passages quoted in extensive theological, apologetic writings actually meant to refute the teachings of Kant, Hegel, Nietzsche, and other "heretics." Contrary to those around him, Joseph immersed himself in their way of thinking and argumentations. He was simply not able, like many others, to grapple with something merely peripherally. This was a strength and a weakness at the same time. Everything he did, he did completely! But this augmented the drama of his confrontation with modern thinking. It soon dawned on him that the arguments of modern philosophers could not be so easily dismissed. It didn't do justice to the matter to simply refer to Kant as an "idiot," as one apologetic book stated ... According to everything that Kentenich had read so far, Kant and other modern philosophers considered truth something relative. For them there was no absolute truth, only a relative one. The world is only as it appears to us. We cannot say whether it really is so. Thus nothing is really certain. *"Our faith,"* as Joseph concluded, *"is also not certain. In faith, we walk on quite unstable ground. Faith is actually a great risk."*

Now everything within him began to waver—everything upon which Joseph had thus far built his life. And he didn't know of anyone in whom he could confide. On the contrary, most professors got scared when the gaunt student on the far right side of the last row of the lecture hall raised his hand yet again to pose a critical question. Father Franz Behrendt was an exception. He examined and discussed social teaching and Marxism with the students. He was not afraid to have a real debate about modern trends. But after the first two semesters, Joseph no longer had him as a professor. This professor's name only reappeared at the end of his studies—at the bottom of Joseph's diploma.

Joseph Kentenich was a first-class *"fanatic of the truth"* and could not live "as if." He read late into the night and later acknowledged, *"But I did not become more mature because of it."* Joseph made no progress in arriving at an understanding. The questions accumulating within him affected him existentially. They didn't only shake the basic pillars of faith, nor did they remain merely on a spiritual and intellectual level; they affected the entire inner life of his soul. Later it became clear to him that he wasn't the only one affected. Philosophical notions generally find expression in life approximately 150 years later, influencing the household of the soul and the living environment of human beings more than one is usually aware. As Joseph Kentenich later emphasized, the emergence of atheism became the cause of much spiritual insecurity, anxiety, and loss of attachments. He even claimed later on that it was the cause of brutality and disrespect for human dignity ...

It was one of those warm, late-summer days. Right after the lecture, Joseph silently walked through the French doors that led to the courtyard. He took a deep breath, soaking in the fresh air. He closed his eyes for a moment. "My God, they simply don't understand what's actually at stake here!" The scene passed through his mind again, how the students had superficially, overconfidently, and naively ridiculed the philosophical material that had been presented. "Do they not understand what this means? A completely new time is dawning! We can no longer return to an absolute security in an undisputed faith. We can't just sweep this under the rug and make fun of it!" He stared into the distance, deeply distressed.

Joseph had repeatedly tried to secure the reasonableness of the whole edifice of faith through logical arguments. His "*whole complex of faith*" had been shaken, and ultimately he could only compulsively cling to it with his will. In written examinations he had strung together a whole gallery of proofs of God's existence according to the model of St. Thomas Aquinas, and still, he had run his head into a wall. At every confession he accused himself of "*brooding.*" It pressed upon him like a "*compulsion.*" It increasingly became clear to him that if truth didn't exist, then neither did God exist, and if God didn't exist, then our life is absolutely meaningless! He had now reached his limit; he had arrived at the threshold of his spiritual and psychological existence. Everything that had shaped his life so far, the strength that had carried him through all of life's hardships from childhood on, was now shaken to the core. A professor had described him in his workbook with the words, "Periculosam incedit viam!" "He is treading a dangerous path!" Joseph had gotten into playing with fire. He was moving about precariously on the crater's edge and had the feeling that he could fall into the abyss at any moment and end up in a state of mental derangement. *"The struggles were dreadful!"* as he later described those years. But Joseph didn't capitulate. He fought and struggled for the things that held his life securely. For there was no doubt: If this volcano finally did erupt, he would no longer be able to escape. There had to be a way out. But as of yet, there was no rescue in sight.

The struggles left their mark. It came as no surprise that Joseph Kentenich seemed strange, consistently serious, and mysterious to others. But instead of prudently and diplomatically keeping to himself during his studies, he posed never-ending critical questions, irritating not only his professors but also some of his fellow students who preferred a more peaceful life.

During these years, Joseph suffered the *"modern person's torments of Tantalus,"* as he called them. Later, it was precisely this that helped him understand people's "*doubts of faith,*" *"skepticism,"* and *"mechanistic way of thinking"* that analytically separated, as with a "scalpel," things that belonged together. But this also put him in a good position to expose dangers. And he could think his way into the man who was considered the great *"hater of God"* and who simultaneously became the protagonist of a new age: Friedrich Wilhelm Nietzsche. Joseph Kentenich often spoke about him; he never demonized him, since he himself had experienced similar intellectual afflictions. But contrary to Nietzsche, Kentenich—already at a relatively younger age—stumbled upon a personal solution to the tormenting question of God's existence, a question that plagued Nietzsche until the end of his life.

An Incident with Repercussions

Because of his indisputable intellectual giftedness—his achievements were "worthy of the highest praise"—he was summoned multiple times to take part in disputations. In one of these, in May 1908, he presented such serious counter-arguments to dogmatic truths that he defeated the three students acting as "defenders." The dogmatics instructor, Professor Johann Hettenkofer, also a member of the provincial council, had to jump in. Ultimately he, too, ran out of arguments. He invoked his authority—after all, he was the reigning expert in his field! Joseph countered him with unwavering steadfastness using a Latin axiom: *"What is presented without proof can by implication be contradicted."* A general murmur went through the hall—a collective "Oh!" of both shock and amusement among the students and a horrified "That is unheard of!" from the ranks of the professors. Brother Kentenich recognized later that at that moment he had been fixated on truth alone. He had never even given it a thought that the professor was so sensitive. He admitted that he had overstepped the line of tact and had publicly embarrassed the professor. A sign of his immaturity ... The incident also had alarming repercussions.

At the beginning of August 1909, when the time came to vote on admission to the so-called final profession, three of the five council members, including Professor Hettenkofer, decided to vote against Joseph Kentenich. They thought he had shown too little submission to authority and that his faith stood on a weak foundation. Who could be sure that he would persevere once he was ordained a priest? Father Kolb, a member of the provincial council, immediately summoned the young brother and asked him, "Have you already heard the results of the meeting?"

He gave a short answer: *"Yes!"*

"What do you think about it?"

"God's providence!"

"What are you going to do now?"

"First get my high school diploma." Yes, if he wasn't admitted to the priesthood, a state-approved high school diploma was necessary for an academic career.

Father Kolb was amazed by the young man. "He stood there gaunt, pale, and sickly, and still, he was rather dry about the whole thing." Tears came into Father Kolb's eyes. He dismissed Joseph with the instruction "to do nothing for the time being." Now everything was really balanced on the razor's edge. All Joseph had lived for was the priesthood—and now it was called into question. No seminary would accept him if he were sent away from here. By 1909, Joseph Kentenich already had such hard years of battle behind him that he was basically certain that there was only one lifeline for him. He had to surrender himself unconditionally to the God he had searched for and questioned, playing all the cards in his hand and, as he put it in his diary, taking the next steps *"like a child holding the hand of his mighty Father."* It was the only way to escape despair. *"God's providence!"* Now he suddenly became calm in the midst of this delicate situation. Something was carrying him. No, someone was carrying him. He sensed a power within himself that wasn't his own. He himself was amazed ...

Father Kolb slowly and thoughtfully closed the door, still fighting back the tears, and returned to his desk. What a tragedy! He had known Joseph Kentenich since his novitiate better than any of the other brothers, and he was convinced that he was being treated unjustly. After all, he was Joseph's confessor and knew about his serious struggles, his faithful adherence to everything important to him from novitiate on, the noble-mindedness of this young man, his sincere intentions, and his extraordinary talent. Such people are often misunderstood and alone. They are easily misjudged. But why was he so headstrong and honest, too, even to the point of self-destruction? What mess had his know-it-all attitude gotten him into? Father Kolb was at a loss. What should he do? What about writing to the general council in Rome to appeal the decision? The mail would take too long, and it would be far too late by the time an answer came. No, there had to be another way out. He had to try to speak with the individual council members one more time and convince at least one of them to change his opinion, making it clear to him that an injustice had occurred.

Father Kolb did just this. Through a personal conversation he was able to straighten out a few things. Four weeks after the initial decision, and without further ado, Father Kolb called for a meeting once more and asked for a re-vote—something that only happened this one time in the history of the Pallottines. The balls rolled out of the ballot box, this time three white balls in favor and two black balls against. With this, Joseph Kentenich's priestly vocation was saved. Father Kolb summoned him yet the same day and, full of joy, shared the new results with him. But he also advised him to be more prudent, admonishing him above all to show more deference and greater respect toward authority. This gave Joseph Kentenich the idea to ask two fellow students for help. They should pay attention to whether he came across too strongly during the lectures, either in tone or in content. After the lectures, he would then go to them to listen to their critiques. He was firmly determined to improve. In his composition notebook he scribbled the resolution, "*At lectures I will completely suspend my judgment and rather simply adhere to the views of the professors.*" As if it were that simple!

The Solution

In the end, Joseph himself didn't exactly know how he came out of the tangled mass of questions, struggles, afflictions, and compulsions unharmed. What he did know was that "*an intimate, profound love of Mary*" had kept his "*soul in balance to some degree.*" His early childhood experience of being consecrated to Mary carried him over the intellectual abyss. Once again, it was Mary's arms that caught him and took him away from the abyss. And it was through Mary that he came to a deeper understanding of the phenomenon of *love*. The experiences he had had with her were something no one could ever take away. Her person represented, embodied, and guaranteed the whole cosmos of faith. As he later acknowledged, she *had a far-reaching influence on him and his development* and *on the subconscious life of his soul ...* Through her he could somehow sense how tremendous the reality of God was, even if human reason powerfully came up against its limitations.

Maybe it was also Mary who gave him the push to dare the way of faith at decisive moments, to risk everything in *"a death leap of the mind, the will, and even the heart."* He had noted in his diary, *"Do it like a child holding the hand of his mighty Father."* Only when he had reached the peak of the volcanic mountain and no longer knew where to go—when there was no way out to the left or to the right and he experienced his total spiritual powerlessness—was he able to let go, renouncing intellectual security and daring to take the risk of love. He fell not into the abyss but into the arms of God. Through this fundamental experience, faith became a hard-won, imperishable treasure and the unshakeable certainty of his life.

Once again he had become aware of the reality of God, this time existentially. He had been guided along a way that spared him no struggle but that made it clear to him that faith doesn't inevitably have to exclude reason. Rather, faith can illumine reason. Moreover, the intellect is not the only human capacity for knowledge; the heart, too, is an "organ of knowledge." These experiences gave him a new assurance of faith. The stormy struggles and fights within him subsided. Gradually a great peace settled into his soul. But it was only when he *"became immersed in life"* and could be active in educating and caring for souls that he became aware of the deeper meaning of all the struggles, afflictions, and sufferings and found the necessary balance for his one-sidedly intellectual orientation. Above all, he now had the chance to give others the knowledge and experiences that had matured in him over all those years. Much later he acknowledged in a personal testimony: *"Hominem non habeo ('I have no one,' John 5:7)—that's what I experienced. And therefore the great principle: What happened to you should never happen to anyone else as far as possible. The strength to simply renounce oneself grows from this. We want to offer an inner home to others (even) when our own heart is crying for a home."*

3. Educator with Heart and Soul

After all the inner and outer difficulties, Joseph Kentenich's ordination day on July 8, 1910, was the fulfillment of a long-awaited life's dream he had fought hard for in every way. The day also became a very special high point in his life ... From an outside perspective, the day was inconspicuous. Pallottine Bishop Heinrich Vieter, Apostolic Vicar in Cameroon, happened to be on a home visit and ordained the eight candidates to the priesthood. The small house chapel of the Limburg Mission House was filled with so many guests that there was barely enough space for them all. Joseph's mother had sent her son a list of suggestions as to whom he might invite to the feast day. He had selected a few relatives, Peter Hessler—his vacation buddy and second cousin, Peter's father, and of course also Father Savels. Unfortunately, his grandmother had passed away a year earlier, as well as his aunt Sibilla, his mother's eldest sister. His relatives were impressed by the large, modern building and the spacious rooms that even had electric light, something they weren't familiar with at all back home. And then of course the ordination itself! It touched them deeply at the beginning to see these young men, including their Joseph, lying prostrate on the ground. They could hear his answer loud and clear: "Adsum! Here I am, I am ready."

Joseph's mother and his cousin Henriette stayed in Limburg for a whole week, especially since Joseph's first Mass as a newly ordained priest took place two days later. Both of them enjoyed their time with him. It was hard to tell what was happening inside him. Henriette was the first one who had noticed a change in Joseph. He did look just as slender and serious as always. But even though he had just been ordained, he radiated a priestly fatherliness that awakened her courage to go to confession to him a few weeks later and confide very personal things to him. Although he was five years

Photo 5: With Bishop Vieter on the day of his priestly ordination, July 8, 1910

younger, she experienced such maturity and empathy from him in the face of her spiritual distress that it was easy for her to unburden everything that was on her heart. She had carried this spiritual burden around with her for a long time but had never found a priest to whom she could say it so openly. In a thank-you note, she wrote to her "brotherly" cousin that even if she hadn't become entirely peaceful yet, he was able to give her much help and consolation. Henriette thought about how kindly and lovingly he had responded to everything and how different he was from so many other priests she knew. Of course, she never told her aunt why she had gone to Limburg that day or what had made her so happy. The young priest simply understood the experiences of human weakness and limitation. He was very familiar with the inner distress of many people that came as the fruit of an exaggerated fear of sin. He had already shown his empathy and understanding in his written examinations, in which the students were supposed to discuss and evaluate moral theological cases for their future work as confessors.

After his ordination, the newly ordained priest helped out on Sundays in parishes all over the Hunsrück region, up and down the Rhine River. He hadn't finished his studies yet; after his ordination to the priesthood, he still had one more year to go. So far, his years of study had been extraordinarily fruitful, as far as formation and theological knowledge were concerned, but the actual completion took place only in the summer of 1911. Until then, the young Father Kentenich once again enjoyed the lectures by Father Franz Behrendt, who spent time discussing Marxism just as intensively as other social-political topics such as the ongoing women's issues. The lectures of this Pallottine Father, who confronted many modern trends in an uninhibited and knowledgeable way, was somehow liberating for Joseph Kentenich.

With great zeal the young Father prepared his sermons for the various parishes. In doing so, he developed a preference for certain topics: the *Eucharist* and the *frequent reception of Holy Communion, mission and community* such as that of *the Marian sodalities, self-education,* and of course, *Mary.* Whether he spoke at the prisons, hospitals, or parish churches of the Eifel region or along the Moselle or Rhine Rivers, or to associations of unmarried women or religious communities, he always preached in a simple, understandable, down-to-earth way, trying to adapt to his listeners and their situation. He tried to connect whatever seemed especially important to him with the one central value: love. Even when he chose conventional terminology, he associated other thoughts and intentions with it. As he proclaimed the faith, he suddenly experienced himself mysteriously strengthened and secure. Having been tested in his own difficult doubts of faith, he became for others an enthusiastic "missionary of faith" and "of love." He was a pastor in body and soul, and like his favorite saint, Francis de Sales, he tried to take the people in front of him into account and convince them through clear arguments and human empathy, not through fire-and-brimstone sermons. He presented great theological connections with the help of simple images, making them easier to understand. During Saturday confessions he especially liked to hear those who seldom came, those who—as he lightheartedly revealed later on to his students—came *"so heavily laden with the old refuse [they] had collected over the years that the confessional creaked."* He made it a personal principle never to enter or leave a town without having made a visit to the Blessed Sacrament in the church.

After he had completed the rest of his studies with flying colors, his superiors decided not to send him to Africa because his health was not in the best condition. Due to the hesitations before his final profession, it had been decided that he should not be sent for further university studies by any means, despite his talent. However, his pedagogical aptitude had not escaped unnoticed. So they placed him in Ehrenbreitstein as a Latin and German teacher for their seminarians. On the side, he should continue to offer temporary pastoral help in the nearby area.

Father Kentenich, barely twenty-five years old, packed his few belongings and moved back beneath the fortress on the Rhine River. He took over the third class, teaching in one of the two rear courtyard buildings. From the very beginning he chose to go the way of a new type of pedagogy. Perhaps it was his own experiences that led him this way, perhaps also all that he had ravenously read and taken in from pedagogical literature whenever the opportunity had arisen. But maybe it was also simply in his blood—the ability to lead people, especially young people, and foster their personal growth. Before his first hour of class had even begun, he had made one thing clear to himself: *"You are more than just their teacher; you are also their educator."* Based on this view, he drafted a list of personal resolutions and principles for his teaching activity. He quickly realized that he could only be an educator for the boys if he understood them on the background of the developments of the time and if he succeeded in gaining a deeper insight into the condition of their souls. During his first experience as an educator, it became ever more apparent to him—not least of all because of his own early life history—that the modern person must be educated differently and learn to find the way to God and self differently than in times gone by.

He stood at the podium in front of his students for the first time and greeted them in a friendly tone of voice, with a somewhat mischievous smile around the otherwise serious corners of his mouth. *"So, now we want to work together. I will demand a lot from you. But you may also make the highest demands on me. And so we will surely become good friends this year."* The boys liked his cooperative style; in fact, they were soon completely delighted with his classes. They gradually developed a special liking for "the new one" who always wore his "biretta somewhat toward the back" and who walked purposefully but with a spring in his step. Whenever they talked enthusiastically about their Latin or German class in the courtyard during break or on a long walk, the students of the other classes cast an almost envious sidelong glance at them. As soon as they saw the young priest walking in the hallway or crossing the courtyard, a peculiar change happened in them. Their high bar performances became even more spirited, their jumps higher and longer, their gymnastic moves more flexible. The boys valued the human, natural way he related to them while making the obvious effort *"not to have favorites."* He had added this to his list of resolutions. Even in Ehrenbreitstein he couldn't entirely stifle his sense of humor and his inclination *"to kid"* or tease one or the other boy. So he admonished himself in his diary-like notes to maintain a greater *"dignified seriousness." "Bend down to them, but in such a way that you still always stand above them!"*

During tests, the young teacher pointedly left the room in order to show the students his trust and to cultivate their *"moral self-reliance."* By doing less monitoring and supervising, he awakened a decision in the boys in return. None of them wanted to disappoint the trust they had been shown. Indeed, no one cheated. Father Kolb, who had meanwhile become the provincial superior, didn't miss the chance to visit the young priest's classes whenever he was in Ehrenbreitstein. He sat in the back and watched the exciting hours in which the teacher awakened independent thinking, a kind of "intellectual competition," and at the same time genuine solidarity among the students. In this way, Father Kentenich fostered a climate of mutual trust. He succeeded in mobilizing the inner strengths of the boys while simultaneously giving personal attention to each individual. Some of the students who didn't belong to the third class lamented Father Kentenich's reserve toward the rest of them. However, one time they were able to visit him in his small, modest office to wish him a happy name day. He immediately passed around a large tin filled with tasty, homemade cookies from his mother. They all helped themselves generously!

Each student was important to Father Kentenich, as was each one's individual development. So, for example, he made the suggestion to the provincial government that Ferdinand Kastner—who was extraordinarily gifted but whose health was weak—be sent to a public high school. He believed this would give him opportunities for further study later on and free him from having to follow such a strict daily schedule. The superiors took up his suggestion. Ferdinand Kastner, like other students who were sent away or freely chose to go, maintained active contact with his former teacher through letters. Father Kentenich followed their further development with genuinely human interest and didn't lose sight of a single one who kept contact. This also included Hubertus Mohr, who was sent away from the boarding school unjustly one day. Hubertus confided in his former teacher, telling him all the details of the hard fate that had befallen him. He was expelled from the school without warning or prior consultation, only on the basis of a false accusation from outside the school. In this difficult situation, he trusted Father Kentenich more than his own father. Hubertus didn't keep it a secret from his teacher how he had stood at the edge of the Rhine, tempted to hurl himself into the water for sheer despair.

Joseph Kentenich immediately sat down at his desk and wrote an answer, advising Hubertus to request a conversation with the rector to clarify the situation. But the attempt failed. Months later, Hubertus, deeply disappointed, wrote that as of yet he had received no response from the rector to his letter. His father had quickly found him an apprenticeship with a merchant, where he had to tackle nine hours of accounting each day. But he longed so much to be a missionary—so he kept studying every day until late at night.

Early on, Father Kentenich had to deal with the opposing pedagogical views of his confreres and superiors and get used to the fact that their style of relating to the boys was completely different from his own. He resolved to keep a simple strategy toward his colleagues. As much as possible, he would avoid criticizing or engaging in counterattacks while at the same time never letting himself be pushed into a defensive position. He considered it imperative simply to keep following his own pedagogical way quietly and unwaveringly, never to get unnecessarily caught up in discussions, and to follow his pedagogical ideal with determination. He recorded in his diary notes, "*Speak less and work more!*" He summarized this independent way in the admonition, "*You must soon become a person with a deep inner life who finds his stronghold in himself and in God.*" This self-educational inspiration didn't come from out of nowhere. Thoroughly self-critical, he believed he had discovered that he was too strongly dependent on his confreres, and he interpreted this as a consequence of his "*main passion: sensitivity and sensuality.*" Whatever he meant by this, it doesn't seem to be a matter of sensuality in the sexual sphere, because he continued, "*Both have me so strongly in their chains of slavery that the majority of my actions are determined by the character of my confreres. That means I must use all my strength to apply the lever.*" He resolved to stop the constant "*gushing praise*" toward his confreres, not to be "*effusive,*" not to constantly disclose his "*whole inner life,*" but instead: "*In moments of difficulty, go to the chapel and ask for advice there.*"

Many witnesses testify to the fact that both students and colleagues perceived him differently than he perceived himself. A former student who later had a critical opinion of Kentenich wrote about what he was like at that time: "Hardly anyone suspected that this was a man who consciously oriented himself on the one great goal of becoming a reformer of ecclesial and religious education in a new era. He withdrew into silence to study the writings of a saint, St. Francis de Sales, but also Nietzsche's *Thus Spoke Zarathustra* and

Photo 6: As a newly ordained priest

the educational teachings of Friedrich Wilhelm Foerster." Father Kentenich did indeed love the writings of Friedrich W. Foerster, one of the few Catholic authors who developed pedagogical reforms. One year later he even read them with his students in order to train them in pedagogy. However, the young teacher could not foresee that he himself would become such a "reformer." Already during his studies he had discovered in Nietzsche's writings a spirit that heralded a new era. Father Kentenich wasn't afraid to take a close look at the great thinkers of his time. In fact, by discussing them with his students, he wanted to enable them to arrive at an independent judgment.

In the meantime, a stately boarding school building was being constructed in the town of Vallendar on the Rhine River, where the Pallottines had made their third establishment in Germany. It was a great joy for everyone that the two lower classes, who had been moved into the "Old House" there due to lack of space, could finally come together with the older students from Ehrenbreitstein into one new building. The small property that was part of the town of Vallendar had the name "Schoenstatt" because of its beautiful location—"eyne schoene Statt [a beautiful place]," as a document from the twelfth century states in old German. An Augustinian cloister had once stood there; now the only things that remained of it were the two church towers, a few farm buildings, the so-called Old House, and the little cemetery chapel originally dedicated to the Archangel Michael as the escort of the dead.

A Revolution Makes Headway

The construction of the boarding school had made fairly quick progress and it now proudly stood out above the wooded heights of the old cloister grounds in the valley. The new building finally offered all 170 students enough space. It included dormitories, classrooms, a magnificent house chapel, a large dining hall, a gymnasium, and even a swimming pool close to the Old House. The Pallottines were proud of their new "House of Studies." During the vacation, a committee of teachers had drafted a handbook for the teaching staff as well as so-called "house statutes" with 120 individual regulations to be placed into the hands of each student right at the start of the school year. After all, they wanted to keep pace with other boarding schools. The students were told to memorize the statutes and strictly adhere to these house rules. This was actually not uncommon at that time, and initially there was no hint of the storm that would begin to brew in the boarding school in the coming weeks.

October 27, 1912

Reverend Father Provincial Kolb!

As you already know, Father Kentenich immediately took up his position as spiritual director in accord with your wish. I personally led him into the dining hall and introduced him to the boys. What surprised me was that the first thing he did was to announce to the students that he was now there to *take their mothers' place* for them. It sounded a little unusual in our very masculine house, but I think—if you will grant me this remark—you have made a good choice. Therefore I would like to permit myself to thank you, Reverend Father, for following my suggestion, especially since you yourself had already thought of Father Kentenich for the position of spiritual director. This evening around 6:00 p.m., he will give his opening address—that is, he will give his first instructions to the students of the middle and upper classes. I hope that he speaks to their consciences and that things will take a turn for the better in the future.

It is a great relief for me as the rector that this solution has been found. Father Panzer's requested resignation as the first spiritual director of our institution is outwardly well-founded because of his weak health.

As for me, I am still trembling a bit from the shock. I can still see the senior class and a few students of the upper classes outraged over a caning administered in the sixth class and infuriated by "the many rules of the new house statutes," the "strict regulations," and the "many punishments." Their complaints also made it clear that they simply couldn't get along with Father Panzer. Indeed, he is overly anxious and likes to have the brother in the stable come with the rod to execute a caning. So it wasn't easy to get him to understand the problems of the students. It was precisely the best ones who had held a gun to my head, so to speak, saying, "Either the conditions change and caning is eliminated or we will all leave the school!" Imagine! What would that have looked like in the public eye after just having sent out the attractive brochures to advertise our House of Studies?!

To be sure, the new regulations were foreign to the older ones because they had been used to something different in Ehrenbreitstein. They had more freedom there. A few of the younger Fathers from there explained several things to me in order to excuse the boys. How happy I was for your visit and the provincial council meeting that was quickly summoned in the midst of this delicate matter ...

I have now urged both the teachers and Father Prefect, who is in charge of discipline, to be more reserved with punishments. Father Kentenich has already come to see me about the caning. He is strongly opposed to any form of corporal punishment. He believes it is a degrading and humiliating practice, not to mention the proof of an educator's incompetence. He's just still very young and inexperienced! We'll grant him that. Discipline, obedience, and order must somehow be maintained at a boys' school! Moderate punishment can't be entirely avoided; every school administrator in our country knows that. Or are you of a different opinion? Then I humbly ask you to share it with me.

Otherwise I am confident that Father Kentenich will guide the boys well. For the time being, peace seems to have set in everywhere. The feast of December 8 will then add its part.

For today I remain, with most humble greetings,

Your loyal servant,
Fr. Franz Wagner
Rector of the Study Institution in Vallendar on the Rhine

If a letter from the rector of the House of Studies to the provincial superior still existed, that's what it might have looked like.

For Father Kentenich, the appointment as spiritual director, as the spiritual educator of the boys, came as a complete surprise. He was just six weeks into the new school year as a Latin and German teacher when he was pulled out of school activity in a mad rush. He had just two days to prepare his first talk to the older classes. For a long time he had been observing them quietly and had perceived the revolution brewing among them. In the hallway he had found one of the notes they purposely left all over: "A house without joy must be closed immediately." Another one said, "We want to be free like our forefathers were!" He had gotten wind of the actual revolt itself only by witnessing the indignation of individual colleagues. Therefore he had preferred to stay back. But what was going on

Photo 7: All students of the House of Studies,
Schoenstatt-Vallendar, 1912

inside the boys didn't escape him unnoticed. There was a hidden longing for more freedom. They wanted to be taken seriously. There was something good behind the revolution that had broken out among them one evening during a recreation hour. It only had to be understood correctly. The powers gasping for air within the boys could perhaps be used, but how? How could he win the boys over for genuine ideals? Actually, they were *"not at all religious from within"* ... Many things were probably only pious practices pasted on, a purely formal fulfillment of duty, hardly rooted in their hearts. They had quickly grown tired of all the many religious devotions in their daily schedule and didn't want to hear any more pious speeches. Many of them were surely only here because their parents wanted it that way or because their financial situation left them no other possibility for education. How could he help them value faith and religiosity and see it as a benefit for their personality and life?

How could he direct the vital and revolutionary powers that had broken forth in them toward something constructive?

These considerations touched something that seemed to have been waiting within him for a long time ... Wasn't the revolution actually a typical sign of the modern time, a sign of the evolution of a *"new type of person"* that demands freedom and self-determination? The boys were perhaps just an example of this ... Couldn't God be opening a door, wanting him to pass on to the boys what he himself had to struggle so hard for and that was burning in his soul? A plan soon matured in him that he would gladly reveal to them right at the beginning of his opening address. Would they understand him and go along?

Father Kentenich took a few sheets of paper and folded them in half length-wise. He wanted to be able to make changes and correct the draft of the speech on the blank left side as he usually did with his sermons. Then he picked up his feather pen and dipped it in the little jar of ink that stood on the upper edge of his podium. He closed his eyes for a moment and imagined the boys before him—what might be going on inside them, what was moving them, what they were feeling. He remembered the way he himself used to think at that age. At first they would surely be eager to see who comes as their new spiritual director. He wrote, *"The news of the new spiritual director caused a general craning of necks,"* making a play on a satire by Conrad A. Kortum that was well-known among the students. The *Jobsiade* was a book that the boys only secretly read under their desks because it poked fun at the clerical state in a humorous but fairly disrespectful way. "Perhaps," thought Father Kentenich, "they will be expecting a totally different Father, one they can admire, like the extra confessor who comes from the neighboring community riding on a horse." Someone like himself, short and of slight build, surely wouldn't make much of an impression in their eyes. Father Kentenich smirked and wrote, *"You are astounded and disappointed."* Only his students knew him from class. He had jokingly asked Theile in the hallway what he should say in his opening address. He had boldly answered in his German dialect, "Oh, say something about the genitivus objectivus!" At the moment, Theile was at war with this particular chapter of Latin grammar. Father Kentenich decided to pick up on this comment. "I don't want to speak so high above them," he thought, "or even reprimand them, as the rector perhaps expects me to do. They should experience that I take them seriously ... And by all means it should also be relaxed! That opens hearts." He didn't want to repeat the same mistakes he had experienced in his own education. Now suddenly everything flowed from his feather pen. He tried to think and feel his way into the boys, but he also wanted to present his project to them, the "*program*" he had in mind. He wanted to show them a youthful ideal. But they should make a free decision! That was important to him. So he wrote on the next page that he wanted to do "*nothing, absolutely nothing without your full consent.*" The boys had been bossed around long enough! Now they had to learn to make their own decisions, develop their self-confidence and self-esteem, and lead themselves. "*Self-education*"—that was the keyword. With that he would orient their overflowing energies and strengths toward a real goal. Their urge for freedom, their desire to be treated as adults—that was the right starting point! If he could succeed in making the goal of "*true inner freedom*" clear to them, an ideal that was so close to his own heart, he would be able to help them become independent of external circumstances which they—he and the boys—couldn't change for the time being. They could make use of them to become interiorly free persons.

In solidarity with the students, he poured his whole program into one single sentence: "*We want to learn to educate ourselves to become firm, free, priestly personalities!*" No, not entirely without education by others. "*Under the protection of Mary*" still had to go in. Mary should take over the part of education by others. What Mary had achieved in him, she could also accomplish in the boys. Father Kentenich picked up his feather pen once more. "*Under the protection of Mary, we want to learn to educate ourselves to become firm, free, priestly personalities!*" He decided that this *program* should occupy them for the whole year—if the boys went along. Therefore he wanted to motivate them, to give them enough arguments about how meaningful such self-education is ... He wanted to make all his intentions transparent to them. That's how he could most honestly prove to them how seriously he took them. Father Kentenich began to list some reasons. *Self-education* is so modern among *educated circles* and so crucial in helping the human person learn self-determination in a time of increasing external control. The boys, he thought, were constantly standing under the yoke of being determined by others in every way: rules that defined the whole day, plenty of supervision and control, the pressure from outside, and the coercion of the harsh penalties. He remembered that only yesterday, as he knelt in the choir loft of the house chapel unnoticed by the boys, was he able to experience what this silly education by rules really looked like. According to the house schedule, the students were supposed to pray the rosary. Instead, some of them pushed and shoved each other so much that one fell out of the pew. "As soon as people who are only dictated by such an education think they are not being observed, the things that really move and direct them will come out." Everything religious was so pasted on! As he observed all this, the thought crossed his mind, "*Well, things can't actually get any worse with my method. I'm going to dare it!*"

Yes, he wanted to take the risk of a pedagogy of freedom, no matter how many disappointments might come as a result. He had to count on this from the start. But he wanted to win genuine, *free personalities, free rowers* for the Kingdom of God, *not galley slaves.* And he wanted to make the boys capable of this as well as he could. Only such priestly figures could be convincing in the future. He knew that from his own bitter experience.

Father Kentenich put down his feather pen once more for a moment. As the spiritual director, he didn't have many possibilities to make changes in the daily schedule or the exterior rules. The teacher statutes forbade him from doing so. He couldn't even change the caning! But he wouldn't ease up on that particular topic, and he would approach the provincial superior about it. As for the rest, how would it be if he would help the boys to accept the house statutes and rules in inner freedom and use them as a training field for educating their personalities? *"Difficulties are tasks,"* tasks that one can master and that make a person strong. He had experienced that himself. If he could succeed in focusing their attention on growing as persons with a deep inner life, they would become truly free and *not determined by the character of those around them.* It was imperative to direct their attention to the *"microcosm"* of their own personality. Now he had found the right word: *microcosm.* Every human person—an entire cosmos. In the weeks to come, he wanted to show them the entire wealth of this cosmos—first, their objective value as human beings, and then their individual, subjective value as unique persons.

Through the development of their *inner powers,* he would be able to make them strong in the face of a time that presented enormous *exterior technological advances* but that also increasingly suffered under the loss of spiritual capacities. The conquest of their inner world and the mastery of their own drives had to keep step—he continued writing in the draft of his talk—with the technological and scientific achievements. He had recently read about this exact topic in a newspaper article containing statements of an Italian politician. Where had he put it? Father Kentenich looked for the newspaper under the pile of notes and papers. It said that some time ago, an Italian statesman had "determined that the greatest danger of the new developments was that half-civilized nations were increasingly taking possession of the technological means of modern civilization without having been given the necessary spiritual and moral culture to make proper use of these achievements." The spiritual director picked up his pen: *"At that, however, I would like to turn the tables and ask: Are our more developed races able and mature enough to make proper use of the enormous advancements of our age in all the exterior realms? Or has not our time rather become a slave to its achievements? It has indeed. Our command of the gifts and powers of nature around us has not gone hand in hand with the subjection of the elemental and animal forces in our own human breast. The powerful discord, this immeasurable cleft, is becoming ever greater and wider—and in that state we will stand before the specter of social justice, before societal bankruptcy, unless we invest all our strength in initiating a change soon. Instead of becoming masters of our achievements, we are becoming their slaves; we are becoming slaves, too, of our own passions."*

He had read something by Foerster about this. Father Kentenich hurried over to the bookshelf and grabbed Foerster's *Jugendlehre* [*Youth Education*]. He found the passage and worked it into his speech.

He still stood at his podium, writing without stopping. It had long ago become dark outside. The wind whirled the leaves wildly around the area. His glance wandered to the window, lost in thought. *"Yes, autumn storms are not only roaring through nature but also through our school."* Would he succeed in calming the storm in the hearts of the boys—or better said, in making use of the strength of this storm?

New Life Breaks Forth

The first talk was well received by the boys. They were impressed. They hadn't expected anything like that at all. The first sentences had already made them break out in peals of laughter, and after that came so many things worth thinking about. It struck Norbert Theele how often the new spiritual director had used the words *"we"* and *"us."* Not one single time did he say, "you must," "you should," or anything like that. Everything was so open, truly liberating—after everything they had already experienced here. "Let's see," he mused somewhat doubtfully afterwards, "if it stays like this, if things keep going like this with our new spiritual director ..."

After the first talk on October 27, 1912, Father Kentenich gave two more—one on Mary's significance in history and one on the other topic that was just as close to his heart, the ideal of modern holiness. November 1, the Feast of All Saints, offered a fitting occasion for this. First of all, he wanted to free the boys from false conceptions of holiness and then make them aware of how current such an ideal still is even today. He began his thoughts by saying, *"Today, on the Feast of All Saints, the Church shows us a whole gallery of real characters: the saints."* He concluded with the thought that the saints are *"nothing else but the canonized goodwill of the human person."* He described them as totally normal people with weaknesses and strengths, with difficulties and struggles. Since they had the same difficulties to master *"as we do,"* they could certainly be models for our own life. The spiritual director avoided speaking in a way that was too religious. Instead, he first concentrated on ethical and social arguments. In the first talk, he had already established the reasons for striving to become a credible Christian personality by emphasizing the influence that the boys would want to have on other people later as priests. This could only happen *"through the power, through the inner richness"* of their *"personality."* Credibility! Joseph Kentenich recalled his own experiences and disappointments ...

It was imperative not to shy away from any efforts as time went on. The new spiritual director ordered books, for example, Richard P. Garrold's stories about students, brand new and up-to-date, with interesting narratives about teenage boys who had to struggle through all kinds of difficulties at home, at school, or in boarding schools. He read *Die beiden Merks* with his students, a book about two adolescents whose father—after his wife had left him—became an alcoholic and beat his children, causing them to run away and become neglected street children. They had such problems at school that the decision was made at a teachers' conference to subject them to corporal punishment, until a young teacher finally stood up for them with kind understanding. For the boys, these stories worked like a mirror that reflected their own difficulties and questions and paved the way for open discussions. From the beginning, the spiritual director drew them into his own pedagogical processes as if he were dealing with mature soon-to-be teachers and educators, not adolescent youth. He invited them to reflect on their own development. In this process, Joseph Kentenich tried to make deep psychological insights useful to them for their self-education and the guidance of others. Without further comments, it became clear to the boys how respectfully the spiritual director related to them and how much he believed they could do.

Father Kentenich illustrated his talks with examples from the most varied domains so that they wouldn't be boring or dry. Together with his students he read the biographies of Helen Keller, Marie Heurtin, and Laura Bridgman. It was imperative to convince the boys from within of the value and dignity of the human person. In this way he not only motivated them to work on their self-education but also made its meaning and necessity clear to them. They owed it to their originality and dignity to work on themselves. During these weeks and months, nothing was too much for Father Kentenich. While his confreres were fast asleep, he studied chapters from the most varied fields of knowledge in order to further his program with the students. His door was always open to the boys. They soon noticed that they could come to him with all their problems and that confession with him was different than what they were used to. As one of the students said, there were two focal points in the house at that time: "the Most Blessed Sacrament in the chapel" and "Father Spiritual Director."

He dedicated himself to the boys with all his strength and helped them in every kind of difficulty. He set out with them on the way of discovering their "PI," their personal ideal or life's goal. He patiently listened to them and inspired them to say their opinion freely, also among each other. The independence he asked of them was no easy endeavor since they were not used to self-activity or even to speaking freely. They were always admonished to speak only when they were addressed, to "regurgitate" what had been presented to them, to repeat the knowledge they had memorized. Father Kentenich made use of a clever method to encourage them. One day, he purposely asked one of the shyest ones whether he wouldn't want to give a talk on a particular topic. The boy took the book he held out to him, enthusiastically accepting the offer from his Father Spiritual Director. But when the moment came, he fearfully hid behind a hedge, still busy scribbling in his composition notebook.

He might never have appeared in the study hall if a few of his fellow students hadn't dragged him to the podium with gentle force. "But as soon as I had overcome the first frightful moment," he later shared, "the walls of shyness were broken down, not only for me but for our whole class, blazing a trail for self-activity."

For Father Kentenich, it was a matter of getting the boys accustomed to independence as he did in Ehrenbreitstein. He explained to them that only *"what was freely willed,"* people's own decisions, the things people worked through and conquered for themselves, could become a personal possession. Everything else was *"only like a stuck-on label that quickly peels off again."* From his own experience, he knew that precisely what people had struggled hard for and conquered for themselves made them strong and secure, even in the face of resistance and danger. To promote such independence, he needed something that would unite the boys in a common task while granting them more freedom. A genuine community formed in this way would forge them together and unite them in a common goal. Such a community would be particularly beneficial for the development of their personality. A different social space would be necessary for this, one that went beyond the framework of the school and the obligatory class associations.

Back in August 1912, Father Kentenich had taken part in the Marian Congress in Trier with his provincial superior and Father Behrendt. He had come across an organization there that could fulfill this purpose. In his opinion, the Jesuits had rendered a great service to the Church through two institutions: the so-called "Ignatian Exercises" and the "Marian Sodality." The latter had its origins in sixteenth-century Germany, during the Reformation, under the leadership of Father Jacob Rem. At that time, this priest, together with a few young people from the ranks of the nobility, had initiated a renewal of the faith in the entire South German region. This young elite was marked by devotion to Mary and a holy, apostolic life. At the beginning of the twentieth century, the Marian sodalities experienced a new blossoming. Such a sodality was pedagogically appealing to Father Kentenich because it offered the chance to form a free community and to cultivate *"moral self-reliance."* He had already read so much about this. In particular, Marian sodalities aimed at moral and religious renewal by modeling a credible Christian life. It would be a social space in which one could lead a personally and freely chosen Christian life. Membership was voluntary and the boys could choose their own leadership ... He had already proposed the establishment of such an organization to the boys on October 27. If it really happened, a tried and trusted institution would be given a totally new face, even if the central office for Marian sodalities in Vienna would still require a few things. But Father Kentenich quickly had to push these thoughts aside. The college of teachers had already decided that summer that a Marian sodality was out of the question for their school. They held that the Pallottines themselves were a congregation with Marian devotion firmly anchored in their statutes. The spiritual director also knew what the boys thought on this topic. They characterized the Marian sodality as a "pious association" or some kind of "blue ribbon club," convinced that it was only something for girls. It became clear to him that it was still too early to move ahead with it. But something that could prepare the ground was a type of "mission club." Here he could count on less resistance. After all, the missions were one of the Pallottines' key concerns, and this aspect would also be appealing to the boys.

But it was not as easy as Father Kentenich had thought. Considerable resistance stirred among the teachers who were firmly attached to an "old-school" pedagogy. Why these nonessentials? Why voluntary membership? "If, then something that pertains to the whole school," was the view of some. Others thought something like that would only serve to distract the students from their studies. Still others were skeptical of the new spiritual director and his newfangled educational methods already after the first weeks. "He is simply too young and inexperienced!" But some of the youth were soon won over for the idea, and with their spiritual director's support, they moved the cause ahead. Hardly had Father Provincial appeared from Limburg when they approached him with the request for permission to found a "mission club." Although he had already heard a few objections from the other teachers, he ultimately agreed to the plan after several attempts by the boys and the spiritual director. Somehow he trusted Father Kentenich, and above all, he himself saw that the boys had shifted their interest. There was no longer any talk of a "palace revolution." Now it was all about a mission club! This was really a pedagogical success within a short time—something that shouldn't so quickly be undone. Rector Wagner agreed with this view.

So, the mission club came into existence already during the Christmas break of 1912-1913. The leading members gathered other interested students and drafted a type of club structure made up of Father Kentenich as the club leader and a leadership council freely elected from their own ranks. It now moved forward very democratically. Some parts of the debates on the club's topics and projects could've given even the parliament of the German Empire some stiff competition. With this, Father Kentenich had given the boys a totally new field of activity. With ardent zeal they set to work selling mission calendars; collecting stamps; writing to the missionaries in Cameroon; listening to testimonies of missionaries who had returned home; organizing public mission festivals; calling meetings; writing talks; holding common sessions to plan the what, when, and how of all that needed to be done; and of course, managing their own finances. The boys enjoyed their newly won freedom to the full. Some meetings were quite lively. Father Kentenich sat in on them in the back corner and listened. He only intervened when there was no other option or when they asked for his help. Otherwise he supported the elected leaders in quiet work behind the scenes and looked after every individual boy who sought him out. He gave talks for the club, also turning their glance toward *"doing missionary work in one's own heart."* In this way he continued to work on their personality development. Convinced of each one's positive strengths, he reinforced the boys' self-esteem by recognizing their value and letting them experience it.

Relatively soon after he began his task in Vallendar, he had become aware of Joseph Fischer, a real "rowdy"—at least that was the faculty's conclusion whenever the teachers complained about him. But precisely from hearing those complaints, Father Kentenich had perceived qualities in this student that the others were evidently missing. Now he reached out his hand to Joseph, saying, "Oh, you are Joseph Fischer?! I have already heard so many good things about you."

Father Spiritual Director left Joseph standing in the hallway dumbfounded as he disappeared behind the big door. "It didn't sound sarcastic, but sincere," Joseph thought to himself. Later he often had to think back on this first personal encounter that had given him so much courage and self-confidence. Back then, no one could have imagined that of all of them, Fischer was to become the first prefect of the future Marian sodality.

In an original manner, Father Kentenich tried to open the way for the boys to develop into the mature men they longed to be. Already after a few weeks, he explained to them in a talk: *"In Locke's 'Thoughts about Education,' he speaks some nice words, saying that the sooner you treat your son as a man, the sooner he will be a man. The sooner we treat ourselves as men in our self-education, the sooner we will be men."* And toward the end of the school year, before the long break in July 1913, he summarized his conviction in these words: *"It's been a long time now since you were children. Therefore you were not treated like building blocks but like builders. And as far as your education was placed into my hands, I always considered you my co-workers."*

After the first all-school mission festival organized by the boys, several issues of the *Star of Africa*—the newspaper for benefactors and those interested in the Pallottine missions—began to contain individual articles written by Father Kentenich about the new mission club in Vallendar. By doing so, he not only praised the boys' work but also cleverly put the boarding school, the administration, and the teaching faculty in a positive light. At the same time, he defended the mission club because he was well aware of the objections in the background. He emphasized the meaning of the mission club for a community of young people: *"In a club, there's always plenty to plan, to organize, to orchestrate—both for the freely elected council as well as for the individual members who wholeheartedly participate. And what makes a young student happier than when he can label his work—be it ever so modest—with the words: 'I did this myself!'"*

In spite of all efforts, one day a storm of anger broke loose. Father Kentenich had written an article about the mission festival for a Koblenz newspaper that reached a broader public. In it, he had also mentioned the names of the students who had given a presentation. "What's more," as the circle of teachers criticized, "he uses worldly expressions like 'Sekunda' and 'Prima,'" terms commonly used at public high schools—etc., etc. They found many reasons to be horrified. The provincial superior and ultimately also the general superior of the Pallottines were pressured to disband the club. The year 1913 was thus full of tension. The boys were convinced of their good cause, although they had to endure many things. For example, the club leaders were purposely and unjustifiably given worse grades for diligence, conduct, and class participation. Or, their individual good accomplishments were judged less favorably than those of other students. Since the general agitation had now come to a head because of the article in the Koblenz newspaper, Father Kentenich advised the boys to relinquish the next mission festival in order not to provoke the teachers' fury even more, even though it had already been prepared to the last detail. The boys went to the rector with sadness and asked him to refrain from holding the next mission festival. But they wouldn't let it get them down.

What became increasingly clear to Father Kentenich regarding the conflicts with the teaching faculty was that the club had no juridical basis at all. Everything depended on the discretion and momentary mood of the teachers. In the long run, to protect the life that had emerged, the boys needed an institution with statutes and rights to fall back on. Also, mere social engagement wasn't enough if the boys were to make progress in their personality growth. In contrast, a Marian sodality had statutes, promoted independence, and made it possible to work in a markedly religious way. So far, the spiritual director had done his best to avoid working much with religious motivations in his talks. He wanted the boys' faith to be able to grow slowly, organically, and genuinely. But the charged atmosphere at present made it impossible to think of founding a Marian sodality. If, then only when the boys were convinced of the good cause. The spiritual director could worry about the teachers, confreres, and provincial council later. He didn't want to initiate anything that didn't meet with the full agreement of his boys. They were his decisive *"co-workers."* Initially, individuals from the club's leadership began to develop an interest in the cause. Father Kentenich had lent them written materials about the engagement and history of the sodalities. They then worked from man to man to win others over for the idea.

One day, Rudolph Gross, an upperclassman, appeared at the spiritual director's door with a booklet titled *Die Fahne* [*The Banner*] in his hand. The periodical was printed at the central office for Marian sodalities in Vienna and broadly distributed from there. Rudolph told Father Kentenich about his brother, whose school had such a sodality. Father Kentenich passed the brochure around among the students and teachers. A few from the ranks of the students, above all, were won over. But the teachers mostly remained skeptical. They didn't want to have a "sodality within a congregation." "The members might imagine themselves afterwards to be some kind of 'elite' and let the others feel it. That would really cause a division in the school! Moreover, their academic achievements would surely suffer. Furthermore, the novitiate shouldn't be anticipated." The chain of objections got longer and longer!

Against all expectations, a special circumstance came to Father Kentenich's aid. Together with the provincial superior, Father Kolb, and the rector, Father Wagner, he took part in a pedagogical conference in Donauwörth during the summer of 1913. At this conference, Father Johann Eckinger, a well-known Jesuit and pedagogical author and the long-standing general prefect of the Marian sodalities, gave a talk on the advantages of sodalities in boarding schools. This shared experience opened the decisive door for Father Kentenich to found a Marian sodality in the House of Studies. He was able to refer to these arguments and submit a proposal to Father Kolb to request a written professional opinion from Father Eckinger commenting on the experiences with Marian sodalities in other schools. This professional opinion could then be shared with the teaching faculty and the provincial council. Encouraged by this circumstance, the boys submitted an application to the provincial government in December of the same year with the petition to found a Marian sodality. Joseph Kentenich attached a detailed letter to Joseph Fischer's application, documenting in long sections the independent and creative development of his pedagogical concept, which remained largely alien to his confreres.

The requested professional opinion answered all open questions in a very positive way. Still, the teachers called for a second professional opinion. When this turned out similar, the provincial council granted permission at the end of December 1913 to found a Marian sodality at their school.

4. Daring to Found

End of February 1914. The boys worked vigorously on the statutes of the Marian sodality to be submitted in Vienna. They even had a heated discussion on Carnival Sunday. Now Father Kentenich stood on the icy path leading from the House of Studies down into the valley and looked through the bare trees at the little St. Michael's chapel right next to the Old House. He realized that the statutes needed to specify the sodality's meeting place, either a church or a chapel. The little chapel down below would be a fitting place. However, Father Kolb had advised him to be satisfied with the far more beautiful house chapel or the brothers' prayer room. But the idea wasn't to Father Kentenich's liking because those places were too public. Any teacher could overhear what the boys discussed, what they expressed in their talks and meetings, and what they wanted to strive for. Father Kentenich wished to safeguard the newly budding life and the autonomy of the boys. Much had already happened in a short time—many of the boys had the increased desire to work seriously on themselves and to prove it in everyday life. Father Kentenich didn't want any of this to be stunted now by unfortunate remarks or interventions that would cast a cloud over the boys' joy and commitment. He already had enough of a balancing act to do in this regard, asking for their understanding and having a positive influence on them so as to stay on good terms with the teachers.

Father Kentenich went back into the house. On the stairway he suddenly felt a piercing pain in his chest. A cold had already been lingering for weeks, but he had been ignoring it. There had been so many things to settle. The boys needed him—one had tears in his eyes because he was homesick, another one because he had failed an assignment, and a third one because he had been treated unfairly by

Father Prefect. There were disputes among them that he helped to settle. One youngster stood sobbing in the corner of the hallway, his hands wrapped in bandages. As soon as Father Kentenich noticed him, the boy went with him and let him take off his bandages. Underneath were bad wounds caused by frostbite. He so lovingly consoled the boy that some others almost got jealous and wished they could be in that little one's shoes. Then he sent him to the infirmary to have his wounds dressed. A harsh winter had set in. Father Kentenich had heard from Alexander Menningen that one of the younger boys next to him often cried at night because he was freezing. Father Kentenich took his own second blanket, allotted to him for health reasons, and asked Alex to take it to the little one—but without saying where he got it. He could give it back to him in the spring. The spiritual director, as Alex later shared, had become both father and mother to the boys ... He smiled quietly to himself as he thought of the boys. But as he climbed up the stairs, he pressed his hand again to his chest, wincing with pain. He had probably taken his health too lightly in the midst of everything. He had been fighting with a fever for days. Suddenly he had a bad coughing fit and quickly grabbed his handkerchief. But when he took it away from his mouth, he was shocked—it was full of blood. He immediately went to his room and had a confrere inform the rector that he wasn't doing well and that he needed to lie down. Concerned, the rector immediately sent the brother responsible for the sick. Casting a glance from his ashen face to the handkerchief, the brother suspected the worst. He informed the rector right away and called for medical help from the local hospital. A doctor arrived shortly after that with two paramedics. Father Kentenich had an acute hemorrhage. Pulmonary tuberculosis had broken out again, but the doctor initially guessed it was a "serious pneumonia."

Pale as a ghost, the patient was already lying on the stretcher when Joseph Fischer—who had in the meantime become the leader of the mission club and a committed collaborator toward the future Marian sodality—stormed into the room. "Father Spiritual Director, for goodness sake, what has happened to you?" Fischer was tough, but it was shocking for him to see his spiritual director lying on a stretcher.

Father Kentenich answered in a weak voice, "Joseph, I'm sick. I have to go to the hospital. But take care that the statutes get finished!"

Joseph nodded but could no longer make a sound. He stood there stunned, his eyes following the paramedics as they left. The bad news spread like wildfire among the students. A few of them stood at the windows, others outside, as the stretcher with their Father Spiritual Director was pushed into the horse-drawn carriage. One boy slipped into a little hiding place outside and cried bitterly. What a dark day, and it all started on Rose Monday!

A few confreres now hurried to see Father Provincial Kolb and advised him to remove Father Kentenich from his office as spiritual director because of his health condition. However, it was doubtful whether this was really only done out of concern for his health, because still that same year they sent a long letter of complaint to Father Kolb, fiercely criticizing the methods and pedagogical practices of the spiritual director.

The boys' pain and great concern about "their Father" paved the way to an inner transformation. Suddenly the house chapel was filled with students even during the day, whereas before, no one had ever seen them going there freely. They prayed from the bottom of their hearts that God would please let their Father Spiritual Director get better again. A few of the leaders, including Alfons Weber, were initially paralyzed. It was said that Father Kentenich's life was still in danger. Perhaps it was precisely this situation that drove the boys not to give up now but to complete the common work they had struggled so much for. They vigorously continued to work on the statutes. From time to time, Joseph Fischer marched into the Vallendar hospital to inform Father Kentenich of the newest state of affairs, to show him drafts of the statutes, or just to see him. Father Kentenich was impressed by the zeal and love of the boys. But he disagreed with the draft on one point. "No, the leadership of the Marian sodality, the 'magistrate,' should be solely responsible for decisions of admission. It should not be determined democratically by everyone. After all, the future magistrate is a body elected by the sodality members and must have not only special duties but also special rights! Moreover, if on principle everyone votes, candidates can easily be misjudged. Judgments are very easily made about others through mass suggestion! Majority alone doesn't necessarily guarantee the truth and correctness of something." Fischer listened attentively and passed on the spiritual director's thoughts. The rest of the boys, as well as Father Kaufmann, who by wish of the rector represented the spiritual director in matters of the Marian sodality, gave in to Father Kentenich's wish whether they liked it or not and even if they couldn't quite understand him on this point.

After a few weeks, Father Kentenich was transferred from St. Joseph's Hospital in Vallendar to the hospital in Bad Ems, where he underwent an operation. At that time there weren't many possibilities for therapy. One option consisted of surgically removing the tuberculous part of the lung. In order not to worry his mother, Joseph Kentenich didn't write anything to her about his illness until some weeks later, after the initial crisis had been overcome. She answered right away with a letter that he kept for the rest of his life:

March 24, 1914
Cologne

My dear child!

My goodness, how your letter astonished me! I had wondered back and forth about why I wasn't hearing anything from you. But I really never thought you might be sick. Just yesterday I thought: If I don't get a letter today, something must be up, or you are no longer in Vallendar. Then I decided to write to your superiors. But now your letter has come. I quickly went to see you in my thoughts, dear child, and consoled you—and then I cried myself to sleep about it. Yes, dear child, with outstretched arms I thanked the Sacred Heart of Jesus for your recovery. Anyone who has been so close to the threshold of eternity sees life with completely different eyes. And it will come for all of us one day. How good it is, then, to be prepared. Just do what your doctor says. You write that the bleeding will soon stop. Where did the blood come from? Thanks be to God that you are well cared for. If you like, I will come to visit you on Palm Sunday. Jettchen thinks you would prefer that we come to Vallendar as we had arranged, maybe during the Pentecost break. Jettchen says it's better if Joseph keeps resting for now. She thinks it's better for your recovery. So then, let's settle for Pentecost. Lately I have been constantly restless and I thought: No, you have no suffering at all. I am not used to that. Surely something will come up again soon.

Yes, we both want to give our lives to the dear God, which I will do for you in my daily Holy Communion. I thank the dear God that I have a good child. That makes me so happy. Happier than if someone would give me the whole world. Now, dear child, I wish you new strength and health ... If you have any wishes, please let me know. You know that I am always—always—here for you. Jettchen was with me today. And we had a visitor for lunch and tea. Otherwise I would have answered you sooner. Now I want to close.

With heartfelt greetings,
Your mother who loves you deeply

I warmly recommend you to God, St. Joseph, the holy Mother of God, and your venerable founder, and St. Peter.

P.S. Hopefully you will write again soon ... I sincerely thank all who have cared for you. May the dear God reward them all. Your mother.

After almost eight weeks, the boys could finally breathe a sigh of relief. They immediately began to plan for Father Kentenich to be present at the founding of the Marian sodality. March 25, the original founding day set by the provincial government, fortunately had to be changed, since the official approval from Trier hadn't arrived yet. By April 19, everything was set to go. Twenty-eight members gathered with Rector Wagner, who was supposed to be the president of the new Marian sodality. Father Kentenich gave the festive founding talk. *"Finally, finally we have reached our goal!"* He

Photo 8: Founding of the Marian sodality, April 19, 1914
(Father Wagner in the middle, Father Kentenich next to him, fifth from left)

spoke again about several objections from the side of the house and then about the future tasks that lay before them. "*Per Mariam ad Jesum! Through Mary to Jesus! This is the whole purpose of the sodality in a nutshell. Just as Mary brought the Savior to us, she also brings us to the Savior, and she knows no other concern, no greater concern, than to keep us in the most intimate union with him.*"

After the long talk, a group photo of the young sodality was taken in front of the St. Michael's chapel. In the front row, to the left and right of the rector and Father Kentenich, sat the newly elected members of the magistrate with their prefect, Joseph Fischer. Even a sodality banner had been donated, and each boy proudly wore his sodality medal on a "blue ribbon," which wasn't a problem anymore. In the statutes it still wasn't mentioned which meeting place the young sodality had chosen, but it wasn't by chance that the founding photo was taken in front of the St. Michael's chapel. Because of his illness, Father Spiritual Director hadn't been able to finish his discussions with Father Kolb officially, but ultimately Father Kolb had presented no further objections. Although there were also protests from the side of the teachers about this decision, Father Kolb obtained the permission of the provincial council during the summer and gave the little chapel to the young sodality. Then in June, the official confirmation of this meeting place arrived from Vienna.

Father Kentenich was indeed aware that there had been all kinds of frictions between the future Marian sodality members and their opponents, but he had let them fight it out. In this way their cause became something they had genuinely achieved. Now May was coming, the traditional month of Mary. Now it was highest time, he thought, to say something more about Mary. After all, they were now a Marian sodality. On the first Sunday of May, he began to bring Mary closer to them by sharing—already for the second time—about his early childhood experience in the house chapel of the Oberhausen orphanage, without revealing that he was speaking about himself. He explained to the students that Mary was really their Mother, *"not just an adoptive mother."* But his words about a childlike relationship with Mary didn't click very well with the boys. The next Sunday, Father Kentenich tried it from the perspective of relating to Mary as her knights, and the following Sunday he mixed both accents together. He clearly sensed their inner resistance. Therefore he spoke about the various difficulties and questions that were going through their minds and hearts. Although he had the impression after this May that he hadn't awakened any special interest in Mary among the boys, he didn't give up. In the younger classes, he was amazed to see how much zealous striving there was in a group of students gathered around Joseph Engling. Joseph Engling had wanted by all means to belong to the sodality and was very close to Mary. Already at the beginning of the year, Joseph Engling, from East Prussia, and his friend Karl Klement had formed an alliance with each other with the mutual promise to strive to become "modern saints." But they were still too young for the sodality.

In June, however, Father Kentenich noticed a peculiar change among the older ones, too. Bitter opponents of the Marian sodality like Max Brunner suddenly calmed down and ultimately became friends of the sodality. When the spiritual director dared to propose the possibility that a saint could also come from their sodality, as was the case in one of the first sodalities in Paris, none of them made faces of amusement anymore. Yes, truly, a peculiar transformation had been taking place in the boys since May. What had seemed unattainable despite all pedagogical efforts and well-chosen methods was now suddenly possible. The boys had caught fire for the ideal of holiness—and for Mary. They even walked through the streets of Koblenz proudly wearing their Marian medals, and the ridicule to their right and to their left honestly hardly bothered them. Even during their summer break they were active as apostles in their surroundings.

Whenever Joseph Kentenich was especially inwardly occupied with something, he loved to go out into nature. Deep in his thoughts, he strolled through the magnificently blossoming grounds. Had Mary herself touched the hearts of the boys? Had she perhaps given the impulse for this transformation by opening them more for religious things? Was she now beginning to unfold her educational strength in the boys just the way he himself had already experienced it in his own life?

He didn't have much time to think, because in the following weeks a devastating catastrophe befell "sleepwalking Europe" and its inexperienced monarchs and war-mongering military leaders, young and old, poor and rich. And this devastating tide also reached the House of Studies in Vallendar ...

Signs of the Times

July 31, 1914. In the morning, Rector Wagner assembled all the students in the dining hall with great apprehension and announced,

"Germany is standing before an imminent nation-wide mobilization. We are at war. Please immediately pack your things and get on the train as soon as possible. By tonight and tomorrow morning the trains will already be packed with soldiers. Go home." One student asked when school would start up again. "All of that is uncertain. It has been arranged with the government offices that in the event of war, the House of Studies should become a military hospital. But we're assuming that this war won't last long. You'll be notified when you can return."

Now every semblance of order disappeared. Students made a mad rush to go pack. They got their suitcases from the attic and provisions from the kitchen. They studied train routes and schedules ... Already the next day, the house was completely deserted. In Berlin, Kaiser Wilhelm II announced the full German mobilization from the balcony of the palace. Within a few days, in a kind of tragic chain reaction of political alliances, warring parties emerged, forcing into conflict even those countries that supposedly did not want a violent confrontation at all.

What now? Father Rector and other Pallottines immediately volunteered for "service to the fatherland." All together over the four years of war, 372 "imperial German Pallottines" served in the army, mostly as army chaplains and paramedics. But their seminarians who hadn't yet been ordained priests also served as armed soldiers, as did the brothers. Father Kentenich did not think much of the rampant war euphoria of his compatriots. For him, the war was clearly *"a consequence of sin."* The developments in Germany and the explosiveness of foreign affairs at that time had not escaped him unnoticed. Now he picked up every newspaper he could get his hands on. His greatest concern was for his boys, and not only because of the exterior dangers they would face. What would become of them, of everything they had conquered for themselves, if they now had to live in barracks and enter into the combats of war, defenselessly surrendered to the most varied influences? What would become of their newly flourishing sodality? Most of the members, called "sodalists," were already of age for military service.

The burden of responsibility that he felt for the boys impelled the spiritual director to go to the chapel. There he knelt with his face in his hands before the picture of the Mater Puritatis, the Mother of Purity, and prayed, "Mother, I can't be with them any longer, I can't console them, I can't protect them, I can't advise them. Now it's your turn! You must come! 'Show that you are our Mother whenever our need is the greatest.' Accept from my hands the responsibility for the education of the boys! You have the power to transform; you are the best educator. Now show what you can do. You have already proven it many times! You have so many possibilities ..." After a long prayer, he went back to his desk. The first letters the boys had written from their involuntarily long vacation had arrived. They told about all they had encountered at home, about everyone's surprise when they suddenly stood at the door, about their fathers and brothers who had already been drawn into the war, about the agitated mood or state of emergency in their hometowns—but also about their own thoughts and feelings. Many told about how they had tried to uphold their sodality ideals even in the changed circumstances. Father Kentenich answered each letter. Every line the boys wrote was important to him.

Joseph Fischer wrote to him often. He longed for nothing more than to be freed from military service and now—after graduation—to be able to start the novitiate, or at least not to have to serve as an armed soldier. After all, that didn't fit to someone who wanted to be a priest! He would have preferred, if anything, to serve as a paramedic. Other sodalists from Vallendar were already in the military barracks or on their way to the Western Front in freight trains. Barely eighteen years old, they had been overtaken by the horrors of a cruel war which was beyond anything they could have previously imagined. By October, when the first transports of the seriously wounded already came rolling back home, there were no enthusiastic crowds at the train stations anymore, holding flower bouquets and waving hats. The first war euphoria had given way to disillusionment, and any hopes for a rapid end to the war had gradually been buried. From the beginning, Father Kentenich didn't believe it would be a blitzkrieg limited to a particular region. He saw the real threat of an all-encompassing world fire. In an answer to a letter from Joseph Fischer at the beginning of September, he already wrote of a *"world war."* In his concern for the boys who had become so dear to him, the only refuge he found was in the person of the Blessed Mother and in the chapel before the tabernacle, where he knew the Lord was always present.

In the afternoons, Father Kentenich normally went from his office to the library, where several newspapers and magazines could be found lying around on the table. One day, he picked up the German newspaper *Allgemeine Rundschau* [*General Review*] and leafed through it, skimming the headlines. "A City of Life on a City of the Dead." That sounded promising somehow. As he began to read, it suddenly piqued his interest. It was about a lawyer who had actually been a non-believer, a materialist, and a freemason, and who then converted. By way of prayers and sacrifices, he erected a pilgrimage place on the ruins of the ancient city of Pompeii—of all things, the valley of Pompeii, which had been tragically destroyed in antiquity by the eruption of Mount Vesuvius! And now, each year, many thousands of people made pilgrimages to this place—which had become a Marian pilgrimage place only through the trustful praying of the rosary.

Father Kentenich laid the newspaper aside. He went to the window and looked down at the small St. Michael's chapel in the valley. In the beginning, Father Kolb had presented all kinds of reservations about using the chapel as a meeting place—that it was too far away, and it was dirty and neglected. Ever since it was no longer used for sacramental purposes, Brother Gardener had been keeping his garden tools there. But in the end, the provincial superior had given in, also since he felt a little honored—after all, the chapel was dedicated to his patron and namesake, St. Michael. Yes, Father Kolb had even prompted some minor renovations and had a St. Michael statue brought from Limburg which henceforth found its place of honor on the carved wooden altar. What Joseph

Kentenich had just read continued to work in him. A Marian pilgrimage place had come into existence in the valley of Pompeii, based only on a human commitment to prayer and on the initiative of this lawyer, Bartolo Longo. Many conversions took place there. People changed their lives after going there. What if God also wanted something like this here? What if Mary would let herself be "*drawn down*" through prayer and sacrifice? What if she wanted to unfold her motherly education even more from here—the education into *firm, free, priestly personalities* that he so desired for the boys? After all, God had selected the best Mother, and it wasn't for nothing that Jesus had commissioned her from the cross to be the Mother of all humanity. She was interested in being close to people. And what did she like to do more than form genuine Christians after the image of her Son? She would give the boys both security and moral and religious resilience in the midst of this difficult situation where what mattered was to show character and profile! Yes, she had to come and she would come! The spiritual director almost became frightened with these thoughts and quickly pushed them away.

But he couldn't dismiss them. They pressed themselves upon him ever anew and no longer let him go. Whenever he thought of the pilgrimage place in Pompeii, and of the boys, and of what was possible for Mary, how actively she had intervened in his own life, and what had taken place in the boys since May, the same questions filled his mind and heart. The thought was incredibly bold, and looking realistically at the situation, actually completely crazy. The little chapel looked like nothing special. The boys were far away, and they were just a handful of immature human beings. There were already plenty of sodality opponents in the house as it was. Besides, a war was raging—a war that showed its devastating and dreadful face more and more. Who knew whether the boys could ever even return to Schoenstatt? And if so, then it was not a matter of something transitory, a spontaneous, short-lived, peculiar idea, but a matter of far-reaching significance, also far beyond the bounds of the House of Studies, and maybe even beyond the bounds of the

Pallottine province?? The thoughts and questions went back and forth in his mind: But it was also precisely on the ruins of a "city of death" that new life had come about in Pompei. *"How often in world history have not small and insignificant beginnings been the source of great and greatest accomplishments? Why could that not also hold true in our case?"* he thought. A few weeks later he would repeat these exact words in his talk to the boys. Certainly, they were standing before the *ruins* of the newly flourishing sodality, but when he recalled the past history of the development of the young community, he had *"no trouble believing that Divine Providence has something special in store for it."* He would explain his thoughts just like this to the boys as soon as they were together again. *"Divine Providence!"* That sounded abstract, dry, a simple matter of theology. What he meant by it was the personal, loving guidance of God that reveals a hidden plan of wisdom. He firmly believed in it. This God who foresees everything with wisdom and love had led him through life.

Joseph Kentenich didn't confide his deliberations to anyone because it was all still a matter of groping and searching. He moved about on relatively unsteady ground. First, he had to be sure about whether his idea had originated in himself or whether God was behind it. The answer to this question was still long in coming. The intellectual risk seemed like a *death leap* into a dark abyss. His mind had absolutely no guarantee. But in the following weeks, an inner certainty gradually grew within him. "These constantly recurring thoughts don't come from me alone!" As crazy as it sounded, it seemed to him as if Mary herself, driven by compassion with such a battered and broken Europe, was knocking very softly and asking to be let in. And she was looking for shelter at such an inconspicuous place, precisely in Germany. She didn't reveal herself in an apparition or vision. She simply met him at the doors that God's providence was evidently opening to him through little signs and signals. What had been the object of a hard struggle for almost a decade during the years of Joseph Kentenich's studies now suddenly stood before his eyes as an overwhelming reality. We human beings are able to discern the will and guidance of God even without extraordinary apparitions and miracles. Now he paused in his thoughts. What were the boys likely to think of the whole idea? How would they react to it? Their reaction would be a very important indicator as to whether God really wanted all this ...

In the meantime, autumn had set in. It was the third week of September. More than 250 wounded soldiers from the Western Front had already arrived in the House of Studies, and the decision had been made: The provincial government wanted to start school again. The students would be divided into two groups again for reasons of space. This time, the two youngest classes would move to Ehrenbreitstein, and the older ones would move into the Old House. This would work as an emergency solution, but it was clear that it could only be temporary because the Old House was damp and cold, and space was tight. The boys would have to sleep on straw mattresses in the attic, without heating. The building authorities had even advised the Pallottines to tear down the dilapidated house. But it would work as a short-term temporary solution. Everyone was still naive enough to think that the war would end quickly with a lightning victory over France, and then one could calmly "concentrate" on the East.

It crossed Father Kentenich's mind that the boys' accommodations would be in direct proximity to the St. Michael's chapel, and he caught himself thinking of his *"favorite and secret idea"* again, as he called it. He continued to keep his considerations to himself. By no means did he want to disturb God's plans by acting rashly or talking too much. If, then God would have to open more doors—just like in Pompeii. He would have to communicate through the reaction of the boys. They were the key to his final security in this question! The moment to share it with them came closer. Joseph Kentenich didn't let a single night pass by without thinking about it. What kind of a daring adventure was he actually setting out on?

By the time the hour came for the boys to return, he had spent a long time struggling his way interiorly to a firm decision. He would proceed carefully, confiding his thoughts to them just once, while trying not to let the weight of his authority and influence bear down on them. Even more than with the founding of the Marian sodality, he wanted to step back and leave the boys as much space as possible to respond to this idea, dismiss it, or even completely ignore it ... As far as he knew them and their development, he was almost sure they *would make his plan their own,* if God willed it. And so he began drafting the talk that had been maturing for so long within him. He polished every sentence, crossed things out, added things, and then let it rest for some days before picking it up again. It was as if he sensed what a far-reaching significance this talk, which he planned to give at the first Sunday meeting of the sodality, would one day have.

Little by little, the first students trickled in and started preparing the Old House for the big move. Father Kolb ordered one of them to clean the little chapel, but the boy wasn't especially enthused. Most of the students had been informed that they were expected back by the middle of October. A few of the older ones were not able to come right away because they were still needed at home. Of the twenty-eight founding members of the sodality, only ten arrived in the end. *"The war has taken the best from us,"* Father Kentenich commented in his first talk after the twelve-week vacation. A few of the sodalists stood before the gates of the novitiate they had decided to enter; others were on hold for military service. Still others had already been drafted and were in boot camp training at one of the German military bases.

A Day like Any Other: October 18, 1914

The relatively small bunch of sodality members sat excitedly in the newly refurbished little chapel on this late Sunday afternoon of October 18, 1914. They were ready to listen carefully to the first words of their Father Spiritual Director after such a long time. A few "new ones" were also there; they would only become members of the sodality at the beginning of December. To their surprise, Father Kentenich didn't begin as usual with a look at the current situation of the times. He spoke no word about "the state of the nation," or the war, or what they were experiencing. He began by speaking about the joy they shared over the gift of the chapel and the fact that their sodality now had a home that should belong only to them, the *"small sodality family."* He praised the beautiful renovations. Then he purposely turned to the ideal of modern holiness. It would not be enough for a *"genuine sodalist"* to settle for mediocrity. Great times, as he had often explained to them, need great people. They had to give their all; no world could be redeemed with mediocrity. *"Each one of us must achieve the highest conceivable degree of perfection and sanctity according to his state of life. Not simply the great and the greater, but the greatest heights ought to be the object of our increased efforts."* Almost apologetically, he explained that he dared to *"express such an extraordinary challenge only in the form of a humble wish"* and continued, *"But if you want to know the reason for this wish, I must tell you of a favorite and secret idea of mine."*

And now he revealed the actual idea that had been on his mind for weeks. Alfons Weber suddenly listened up and looked over at Albert Eise, but he had his eyes closed. "Is he even getting what the spiritual director is saying here?"

Alfons noticed that Father Kentenich was firmly clutching the manuscript of his talk. He seemed to have meticulously worked it out. But neither Alfons nor any of the others understood how significant this talk would one day be. Although he was pretty tired from the long walk, he made an effort to follow the spiritual director's words. *"When St. Peter saw the glory of God on Tabor, he called out with delight: 'It is good for us to be here. Let us build three tents here.' These words come to my mind again and again. And I have often asked myself: Would it then not be possible for our little sodality chapel to likewise become for us the Tabor on which the glory of Mary would be revealed?"*

But what kind of glories was Mary supposed to reveal here? The spiritual director continued, calmly and dispassionately, but clearly engaged, *"Undoubtedly, we could not accomplish a greater apostolic deed nor leave our successors a more precious legacy than to urge our Lady and Queen to erect her throne here in a special way, to distribute her treasures, and to work miracles of grace."* Miracles of grace. What kind? Alfons could hardly believe his ears as Father Kentenich continued, *"You gather what I am aiming at: I would like to make this place a place of pilgrimage, a place of grace for our house and for the whole German province, and perhaps even further afield. All those who come here to pray shall experience the glory of Mary and confess: 'It is good for us to be here. Here we want to build our tents, here shall be our favorite place.'"*

Many thoughts crossed Alfons' mind. "A place of pilgrimage? Here? Not only for us but also for others? Not only now during the war years, but for coming generations? What gave Father Spiritual Director such an idea?" Alfons flipped his student's cap over and over again in his hands. "How is this supposed to work? Father Kentenich radiates so much security."

His voice revealed the firm conviction that they would go along. *"Even as I speak, my dear sodalists, I feel that I have struck the right note. Your hearts have caught fire. You have made my plan your own. With confidence I place it and its fulfillment into your hands and will not hesitate to enter it into our chronicle. Future generations may then pass their judgment upon us."*

Like many others, Alfons could hardly follow it all. He heard the comparison the spiritual director made—the calling of St. Joan of Arc, her modest way, and the commission God gave to her. He heard other examples of how God arranges everything and can use human beings for great things. Suddenly it almost seemed as if Father Spiritual Director lent his voice to Mary and spoke for her, in her name. Alfons' thoughts wandered elsewhere. At some point he began to pay attention again and suddenly became excited to hear what Father Spiritual Director was saying about the war, its disastrous consequences, and what God might want to say through it. *"Without sin, there would be no war. That is true in general, but it can also be especially proven beyond a doubt by the current genocide."* He called the war a *genocide* and so left no doubt that he saw it as a criminal injustice. No one else ever dared to speak that way. Alfons was amazed. The spiritual director didn't present Germany's opponents as enemies but as nations who were just as much at the mercy of the senseless murders as their own fatherland. He spoke of the "*unspeakable misery ... that the war [was] bringing upon the nations.*" He didn't sugarcoat anything. His depictions of the reality of war turned out to be pretty drastic. "*As the effect, so also the cause.*" He described this horrible war as the result of sin, an exaggerated desire for power, insatiable greed for prestige and honor, and the modern person's boundless arbitrariness and arrogance. As he saw it, the war was a visual aid for the consequences of turning away from God. It was a call to humanity. "*If we now succeed in reaping from this time of need the incredible religious benefit it could bring, it will become a real time of grace and of God. But if we let this great and downright decisive moment pass by unused, no other quite as favorable will recur in the foreseeable years to come ...*"

Joseph Kentenich's statements were not dominated by propagated images of the enemy, but by the question of the human person's ultimate destiny in God. The questions that moved him were not superficial: How will we win the war? Where have we chalked up victories in battle? How soon will the war end? His central question was: What does God want of us through this whole thing? At the very end, Father Spiritual Director came back to the one condition under which Mary would let them "*draw her down*" among them by "*gentle force*": "*In the end, no more doubts can prevail as to the intention Divine Providence is pursuing with us: the acceleration of our self-sanctification.*" With that, he came full circle in his thoughts. This seemed to be the new, extended program, as he wrote at the top of the manuscript of his talk: "*Program: Acceleration of the development of our self-sanctification as a means of transforming our chapel into a place of pilgrimage.*"

After the talk, the boys left the chapel somewhat bewildered. "Did I understand that right? Father Spiritual Director really wants to make our St. Michael's chapel into a place of pilgrimage?" For a long time, this question was the listeners' only reaction. Many who later became totally committed to the spiritual director's *"favorite idea"* and even offered their lives for it, like Joseph Engling, weren't even present on that day. The first one inspired by these thoughts to offer his life to God for the realization of this aim was the second prefect of the sodality, Franz Xaver Salzhuber, who was drafted into military service shortly after October 18.

The Time Thereafter

As a matter of fact, right after the talk everything remained very quiet. The young people were completely occupied with other things. They were pulled into everyday life and its extraordinary challenges. Life went on ... Out of love for Father Spiritual Director, they stopped their warlike drills and games in the courtyard. He had said in the talk that he wasn't very happy about them. Otherwise, no one uttered a single word more about the talk for months. Father Kentenich, too, kept silent—about his talk. Instead, he tried to continue encouraging the boys in their personality development, enthusing them to give a personal touch to their religious life and to make firm decisions in everyday life. In this regard, he liked a particular thought he had heard at the pedagogical conference in Donauwörth and now picked up on it. He inspired the boys to say private morning and night prayers, independently of the community prayers. He knew that the time would soon come when exterior cloister walls would no longer protect their religious and moral life, and then everything would depend on how much *"moral self-reliance"* they had acquired in this regard.

At the beginning of December, the next sodalists were admitted into the sodality. At the same time, a so-called "congregatio minor" was founded so that the younger ones, too, could cooperate. The contact with Father Spiritual Director intensified; it was precisely also the "long-distance members" away at war who sought his advice.

During the war years, more than 1,600 letters reached him. The young people wrote openly about everything they experienced in the barracks and on the front: the moral depravity and noble humanity they encountered, their own temptations and weaknesses in this line, their daily efforts to begin anew, the struggle to survive everyday life in the war, hunger, deprivations, miserable living conditions, the death of young comrades who had become dear to them, the dismembered corpses they had to gather and bury, the constant terror of cannons and grenades, and people dying to their right and to their left without their being able to do anything. All these experiences were written, so to speak, into the heart of their Father Spiritual Director, who accompanied them from Schoenstatt. Many wrote about experiences that only confirmed the advice Father Spiritual Director had once given to them. How quickly all stuck-on forms and customs, every sense of value and nobility, crumbled away if they had not grown and been cultivated within, and with how little resistance some were inclined to adapt and submit to the character of their surroundings. They were struck by the disparaging talk and the way many lowered their standards as soon as they were forced into the primitivity of the trenches. In the struggle for their very existence, even seminarians had thrown their ideals and religious convictions overboard. They encountered a *mass humanity* in which individuals stopped thinking and deciding for themselves—a bandwagon behavior that posed no more questions and questioned nothing. Father Spiritual Director had warned them about this from the beginning.

Many of the Schoenstatt sodalists were urged all the more to prove their moral self-reliance and remain true to themselves. They fondly recalled their sodality. They longed for Schoenstatt, which had become a real home for them. How hard it was for many of them to have to pass through Koblenz by train on their way to the Western Front without being able to speak with Father Kentenich or visit the little chapel that had become dear to them.

But in the midst of the horrible chaos, there were also joyful things to report: for example, that they were able to meet in twos or threes, or that they had succeeded in a small deed of self-conquest or an apostolic effort. They organized so-called "sodality days" at various places and held common discussions in small groups to mutually encourage one another. Father Kentenich was happy to see that a genuine sense of responsibility was growing among one another and for one another. While some had to face the harsh everyday war life, others at the boarding school felt like their "guardian angels" and began to represent them by praying for them in the little chapel and expressing their opinions at meetings. The "long-distance members" developed into the so-called "external organization," which included all who were attached to Schoenstatt's ideals, the little chapel, and the sodality, even if they didn't officially belong to the boarding school or had left. Through their apostolic efforts, individual sodalists began to win over students and some others who were interested and formed new groups that met regularly. It was important to them to win over collaborators for the aims that Father Spiritual Director had brought home to them and which they had made their own in their discussions. What especially set them on fire was the thought that they could really set something in motion just like the first German Marian sodality in Ingolstadt had done—to bring about a spiritual and moral renewal through faith. When Ferdinand Kastner was admitted into the sodality at the end of May 1915—the first one from the "external organization"—Father Kentenich gave a speech in which he articulated the idea, *"How would it be if the Ingolstadt of the Middle Ages would become a Vallendar of the modern times?"*

Just recently, in April, the sodality had received a copy of an Italian picture of Mary for the little chapel from one of the teachers who had found it in an antique shop in Freiburg and purchased it. Initially, nobody liked it—the somewhat "sweet" features of Mary didn't quite suit their taste, and what's more, it was a Madonna and Child. No, that's not how the boys had imagined the picture of Mary for their meeting place and their sodality. Not Father Kentenich, either, actually. But if "Divine Providence" had now placed this picture into their hands, then it must have somehow been the right one. Father Kentenich tried to help the boys find a connection to the picture by pointing out how it showed the special unity between Jesus and Mary, how the heart of the Child rested on the heart of his Mother, and how the glance of both was directed at "us" and the world. Both of them clearly had their sights set on us. The picture, which now hung in the middle of the sanctuary above the altar, while the statue of St. Michael the Archangel "reverently and politely" moved to the side, conquered their hearts little by little. It became precious to the boys. Soon they looked for a new name. The Italian painter, Luigi Crosio (1835-1915), had titled the original painting "Refuge of Sinners," but neither the boys nor Father Kentenich felt that it fit to the activity the Blessed Mother was to unfold from this little chapel. They recalled the movement of renewal started by Father Jacob Rem SJ (1546-1618), whose picture of grace had been titled "Mater Ter Admirabilis," "Mother Thrice Admirable." This gave rise to the wish to call their picture of Mary in Schoenstatt by exactly the same name. It quickly became a custom to use the abbreviation of the Latin version "MTA"—not of Ingolstadt, but "of Schoenstatt."

Father Kentenich observed with amazement the striving that had broken forth among the boys. One secretly polished another's shoes. Another waited respectfully when the horde of hungry fellow students swooped down on the jelly sandwiches at the morning snack. Whatever was left didn't look particularly appetizing anymore. Many studied very diligently and kept the house schedule faithfully—something that had caused them so many problems before. Even the teachers who had many things to criticize about Father Kentenich's pedagogy and the sodality were impressed because they only very rarely had to reprimand a boy now.

The boys visited the little chapel and the new picture of Mary more and more frequently, but the "long-distance members" also expressed their inner attachment. Some asked to be remembered there in a special way, while others sent Father Kentenich a photo of themselves, asking him to place it in the little chapel. The little chapel soon became a special attraction for them and the secret heart of their community. More and more they began to use the term "shrine" in their letters because they really believed they could sense the nearness of God and Mary in a special way. They accepted without complaint the harsh realities of the primitive lodgings in the Old House, where the bread was so scarce, the straw mattresses so uncomfortable, and the half-frozen water in their wash bucket every morning so ice-cold. Every little sacrifice counted! Every one became for them an expression of their love. They called them *"contributions to the capital of grace of the MTA."* Father Spiritual Director had told them about how the merits of their good works could benefit others. Youthful imaginativeness turned this into a "capital" into which deposits could be made; money was a daily table conversation topic because of the war bonds. The way they understood it, Mary was God's treasurer and so, just like the well-known world banks, had disposal over a large capital—an endless wealth of graces given to us by Christ through redemption. As genuine collaborators in the Kingdom of God, they wanted to help make this capital overflow for others, so to speak, through everything they gave their Mother in the shrine. Joseph Engling had begun with these contributions to the MTA's capital in May 1915. They could show the genuineness of their love by the things they were ready to give and sacrifice. Their prayers took on a different quality, partly because they were concerned for their comrades on the war front and their families at home. Love for Mary, for the shrine, and for Schoenstatt as a place, as well as the sense of responsibility for one another that grew among the Schoenstatt sodality members—intern and extern alike—unfolded new life that was completely original. And Father Spiritual Director remained the "soul of it all," as one of them expressed in a letter.

The boys in Schoenstatt were amazed to read the letters from those on the front. They told about how they tried to maintain their spiritual life amid the danger of death in the trenches, spending months at a time in miserable foxholes. They described their efforts to speak with others about their faith and to be there for their comrades in a spirit of fraternal love. The boys in Schoenstatt heard what Father Spiritual Director read to them from many letters. They listened intently to the reports of how their fellow sodalists out there fetched the food for their company even amid volleys of bullets and grenades, or how they ventured onto the battlefield under fire to assist at least one dying man and pray with him. It obviously didn't bother them when they were ridiculed for their faith or for attending holy Mass. Franz Xaver Salzhuber was even so bold as to ask his superior in front of the assembled troops if he could attend holy Mass—right after that same superior had gotten infuriated with another recruit. To the surprise of all, the master sergeant had responded, "Yes, you may go, but only on the condition that you also pray for me." In the end Franz Xaver was even allowed to go to holy Mass daily.

The mail unceasingly piled up on Father Kentenich's desk in the Old House, where he had moved in with the boys. He asked his mother and his cousin Henriette for help, and so the two of them sent knitted head warmers and earmuffs, kneepads, socks, and money "for his boys on the battlefield." Besides the many letters, Father Kentenich sent all kinds of care packages to the various war fronts in Europe. The boys had asked for rosaries, medals, books, and pamphlets for themselves but also for their apostolate. He also sent other things by way of the army postal service: ham, hard cheese, cookies, and tobacco products. When the quality of the cigars was not so great, the spiritual director apologized, saying that unfortunately he hadn't received any better ones lately. At the end of many letters he added the question, *"Do you have any other wishes I can fulfill?"* He was concerned about their wellbeing in an almost motherly way since he was often their only spiritual shelter amid the harsh realities of the war time. They utterly longed for a greeting from him. Every sentence he wrote became so precious to them that they kept his letters for many years afterwards. His pastoral care and educational guidance never ceased, even from hundreds of kilometers away.

Father Kentenich lost twenty-six pounds in the summer of 1915. His health was so poor that he had to go to the hospital in Dernbach. Meanwhile, he observed an unprecedented religious breakthrough in his boys. Many developments could no longer be explained in purely natural terms. The Holy Spirit seemed to be inspiring the boys. The spiritual director finally made the decision, "They have to know more about each other and support each other mutually!" In the spring of 1915, he had already begun to copy individual personal reports in circular letters with the sender's permission. But that was obviously not enough. In March of the following year, Father Kentenich started a little magazine called the *MTA*. Its subheading read, "Mutual inspirations in the struggle for our threatened ideals in a difficult time." Many things, especially the feature article, were written by him personally or by one of the sodality leaders. But the main part consisted of excerpts from letters, which helped the magazine—soon read by outsiders, too—to quickly reach a total of 1,000 copies in circulation, and by the following year, 2,000 copies. Dr. Arnold Rademacher, theologian and professor from Bonn, heard about it and collected individual issues. In a talk for religious educators, he called "Schoenstatt"—as the young movement was called from then on—an "outstanding case." Other sodalities subscribed to the *MTA*, while the boys' own Pallottine community in Limburg forbade their novices from reading it. But such resistance did subside again. At the beginning of August 1918, the general superior informed the rector in Schoenstatt that they were again permitted to send the *MTA* to the novices and students.

The magazine was a true spiritual and moral support for the young movement, which through the "long-distance members" had long gone beyond the protecting walls of the Pallottine Seminary in Vallendar, also organizationally. At the same time, the magazine was a valuable means of apostolate. It was no surprise that the new life within it didn't only appeal to seminarians or interested soldiers. At the military hospital in Mons, Belgium, Franz Xaver Salzhuber met the young countess Gertraud von Bullion, who had volunteered to help with first aid. At the weekly choir rehearsals in the military hospital, she noticed the young men who gathered for group evenings with Salzhuber. They impressed the countess above all by the radiance of their personality. Gertraud von Bullion became curious and turned to the young lieutenant with her questions. Readily and with interest, he not only tried to satisfy her curiosity but also suggested working in a similar way with the young women. He gave her written materials to read for this, including the *MTA*. This soon wasn't enough for her. She wanted to get to know Schoenstatt as a place and the young founder Father Kentenich at close range.

During these years after the significant talk of October 18, Father Kentenich was in such high demand that one of the leaders in Schoenstatt wrote to Joseph Fischer, "I'm amazed at how well he has managed it so far. The leadership of two sodalities, the office of spiritual director, the direction of the magazine, the extensive mail correspondence with the students who are away—these are no small things." Father Kentenich was active not only on an inspirational level but also organizationally. In a letter to Albert Eise in August 1916, he presented an organizational plan for the "external organization" that divided the growing groups into sections and districts by regions. He himself frequently felt physically weak during this time and had to struggle with a lot of opposition.

In 1915, when the general superior of the Pallottines made it known via third parties that he wanted to ban the Marian sodality because many objections had been brought to him, Father Kentenich followed him all the way to the train station to ask him not to carry out the threatened ban. Outraged, Father General responded, "I can no longer answer to our founder for what you are pursuing."

Humbly but resolutely, Father Kentenich answered, "But I can!"

The general superior was speechless but also impressed at the same time. The ban never happened. From then on, Father Kentenich studied intensively wherever he could get his hands on material about Vincent Pallotti and his intentions and teachings. He tried to prove how much the emergent movement corresponded to

Pallotti's actual apostolic aim. *"Difficulties are tasks!"* These words became not only the guiding motto that the spiritual director had passed on to the boys, but also more and more his own principle of life. The tenacity and persistence with which he pursued these tasks were connected with the unique divine commission he sensed within himself and which he could not evade.

As he studied Pallotti, he realized with astonishment how much the founder's original intentions, which had largely been forgotten, were consistent with the development of the young Schoenstatt Movement. He now tried to point out this consistency on various occasions and to illustrate how much the young Schoenstatt Movement had been guided by the Holy Spirit. Over the course of the years, a number of Pallottines subscribed to this conviction.

During these founding years—from 1912 on—Father Kentenich experienced himself as an instrument in the hands of another. In 1914, he wrote among his few diary notes, *"I feel so much now like the administrator of Our Lady's goods."* This awareness that he actually no longer belonged to himself became deeper in him. There was no time left at all for him to think much about his own physical constitution or state of health. His superiors sent him to various recuperation places where he was able to work more peacefully. In 1917, he was supposed to spend some weeks in Kolberg, on the Baltic Sea, to remedy his tuberculosis and its long-term effects once and for all. He wrote from there to his former prefect Fischer, *"I'm here until the end of the break in order to freshen up my nerves a bit. They have been strongly worn down. My concern for all of you simply presses hard upon me and far exceeds my strength."* He had already written to Fischer in April of the same year, *"Our endeavors have become a movement that draws ever larger circles. I've been toying with the thought of asking Reverend Father Provincial for some help. ... The work has doubly and triply outgrown me."* His petition was granted. Father Schneider became one of his first collaborators from the ranks of his confreres. He mainly took charge of the entire editing of the *MTA* Magazine. Father Kentenich's ailing health was also the reason why he only had to complete one week of military service as an orderly in Trier after having been drafted in the fall of 1916. Due to his lung condition, he was dismissed as "unsuitable for service."

Father Kentenich devoted himself to the matters of the young movement in such a way that he hardly had a private life anymore. During his retreat in 1917, he noted, "*Meanwhile, the dear God and my heavenly Mother seem to have chosen me to be their instrument in a way that makes my weak nature utterly tremble.*" Wasn't he actually completely unsuited for the great task that stood before him? His diary was the witness of his critical self-inventory: "*My health is weak, my appearance clumsy and awkward—a consequence of education and nervousness. My knowledge is insignificant, both my general education as well as my classical formation. All in all, I lack the most necessary natural prerequisites, and I lack the time and opportunity to acquire them because of the enormous amount of work.*" Questions stirred within him. "*Is it not madness to adhere to the plans? What a contented, peaceful, and yet priestly life you could live if you kept to your actual office, that of spiritual director, and gave up everything else. You could care for your health, enrich your knowledge, and move around more easily in society.*" But none of that was decisive for him because someone else was doing the deciding ... "*And still, if the dear God and our heavenly Mother want to use you—at least until someone more useful appears on the scene who can keep working energetically. 'Here I am, Lord; send me where you will!'*" This disposition increasingly marked his self-understanding. The experience of limitations didn't keep him from continuing along his way. But in all important questions and decisions, he involved his provincial superior, Father Kolb—whether it was a matter of the founding of the mission club, the Marian sodality, or a circle of seminarians in 1916. He wrote to Joseph Fischer about this, "*The seminarians are getting interested. I also consulted Father Provincial. He would be happy if a sodality for seminarians would come into being.*"

Father Kentenich didn't only stay in Schoenstatt. He attended conferences and courses in Düsseldorf, Cologne, and Bonn, and made new connections everywhere. In many places, people were becoming aware of the young Schoenstatt Movement and what was spreading from this little spot in the valley of Vallendar. But more than big numbers, what mattered to him was what was happening in individual souls through the contact with the shrine. Joseph Engling was one of the ones who followed every inspiration of his spiritual director in a special way. He had written in his diary, "I want to become a saint through my spiritual director." He became a kind of "model" of *"the idea of the new person in the new community"* for the young Schoenstatt Movement.

It must have been shortly after October 4, 1918, when Alfons Weber came storming into Father Spiritual Director's office to bring him the shattering news: "Joseph fell in Cambrai."

Father Kentenich stood quietly for a while at the window and looked at the little shrine. Then he said softly, hardly audible, *"Now the sodality has its first saint!"* He had closely experienced this boy's development for too long and too intensively not to notice the workings of God's grace in him and through him. He closed his eyes. This farewell had been hard for him with each of his fallen boys; he had grown so fond of all of them. But Joseph was one of the supporting pillars of the young movement. Father Kentenich went to his desk, opened the drawer, and pulled out the last personal dedication prayer that Joseph had sent him from Flanders in 1918. He unfolded the sheet of paper and read once more, deeply moved, what Joseph had formulated in this prayer: "Dispose over me and what is mine completely as it pleases you. But if it can be reconciled with your plans, let me be a sacrifice for the tasks you have given to our sodality." Joseph would become a glowing example for many who followed him.

Years Pass–Life Blossoms

Years had gone by. Father Alexander Menningen, formerly a student in the House of Studies and now a young Pallottine Father and one of Father Kentenich's closest collaborators, had settled down on a bench right next to the founder. He cast a sidelong glance at him. He had known this man since he was twelve years old, and this man knew him like hardly any other. How much he owed to this priest, like so many others from their ranks! "He looks like a Jewish rabbi—with his long beard and the black hat on his head!" thought Alex Menningen, amused. For about ten years, Father Kentenich had let his beard grow. "Did he perhaps want to look more mature or keep himself warm?" thought Alex further. Involuntarily, both men now looked in the same direction, from the little shrine in the valley to the opposite hillside, where the large retreat house, also called "Bundesheim [Home of the Federation]," had been finished one year earlier. The blossoming movement had needed space. The ongoing courses for priests and seminarians, the conferences for students and university graduates, and the many talks and seminars held by Father Kentenich for hundreds of interested attendees required a house set aside for this.

"So much has come about since October 18, 1914!" Father Kentenich looked into the distance, lost in thought.

Alex Menningen nodded. "I can still remember when I came here in 1924 during my studies in Rome and Ferdinand Kastner called the talk of October 18 the 'Founding Document' of the movement for the first time. Back then I was filled with indignation. Founding Document? I thought, 'That fits to the talk of April 19 at the founding of the Marian sodality!' But you said Kastner was right! Then why was it only in 1919 that you published the talk of 1914?"

"At that time, the war had just ended. There were many political and economic ruins left behind in Germany, but also spiritual ones. No one had any idea how the dice would fall after the forced abdication of the emperor. There were no more letters from daily life in the war that could have been published in the *MTA*. The situation of the times demanded a new orientation. I then tried to interpret the signs of the times in the *MTA*. What had actually been our guiding idea since 1914? How had we been led? By 1919, I was sure that Mary had accepted our offer. And I published the first main part of the talk under the heading *'Views from the Heights.'* At that time, contact with one another remained possible only through the *MTA*. It circulated everywhere."

The situation in Germany after World War I made him realize more and more what he had formulated in the *MTA* in December 1918: *"In a democratic state, we as Catholics will have to get much more accustomed to representing and asserting our demands before the general public by ... means of a well-developed organizational method. We just may not overlook one warning sign as we do so. Christianity esteems and values the soul of the human person above all else. It bears the motto on its brow: 'What profit is there for one to gain the whole world and forfeit his soul?' This measure must be ours, too. That's why our work may not disintegrate into a restless hustle and bustle of outward activity—otherwise our own soul becomes merely outwardly oriented and impaired. Our collaboration must flow from the right spirit. To be sure, the right spirit is best acquired and cultivated through attention to detail and individual influence. If the individual members are healthy, the whole organism will be, too. It will become more resilient and proficient. So, the call to move and organize the masses may not completely drown out the call for attention to detail, otherwise we will have a body without a soul, an ugly monster."*

After the war, the long-distance members urgently needed an organizational entity beyond the Marian sodality that would work precisely in this direction—with a special community structure and personalities capable of leadership who could receive continuing formation in it. But the question as to how this could be concretely implemented was initially left open. Over time, the idea began to take on more precise contours in Father Kentenich's thinking. He waited and observed what took place in the individuals. One of the long-distance members wrote to him in December 1918, "Your sodalists must have returned home by now. A burning question arises for us who aren't in Schoenstatt and weren't educated there: ... What will become of our organization? Will it continue to exist as it is, take on a different form, or be dissolved?" The long-distance members decided to meet in Schoenstatt and ask him to give them a retreat in January. But this was extremely difficult due to the war conditions. Besides, he wouldn't have considered it a lasting solution! New groups formed starting in April 1919. In the summer, Father Kentenich was relieved of his office as spiritual director in order to be completely free for his work with the movement. Since his health still wasn't good, his superiors sent him to Engers, where, in addition to the movement work, he was supposed to offer little services as the chaplain of the convent of the Waldbreitbach Franciscans and also recuperate a bit. The sisters received him there as "a doomed man." But the work continued. He initiated individuals into his fundamental goals and intentions and did indeed find *"kindred spirits with whom and through whom the organization"* he *"had in mind could be founded."* When a "Sodalists' Day" for all who were connected with Schoenstatt was organized in Dortmund-Hörde, he canceled his attendance at the last minute. If they really wanted the organization as he envisioned it, they should decide for it freely and advance the cause themselves. He had sufficiently chipped in by helping with opinion formation behind the scenes.

Father Menningen interrupted his thoughts. "The 'Apostolic Federation of Schoenstatt' was founded in Dortmund-Hörde in August 1919. Exteriorly, you weren't there, but many of the leaders told me that you were quite present in spirit."

"Yes, through those *'kindred spirits'*! With that, Schoenstatt had grown beyond the House of Studies and the Marian sodality!"

Father Kolb became the sponsor of this Apostolic Federation, which initially only consisted of men, and placed the shrine and the Old House at the disposal of the new organization, "the federation." But long and heated discussions would still be needed as to what the actual goal of this "federation" should be. The current situation of the times raised the first question: "Shouldn't we commit ourselves politically or socially?" However, little by little, Father Kentenich's deeper intention, and one that would be more sustainable for the future, became crystallized. In a time in which monarchies throughout Europe were being pushed back and replaced by democracies, decisions would no longer be made from above by one single head, but determined by the majority through elections. He saw both forms of government as God-willed, but democracy required a type of person who also had to be equipped for it. So for him, much depended on whether a corresponding spiritual and above all moral elite would be there to positively influence the majority ratio of the masses, and whether people who were supposed to vote freely would also be correspondingly educated and formed toward an ability to make decisions. He believed that in the future more than ever before, personalities would be needed across the board. Therefore the newly founded Apostolic Federation composed the formulation, "Education of formed lay people in the spirit of the Church through the striving for the greatest possible holiness according to one's state in life." This meant nothing else than the cultivation of a profiled, credible Christianity through a new type of community of leaders!

Father Kentenich vividly recalled all these events and continued the conversation. "We always adhered to the goal of *'free, firm personalities' out of an inner sense of responsibility for the world.*"

Alex Menningen leaned back. "After the war, everybody talked about reforms and how everything had to be made new, but mainly with purely exterior means!"

Father Kentenich added, "That stood in complete opposition to the intention we had from the beginning. It was 'the false cultivation of the exterior life to the neglect of the inner life.' For me, it's always a matter of the *cultivation of our inner world,* the *microcosm,* and from there, the transformation of society. Here is the spot," and Father Kentenich pointed to his heart, "where you can accomplish the most—the world that you can and must change first. Wherever there are credible Christians capable of leadership, the world can be changed in every aspect, whether in politics or economics, culture or education. The prerequisite for the renewal of society is not a revolution, but the development of genuine personalities."

"But they don't fall from the sky!"

"And that's why the federation, as a community of leaders, wants certain duties for its members. Those who belong to the federation must practice systematic personality formation, keep a spiritual daily order, and try to work seriously on themselves through their personal ideal and personally composed resolutions."

"But for many people who appreciate Schoenstatt, the shrine of the Mother Thrice Admirable, and the pedagogical ideas, obligations of this kind are pretty hard to meet."

"Well, that's why the 'Apostolic League' has existed since 1920. People have social inclinations that vary in strength. Therefore we need various forms of commitment as a means to the maturation of the personality. There are people who definitely reach out for the highest ideals but who can't unfold with obligations that are too strong. They feel too constricted."

"Both organizations, but especially the league, carry the lifestream and ideas of Schoenstatt into the widest possible circles of the Church and society."

"Yes, but one thing remains central for both forms of community: '*What our time needs most, if not exclusively, are new saints—great, convincing, captivating saints—and if not saints, at least new persons, whole persons, new Christians, true, perfect Christians from within. From the very beginning, we chose not to be a movement of the masses. We must adhere to this. Otherwise our little troop could easily be misled into wrong and discouraging conclusions and decisions. The demands we make are so far-reaching that relatively few will decide to persevere faithfully with us.*"

"Now come on," replied Father Menningen skeptically, "there aren't *that* few of us! The movement has grown quite a bit. Isn't it also a disadvantage to work only on a small scale, precisely in a time in which mass movements are gaining such an influence? If I think of the women's movement, the youth movement, the socialist movement ..."

"Yes, that's possible! But initially it depends on each individual Christian. We have always worked in small cells and groups and spread the word from person to person. That could one day be very beneficial to us if the political situation would change. Think of the Nazi Brownshirts and how they operate among the masses! Who knows what might still come upon us! I'll admit, it does take a lot of courage to do detail work, to take small steps. But if we don't forget the world at large and the vastness of our mission as we do so ..."

Alex Menningen recalled some words written by Father Kentenich in one of the magazines at the end of 1919: *"I must honestly confess to you that sometimes in quiet hours I tremble before the work we have undertaken. But the thought of our heavenly Mother and a wholehearted trust in her quickly and completely drives away all dark clouds. Peaceful contemplation of the developments thus far justifies the conclusion that our Mater Ter Admirabilis wants to use us for the renewal of the world."* "Tremendous words, the renewal of the world!"

"Alex, from the very beginning we bore within us a great sense of responsibility for the world. How important it would be—in the spirit of Vincent Pallotti—to unite the many different apostolic forces and align ourselves with one another! In the shrine Mary offers everyone a source of strength for this. For me, the shrine is the key to interiority, but also to world apostolate."

"You really dared a lot!"

"We, Alex! I didn't do anything without all of you. And we confidently 'built our cities on the edge of Vesuvius,' as Nietzsche expressed it. We are children of war! The Work was born during a war, and we will always remain children of war, surrounded by dangers and accustomed to battle. *'If no more battles come, that will be the best proof that we have fallen short of our task.'*"

"By the way, you have now sparked a lot of bewilderment among the Schoenstatters by saying that in the shadow of this shrine the destiny of the Church will be co-determined for decades and even for centuries."

"Oh, Alex, that can only be understood by those who have followed the developments of the time and the history of our movement. And by those who understand that things also have to be formulated provocatively to awaken life."

"Aha, so you only meant that pedagogically?"

"No, I mean it seriously. I am firmly convinced that God expects great contributions from Schoenstatt for the inner renewal of the Church and for building bridges between the Church and society, between clerics and lay people, between religious orders and people living in the world. You will see, the future will show what a gigantic initiative Mary wants to take from her little shrine. ... But don't we have to go?" Father Kentenich pulled out his watch and unclasped the cover marked with an image of Christ's head crowned with thorns. No, there was still time.

Meanwhile, Alex Menningen looked at him intently again and thought, "Where did this man get such security? How can he assert things that then really do happen? Isn't there something prophetic about him?" A question was now on the tip of his tongue, something that had been on his mind for some time already. It was the right opportunity. "Father, there's still something else—the question of women in our movement."

Father Kentenich smiled. He sensed where his co-worker was going with that. "You are surely thinking of what the Jesuit Father Horstmann said at the conference in Bernkastel, that it was a disastrous development that women wanted to join the Apostolic Federation, and that the federation would perish because of the 'question of women.'"

"Actually, no, that's not what I was thinking of just now!"

"You know, back when Gertraud von Bullion came to Schoenstatt shortly after the war and asked to be accepted into the federation, I initially hesitated. Today I am happy that I followed the signs of Divine Providence."

"In 1920, she and Maria Christmann became the first women to seal their dedication in the federation. It's true—the women's movement grew quickly and works fruitfully. One has to admit that. The members, whether federation or league, represent something—they are remarkable women. But the Sisters of Mary, when I look at some of them ...? Father, don't take me wrong, but when I think of mature women, I imagine something different! If I think of my mother ...!"

"Alex, wait and see! What grows slowly, grows well. What you consider immature is perhaps childlike and original, an important foundation for every personal relationship to God, also for men. The motherly maturity you miss in them will come with time. Think how quickly the community has grown in just three years—there are already almost 200 members in twenty houses."

Already at the beginning of the 1920s, it was clear to Father Kentenich that the Schoenstatt Work needed women who would work full-time for Schoenstatt. The first ones, mostly teachers, came in 1926, including Emilie Engel and her colleague Anna Pries, the first general superior. Both of them had been willing to give up their secure profession, a courageous decision. On Father Kentenich's part, too, the founding was a daring venture. Very soon the first ones were sent out as family assistants, parish workers, and social workers. As far as the organization of the community was concerned, nothing had simply been decided in advance from on high. Father Kentenich let the sisters formulate their own name and their own community rules—or constitutions, as he called them. According to their own wish, they tailored a common dress for themselves—not actually a habit, but something corresponding more to the style of the time. He let them search for their own community ideal, draft their own daily schedule, and determine times and places of silence. The idea of silence had just recently come up. So far, many things were still a hopeless mess, at least that's how it seemed to Father Menningen—but he had nothing to say. Father Kentenich tolerated no meddling in the life of individual communities in Schoenstatt. He didn't want uniformity. So actually, none of this was really his business ...

"You know," Father Kentenich now interrupted his own thoughts, "I would like a new type of community, but they were founded only three years ago. You can't expect too much yet!"

"You dedicate a lot of time to them!?"

"Look, Alex, it's the first community of this type. I'd like to accompany them and train them as much as possible. Then we'll have a model for the '*new person in a new community*.' If that succeeds, Alex—"

"But you still have no legal status for them within the Church," Alex interrupted. "They're not supposed to be a religious order in the traditional sense—they don't take vows!"

"The times and the Church need something new ..."

Pallotti hadn't wanted vows. Father Kentenich had drawn far-reaching consequences from this as the founder of the new community. He wanted only *"free rowers,"* members who made an inner decision for their vocation and their goals. Already early on, he sent the first Sisters of Mary to study at universities, where women were still something new. They should stand *"out in the world"* and get to know it well, *"but without being worldly"*! What he envisioned had no real model in the Church yet and therefore no legal basis, either. "We'll have to wait and see. God will show how it will continue."

Father Kentenich called many of his sisters to mind. Yes, the community had really developed well already in a short time. Many were on the way to becoming genuine, mature personalities, even if this wasn't visible to the outside right away. Sister Emilie Engel was the assistant of the general superior. Despite her excessive anxiety, he hadn't shied away from giving her positions of leadership. She took her tasks very seriously and showed unusual persistence in striving. She had asked him in a letter if she could offer her life for the holiness of the young community. On the other hand, the one who made him worry a bit was the general superior, Sister Anna Pries. Had he done the wrong thing by putting her in this position? He had noticed her great capacities, her friendly and empathetic way of being, her organizational talent, and her genuineness. He saw her "refreshing naturalness" as well as the "human sincerity with which she conquered hearts"—in the words of one of the members of the general government. They had also made some critical remarks about her. Some of the sisters quietly complained about Sister Anna. When she told everyone that the deceased Maria Sauer, whom everyone admired, had appeared to her, he hadn't taken it too seriously. They were all still young, and which of them already knew how to govern such a new type of community? "As much as I can, I want to help her settle into her office as general superior and into her motherly tasks. Everything takes time. I need to be patient," he quietly thought to himself. "When things have come so far, I'll step back more and more from the leadership of the community as I did with the federation."

"And will the Church understand such a type?" Father Menningen picked up the thread of the conversation once more. He knew from the time of his studies that Rome wasn't exactly interested in new things ...

"I want to wait until Schoenstatt has developed even more, and then I will present it as a whole to the official Church. That's why I have already visited several of the German bishops."

"It sure was a great honor that Bishop Bornewasser of Trier officiated at the dedication of the Bundesheim!"

Father Kentenich nodded. "Yes, an honor. But what mattered to me was to present Schoenstatt to the bishop. In my address I deliberately expressed the invitation, also to our Pallottine Fathers, to join the Apostolic Movement in newly taking up Pallotti's original concept out of faith in the efficacy of the Blessed Mother in her shrine."

"That is a totally new beginning and a great chance for us as Pallottines, after our venerable founder died so early. ... Oh, now it really is time!" The shrine bell in the valley was ringing for the midday Angelus prayer. Both of them stood up. "The angel of the Lord declared unto Mary ..." They walked down the mountain heading toward the Bundesheim, taking turns praying the lines of the old prayer. They had to hurry because they were expecting some priests for the noon meal.

One of the many conversations between Father Kentenich and his young co-worker and confidant could have gone something like this, looking back over the past ten years.

The time thereafter was marked by Joseph Kentenich's countless talks, retreats, conferences, and individual conversations. He traveled across Germany, sometimes only to visit one single priest or a small house of the Sisters of Mary, or to make further connections with bishops and other Church representatives. The more his workload increased, the more his physical resilience

Photo 9: Father Joseph Kentenich, 1933

seemed to be strengthened. He dedicated himself all the more to the mission he sensed God had placed within him. He sought to fulfill it whether it was convenient or inconvenient—to some. In the meantime, critical questions had been voiced within the Church in Germany. It was simply unusual that a spiritual movement was growing and gaining such influence in the Church without having been initiated by the bishops or official Church authorities. There were many associations, and those could be integrated, but ecclesial movements? What kind of a thing were they? Schoenstatt was a trailblazer in Germany. Every trend of spiritual renewal was intially viewed with skepticism, since the Church had experienced aberrations and feared them. But official sources also gave positive feedback about this young Schoenstatt Movement. Father Kentenich gave pedagogical conferences all over Germany and was invited as a popular speaker in various circles. The general secretary of the Catholic Young Men's Association wrote to him in 1932, "There were 320 participants at the pedagogical conference—incredible, but glorious! This is something new in Church history." The chronicle recorded that from 1919 to 1932, Father Kentenich gave almost 400 conferences and retreats, not to mention more than 530 individual talks and speeches on the side and countless visits and conversations. The Schoenstatt Movement's sphere of activity expanded year by year.

From the beginning of the 1930s, Father Kentenich increasingly traveled across Germany, even when his superior Father Kolb expressly warned him to look out more for his health, advising him not to accept every request. Concerned, he wrote to him in a letter, "If you collapse before your time has come, who will take over the leadership of the Work?"

However, Father Kentenich didn't spare himself. He visited almost every one of the young federation priests newly assigned to a parish. Several times this meant long journeys by foot, up to eight hours alone from Zwiefalten to Ennabeuren in the Swabian Alps, amid great heat in the summer and icy cold weather during the winter. A Schoenstatt priest, Father Kulmus, reported from this time, "Father Kentenich sent his sincere, fatherly congratulations ... to us young 'federationers' for our priestly ordination. He was with us in all his thoughts, with all the love of his fatherly heart, with his prayer and sacrifice, with his words and example. He gave neither himself nor us any rest ... and waited for our letters about our first priestly activities in the care of souls. ... He looked for us personally.

One time Father suddenly and unexpectedly appeared at my rectory. He wanted to know how I was doing and how I was managing everything. I was completely beside myself at so much fatherly care. ... Once he came to us in the Alps and was utterly exhausted from so much work and the long trip. He settled down on the wicker chair in the rectory living room and said to me, *'My strength has been spent to the last drop.'* Even so, he was and remained the sunniest person and priest we ever encountered."

In addition to the large conferences, retreats, and many talks, Father Kentenich intensively accompanied the beginnings and growth of his Schoenstatt communities. In addition to the priests, there were also the women's federation, the men's and women's branches of the "Apostolic League" that also included the two communities of youth, seminarian groups, student groups, and the Sisters of Mary. As the movement director, he also had tasks in the core leadership circle, the closer team of collaborators later nicknamed "King Arthur's Round Table" to camouflage it from the Gestapo. Beyond that, Father Kentenich was available for the many people who came to Schoenstatt or who randomly met him on his travels. But he also knew how to delegate tasks and so to awaken and cultivate leadership talent. The young Schoenstatt Movement grew and came into contact with the most varied circles in society and the Church. At the same time, dark, ominous clouds appeared on the horizon. Father Kentenich noticed them and they no longer left him in peace. The brown cloud of National Socialism was spreading all over Germany. Who would be able to tame this volcano?

5. Nazi Power and Secret Resistance

Joseph Kentenich saw National Socialism already early on as an immense danger rolling into Germany. Other Catholics, such as his long-time friend Ludwig Kaas, chairman of the Center Party, whom he had met in 1916 at the Trier military hospital during Kaas' short time in the military, still entertained the hope that Hitler and the Nazi movement could be kept in check. People thought they could be kept under control by granting them a few political concessions. In the face of the communist threat from the East, National Socialism seemed to be the lesser evil. Most people's eyes were only opened when Hitler seized totalitarian power, disregarded the concordat, and eliminated all opposition.

Father Kentenich unmasked the godlessness and *"heretical image of the human person"* in both ideologies. He focused his pastoral care on the inhuman danger that emanated from both schools of thought. He skillfully spoke of "Bolshevism" or "the Bolshevists" as cover names. But every listener could easily understand that he was primarily talking about the Nazis. He contrasted collectivism on the one hand and the "master race" on the other with the Christian *"religion of redemption"* that centers on love of neighbor and even love of enemy.

Gaining as Much Influence as Possible!

Meanwhile, the number of German priests taking part in conferences and retreats in Schoenstatt grew considerably. There were 2,184 in the year 1932 alone. The number of participants increased year by year until 1936, when Father Kentenich gave talks in and outside of Schoenstatt for 3,722 priests. Beyond this, the pedagogical conferences were also quite popular, especially among professional educators. In 1932, there were 6,950 listeners, and in the following year, more than 7,040. In late fall of 1932, when one of Father Kentenich's large pedagogical conferences took place in Mannheim with about 450 participants, one of the journalists present wrote about the speaker in the *Mannheimer Volksblatt*. He referred to him as a "distinguished expert in youth psychology" who over the course of eleven talks gave "an impressive illustration of a general theory of principles for a modern youth pedagogy ..." The newspaper report revealed his unmistakable enthusiasm. It said, "The speaker's intellectual breadth and fine sense for the current trends of our time encompassed all essential questions of modern culture and education with extraordinary confidence and integrated them into a system of Catholic educational wisdom. ... In fact, perhaps the most valuable result of the event is that the speaker didn't limit himself to merely enriching the audience with new insights. Instead, by the strong formative power of his thoughts, he also directly uplifted the personal pedagogical ethos of the listener and so proved himself to be an educator for educators in the best sense of the word. Professor Schwall's request that Father Kentenich should return to Mannheim in the not-so-distant future thus expressed the general wish of the listeners and met with spontaneous and enthusiastic approval among all participants of the ... event."

Such public praise was bound to arouse the mistrust of the Nazis, who had begun to spread a surveillance network all over Germany. So, it wasn't surprising that the pedagogical conferences had to be abruptly suspended, both in and outside of Schoenstatt, starting in September 1933. From then on, Father Kentenich incorporated his pedagogical topics into other talks, announcing them outwardly as "Modern Pastoral Care," "Conference for Religious Education Teachers," "Retreat for Religious Education Teachers," or "Pastoral Care Course for Priests." At the same time, he sought to pass on his pedagogical insights and experiences to members of his communities, above all to the leadership circles of the movement, through personal conversations and pastoral accompaniment. In the 1930s, he gave countless talks for the Sisters of Mary, the women and men of the Apostolic Federation, and the leaders of the youth branches of boys and girls. The number of listeners actually didn't matter so much to him. He often traveled long distances, sometimes even all the way to Switzerland, to give talks to a few priests. During the ten years until his imprisonment in 1941, he led approximately 300 events at 107 places in Germany. Switzerland was the destination of his apostolic travels forty-one times, and he visited Austria four times, staying in Vienna, Maria Trost, and Salzburg. He even held retreats for priests in the Netherlands and in Brixen, South Tyrol.

In all conversations and talks, Father Kentenich tried to spiritually immunize his listeners against National Socialism, ensure clarity and the discernment of spirits, and formulate a "countervision" against the Nazi ideology based on the Christian image of the human person. Whenever possible, he encouraged the Schoenstatt priests to work in similar ways, but to act carefully and prudently. They shouldn't be so quick to concede victories to the Nazis where it was possible to get around them, and they should try to avoid direct confrontations and open resistance while continuing to build up the system of their own world of values. If arrests and prohibitions began to take place too soon, there would be nothing else they could do against the Nazis. In this way, Father Kentenich helped build up a secret bulwark of inner resistance. But extreme caution was required. Schoenstatt itself, as a place and a movement, was to become a type of "*island*" or "*ark*," offering a spiritual home and refuge to as many people as possible. There they should acquire inner resilience and be strengthened in their faith amid the fierce conflicts in the making. "*Whenever the great flood comes, our ark must be ready*," declared Father Kentenich among trusted circles. He emphasized the importance of saving human and Christian fundamental values for the Church and society and carrying them into the time "thereafter." Everything vital and valuable was to be sheltered in the *ark*, while any unnecessary dead weight was to be cast off. Therefore, the focus was placed on ultimate principles and foundations that could support people and their dignity in the most difficult situations. In a 1933 newsletter to all members, Father Kentenich wrote the heading, *"Schoenstatt, a Marian center for the religious and moral renewal of the people,"* and from then on, he promoted a broader people's movement.

It was especially a matter of strengthening the Catholic priests who still enjoyed the people's esteem and trust and could therefore give orientation. In Karlsruhe, Father Kentenich spoke before 250 priests on the topic of *"the priest's mission and task in the Church, with special consideration of the needs of the time and the imperatives of the time."* Soon it could no longer escape unnoticed by the National Socialist German Workers' Party that there was a power working against them here—in secret, but to be taken seriously. The party made attempts—at first disguised, but later more and more openly—to ridicule the clerical state and defame it in public. Ultimately they began to spy on priests everywhere and carry them off to prisons and concentration camps with flimsy excuses. After the "Final Solution against the Jews," according to Hitler's explicit order, the next step was to eliminate active Catholics, especially priests.

Father Kentenich advised all collaborators of the Schoenstatt Movement to remain in the background as long as possible and to proceed prudently with any necessary risks. The daring words about the *"shadow of the shrine,"* which he had mentioned several times already back in 1929, now had a totally different depth and meaning. The little chapel in Schoenstatt, as a spiritual center, became a "secret power" and source of strength for the resistance against the Nazi Regime. Contact with the shrine of grace clearly enabled people to become more deeply anchored in their faith and to remain faithful to their ideals even amid life-threatening situations. During the 1930s, the majority of German priests came in contact with this shrine directly or indirectly at some point in time. In 1934, the sacristan joyfully reported to Father Kentenich that on Pentecost Sunday and the following Monday, a national holiday in Germany, a total of 5,845 visitors had come to the little chapel. From this secret center of the movement, the vision of a new world and world order came into being—one which the Nazis could not influence. The Gestapo were not capable of seeing through the original intellectual and spiritual effectiveness that emanated from this place.

Father Kentenich was of the conviction that the struggle against Hitler and his followers could not possibly be handled with natural means alone. He believed that *"diabolical, devilish forces were at work"* here that could ultimately only be conquered with the help of God. He was of the conviction that *"God is more powerful than the mighty ones of this world."* He also radiated this inner security. It was contagious. It encouraged others to take up spiritual resistance. He motivated others toward *"inner freedom."* Yes, the Nazis could take their life, but not their dignity nor this inner freedom.

"Father calls things so clearly by name!" One of the young Sisters of Mary came hurriedly into the dining room and waved her shorthand pad. Startled, the superior turned around—she was just in the process of hiding a few colored Easter eggs. The weather outside wasn't exactly inviting for an Easter egg hunt on this Easter Tuesday in 1934. But she wanted to give the sisters a little joy, even if she didn't have many eggs to hide. The community had only been in existence for eight years and hardly had any income. Their numbers had already increased to 560 members in close to sixty houses in Germany.

"Lots of young spring chickens," thought the superior, "but so little to feed them ..." After all, they lived only from what the individual sisters earned. But many of them first had to be trained and learn some kind of civil profession.

"Here, listen to what he said about *them* this morning ..." The sister quoted from her notepad, "'*They intend to ruin the freedom of the human person more and more, human nature as God created it, so that with time we acquire a mass psychosis in the midst of the civilized world.*' And then, what he said yesterday ..."

"That it is meanwhile considered shameful to be Catholic, and that as Catholics our honor will be taken from us more and more?"

"Yes," responded the young sister zealously, "and Father said it even though one of the leading Nazis had suddenly appeared at his door and flatly stated that as National Socialists they also constantly respect 'exactness, cleanliness, honesty, and patriotism.' He said all these things were also Christian! Father then explained to us what the core of Christianity is, and that it has nothing in common with Nazi ideology. Here, I wrote it down: *'Christianity is life, real life, divine life, life in likeness to the divine. ... And in today's spiritual trends, something entirely different resonates.'* They think: *'We only have to see to it that healthy blood becomes a reality once again, then we will have before us a healthy humanity that needs no redemption, that redeems itself. ... How sad these errors might make us! ... The human person who doesn't want to be divinized, to be redeemed by the divine, will become animalized with time! Humanity without divinity becomes bestiality! ... Today you must have a fine sense for realities so that you can go your way securely wherever our German fatherland rejects the supernatural and wherever our fatherland rejects Christ as the divine Redeemer. Do you know where we will then end up with time? In the most horrible barbarianism.'*"

The young sister closed her notepad. Her eyes now reflected real anxiety. "Do you believe that, too? What does Father mean by this? What kind of barbarianism?"

"Things are told about the kinds of atrocities the SS and the Nazi stormtroopers have already committed, how they eliminate political opponents and eventually all who think differently than they do. We don't feel much of that here yet ..."

"Aren't those isolated cases?"

"I think Father sees deeper and wider. *'Humanity without divinity becomes bestiality.'* He says that often. Without God, the human person easily becomes a beast toward other human beings! But did you really write all that down? You have to burn that! If such notes were to be found here, you would put him in danger!"

In December 1935, Father Kentenich gave a four-hour lecture for about 250 priests in the auditorium of the Borromeo College in Muenster and held a conversation with the well-known philosopher

Peter Wust. Afterwards, he visited one of the Sisters of Mary studying there as well as the bishop of Muenster, Clemens August Graf von Galen, who kindly welcomed him. In the course of the conversation, the bishop wondered whether there wasn't really one or the other thing about National Socialism that could still "be baptized." Father Kentenich shook his head and responded, *"I wouldn't know of any spot the waters of baptism could touch."*

Creating New Centers of Life

Father Kentenich looked seriously and resolutely at his former student Father Albert Eise. *"We must consciously focus our work on the renewal of our families ... If we want to save Catholicism in Germany, we have to use all means to aim at the re-Christianization of our families."*

"What you are initiating is a totally new type of pastoral care in the Church in Germany!"

"That's why I have asked the provincial council for your assistance in the core leadership circle, Albert. You are to take up this work with the families. This is extremely important! I don't trust Hitler's Reichskonkordat with the Holy See by any means! For more than a hundred years now, the Church in Germany has been working on developing the structure of its organizations and associations, but Hitler won't adhere to it. He won't allow them their freedom, much less protect them! Soon he will either reorganize and take over the last Catholic associations for his benefit or wipe them out completely. Then the family will be the only cell in which the Christian faith can still survive. We must try by all means to hinder the Nazis from taking hold of this cell of society."

Father Eise sat up straight. "And you believe I can do that? Education for marriage and pastoral care of families?"

"Of course, Albert—why not? You have apostolic vigor and know many families. We can start in various places at the parish level." And he repeated what he had already jotted down for a talk:

"In the midst of heathen surroundings, we must once again climb upward to Christian ideals of marriage ... and build Catholic islands of marriage just as in early Christianity."

"You mean, make Christian marriage and family attractive?"

"Certainly, Albert, and you can manage it even in addition to your task with the university women. There is no doubt about what is at stake for Germany: *'Either it will become a heathen nation through a dictatorship with an inhuman system, or it will become Christian. We have to do everything we can to uphold Christianity in our fatherland.'*"

Their conversation took place a few weeks after Hitler had seized power. During this time, Father Kentenich began to send the first Sisters of Mary overseas in small groups, first to South Africa, then to Argentina, Chile, and Brazil. Very young sisters left everything behind without any guarantee of ever being able to return. Most of them departed with little or no knowledge of the new native language. He gave them the express commission to save Schoenstatt's life and spiritual wealth by bringing it to other countries since no one knew what would become of Germany. Schoenstatt should at least be able to keep growing and unfolding elsewhere.

When the Nazi Regime forbade religious communities from accepting new members, Father Kentenich instituted the so-called "Fliegenden [flying ones]" within the community of the Sisters of Mary. Candidates who could not be released from service came to Schoenstatt at regular time intervals. During one weekend, in a secret nighttime operation, they received the dress of the Sisters of Mary in the shrine—but they left Schoenstatt the next Monday dressed in plain clothes again. They worked as "externs" at some place of employment or in the labor service required of German men and women at home since the beginning of the war. No one was supposed to take any written materials, such as notes from talks, along with them. Schoenstatters were only supposed to meet in small groups at rotating places. Moving targets were harder to hit!

During these years, the desire arose among members of the women's federation to unite themselves into a community with juridical bonds. They would live according to the evangelical counsels but stand alone and unrecognized in the world. They wanted to dedicate themselves entirely to apostolic activity in society and above all in their professional circles. In most difficult times and in surroundings that were becoming ever more pagan, they wanted to work like "yeast" among the people. Father Kentenich worked on this original community form for several years before he could call the institute into existence in 1941. The "Ladies of Schoenstatt" became Schoenstatt's second "secular institute," although as yet—as was also the case with the Sisters of Mary—there was no name or corresponding juridical status within the Church for it.

From the side of the official Church in Germany, increasingly critical questions arose. A theatrical performance by young people in 1933 brought the term "Schoenstatt secret" into common usage—a term that wasn't correctly understood. The rapid growth and expansion of the movement hadn't escaped the notice of the German bishops, and it almost felt like a threat to them, particularly because the movement was developing quite autonomously, without the initiation or control of Church hierarchy. It was especially the original terminology that met with the skepticism of many theologians, as for example the "contributions to the capital of grace" or the "Schoenstatt secret." The "covenant" sealed with Mary was misunderstood as some kind of legal bargain. "How presumptuous," thought many Church representatives, "that this was assumed to be a 'divine initiative' and a 'chapel of grace' ... Mary hasn't even ever appeared here, and the official Church hasn't examined the whole thing yet!" Father Kentenich tried to clarify a few misunderstandings. The covenant with Mary could only be a *"covenant of love,"* not a legal agreement. And the term "Schoenstatt secret" simply meant the innermost core of the place of grace, without which the whole development and effectiveness could not be explained. There were a few moments when things looked quite critical for Schoenstatt, and well-known theologians thought

Schoenstatt was a case for the Holy Office—the highest authority of the faith in Rome, an institution succeeding the Inquisition. But with time the accusations subsided again. There were other things causing problems for the bishops at that time.

Defying the Nonsense

Direct demonstrations began, especially under the guise of pious initiatives, like the Christ the King Festival later in Muenster. Father Kulmus related, "In November 1933, the week after Hitler's election to the Reichstag, we Swabian priests [from our region in southern Germany] left the safe tower as a small, united band ... and took up the offensive from Rechberg, Schönenberg, Rottenburg-Weggental, Horb-Weggental, Rottweil, and Zwiefalten. This daring step was the impetus for a comprehensive pilgrimage movement among the men in Germany." A total of 15,000 men assembled at various pilgrimage places to stage a counter-demonstration to the Nuremberg Rally and to document their resistance through a mass mobilization. "For Father Kentenich, the day I was able to come to Schoenstatt to bring him the news of this successful Swabian strike was counted among the happiest of his life. ... We had taken seriously the words he had spoken on November 20, 1933, '*We have to come out of the tower!*' but also the other statement our founder made, '*We have to pray and sacrifice much so that our dreams come true.*'"

Since Father Kentenich increasingly counted on persecutions, he began to systematically "*prepare*" the members of the Schoenstatt Movement intellectually and spiritually "*for martyrdom.*" He made every effort to free them from the terrible fear of suffering and of the tortures that could befall them. By *inscribing themselves into the heart of God—the "inscriptio"*—they could surrender themselves entirely to God's will and God's love. Father Kentenich wanted to immunize himself and them against intimidation and campaigns of violence by seeking to deepen their "*love of the cross and the Crucified*" and strengthening their will for total surrender to God. At a solemn nighttime reception of young women into the community of the Sisters of Mary, he thus spoke about the words of Jesus: "No one has greater love than this, to lay down one's life for one's friends." Similar words of holy Scripture emerged ever more frequently in his sermons: "Behold, I am sending you like sheep in the midst of wolves," and, "Was it not necessary that the Messiah should suffer these things and enter into his glory?"

He looked for topics that were especially suitable for strengthening the inner powers of the personality. For example, he emphasized the formative power of a consequent life according to the personal ideal. Right before opening new houses of the sisters' community or before sending young sisters into new areas of work, he would speak on the topic *"Dilexit me—he (God) loves me,"* underlining that this conviction would enable them to master all dangers and difficulties. For priests, he held large conferences and retreats on topics such as *"Priestly Joy of Life"* (1934) and *"Childlikeness before God"* (1937). More and more, he unfolded the reality of our childhood before God, *childlikeness,* as an essential part of Schoenstatt's spirituality and as an answer to an arrogant, power-hungry regime that propagated the "master race." In this way, he covertly undermined Nazi ideology wherever he found open ears.

January 1939. Mrs. Marie Kahle sat across from Father Kentenich, pale, exhausted, and despairing. She was actually only forty-six years old, but the last months had left their mark. She was a mother of five sons and the spouse of Paul Kahle, a university professor, renowned specialist in Middle Eastern and oriental studies, and art historian at the University of Bonn. While Bonn was in complete darkness for three nights, she had secretly ridden her bike along the Rhine River to Schoenstatt with her oldest son Wilhelm. Marie had already received advice and help from Father Kentenich many times here in Schoenstatt. She had gotten to know him through Father Rademacher, a theology professor in Bonn. She herself was a Protestant, but Catholic prayers had appealed to her, and she came to esteem both priests as "good friends."

But this visit today was not like the others. She came to Schoenstatt in the midst of an extremely difficult situation. For the first time since November 10 of last year, she spent three restful nights with the Sisters of Mary in "House Marienfried." The house really became a place of peace for her. "The sisters are very nice," she told Father Kentenich, "and the superior assured me that I could be very calm. She told me that if the doorbell rang, she would let me know before she opened the door. It did me so much good to have some nights without any threatening noises and only the soft rustling of the pine trees and the rushing of the little brook nearby."

And now she began to tell her story. She and her husband didn't belong to the Nazi Party because of their Christian convictions, and none of her boys were members of the Hitler Youth. Until recently, she had Jewish friends living on Kaiserstrasse in Bonn. A few Jewish scholars were colleagues of her husband, and they had also shopped for years in Jewish businesses. The evening before the horrific "Night of Broken Glass," her boys had tried to warn the Jewish merchants, but the warning came too late for most of them. After that gruesome night of destruction, her sons had helped Jewish shopkeepers with the clean-up work. The next day, she, too, went with her oldest son Wilhelm to visit an elderly Jewish lady, Mrs. Goldstein, in order to console her. A police officer appeared and later denounced Mrs. Kahle before the Gestapo. Since then, she and her family had been the object of uninterrupted harassment and persecution campaigns. The Gestapo patrolled in front of her house every night. Five SS men drove up in a black limousine and shattered her windowpanes. But that was only the beginning. She handed Father Kentenich a newspaper clipping. He read, "That is a betrayal of the people. Frau Kahle and her son helped the Jewish woman Goldstein with her clean-up work. ... The people of Bonn, with their honest and pure sensibilities, are speechless at such baseness."

Mrs. Kahle began to tremble as she continued to report, "Ernst came home crying and related how the Hitler Boys had beat him because his mother had committed an offense against German blood. ... At home we found everyone greatly upset. About twenty people had called and said that pigs like me and my son should be killed, and that we would be tortured and our house destroyed. ... Then my husband came home. The president of the university had asked him to leave the university. He was forbidden to set foot in the building or enter the library or the lecture hall. Stones flew with such force into the rooms on the upper floor that even the marble windowsills cracked. They painted on the sidewalk in big letters, 'Here lives a traitor of the people, a friend of Jews.' The Nazis put up posters in our urban district that said, 'Frau Kahle and her son call themselves citizens of Bonn; how long will this still be permitted?' Then my husband was asked to bring me to an interrogation. But I was fortunate because some years earlier I had once helped the family of the Nazi block leader and could say, 'You know that I help anyone in need, whoever it may be.' He affirmed that, and after some time I could go again. My son Wilhelm was quoted in front of the university tribunal. Although a professor is allowed to represent him there, all but one backed down, and eventually he was expelled from the university. Here's the letter of expulsion."

Mrs. Kahle handed Father Kentenich the document. "Wilhelm Kahle, student of music, is punished for conduct unworthy of a student at the occasion of a protest activity against Jewish businesses. He is removed from the college and loses all semester credits."

"Almost everybody has kept away from us. They don't come into our house anymore because it has become dangerous for them to know us. The Gestapo threw my husband out of a discussion group, a club he had led for fifteen years. And none of the other members had the courage to say anything." Disappointment and horror marked the woman's face. She was at the end of her strength. "I myself have not been able to leave the house for many weeks. I only dare to go out at night to get a little bit of fresh air. The younger boys run home quickly after school to avoid getting beat up. Our servant girl quit, and the milk delivery girl heard from the leader of the National Socialist Women's League how much she disapproved of her bringing us the milk. 'Traitors and all their progeny must be starved to death,' she told her. People try to trap us by sending anybody, even innocent-looking Nazi girls, to our house to trick me into saying something wrong. Wilhelm isn't even permitted anymore to play the organ in churches where he had always been allowed to rehearse before. I asked my friend Freiherr Erich von Redwitz, professor of surgery in Bonn, for advice. He said, 'Get out of Germany while you still have time, even if you lose everything! There is no hope for you nor any member of your family here in Germany.' But that's absolutely impossible, Father Kentenich! The Gestapo took away my passport and my son's, too. We would need special permission from the police and the Gestapo, and I doubt that our five boys would get permission to leave, even if they were good Nazis. We live in complete isolation. Only now and then am I able to visit Father Rademacher, who consoles me. We speak about the question of love of enemy ... Oh, Father Kentenich, you can't imagine how we are treated. Even my seamstress sent my material back to me because her son would not permit her to work for me. There are only a few friends who stick by us, and I've received a few anonymous letters congratulating me for my courageous deed of help. But now comes the worst part!" She looked at him in despair. He had calmly and attentively listened to her the whole time without interrupting her even once. "You know Dr. Aigner, the neurologist who has belonged to the Nazi Party since 1929. An unflinching Nazi. My husband knows him well because of his studies of Aramaic; he was almost like a family friend. He took up contact with the Nazi control center in Bonn, and what he has now reported to me no longer leaves me in peace. He said that in addition to the official tribunal, there is a so-called Nazi tribunal that judges cases internally and pursues the very definite strategy of systematically eliminating individuals and entire families through harassment, threats, and even torture and murder. He said they were systematically destroying my family and me. Their judgment and their chosen punishments are kept secret. He told me literally, 'Usually we achieve success without publicity. Once we have worn down the person's nerves enough, we take care of the family, one family member after another, and only when we do not succeed do we become violent. We bring the person concerned to the concentration camp, or there is the basement of the Gestapo.' Dr. Aigner asked me, 'Did you know that the Gestapo building in Bonn even has a second basement?' I knew that and said yes. He then said, 'Sometimes they make a person stretch out their arms and they nail them to the wall like this, and then they torture them with burning matches and cigarettes. No one can endure this for more than a few hours.' After everything he himself described to me, he told me literally, 'There is no way out for you personally at all. That is certain. But you can make it possible for your family to be saved; that is also certain.' When I asked how, he gave me a bunch of examples of how women had taken their own lives and so saved their families. And after some back-and-forth, he wrote out a recipe for me with enough barbital for suicide."

Marie Kahle took a deep breath. Father Kentenich looked at her calmly and pensively, silently moved. From the reports of former concentration camp prisoners and prison inmates, he knew what the Nazis were capable of. After a while she breathed in deeply and asked him directly, "Is it my duty to kill myself in order to save my family?" Father Kentenich remained silent again for a few minutes. Mrs. Kahle felt that he deeply understood her distress and concluded to herself, "He knows all too well that this is a real decision for a mother who fights for her children."

After a long silence, Father Kentenich said firmly, "No! Don't commit suicide! Come here instead. Come here and I will accept you *pro forma* into my community of sisters and have you brought into Switzerland by another name. ... But I would think you have enough character and courage to take a risk. Therefore I would advise you instead to go home and try to get out of Germany with your husband and family. Put all your powers at the service of this risk: your heart, your mind, your will. Try to go to England, where your husband is known and has many friends. Yes, I know, it looks completely hopeless that you and your loved ones could succeed in fleeing, but God is also there and protects those who trust him and suffer for him. You know, I think you will safely get to England or another country. It's another question whether you will succeed in keeping your property. But I think you know that honor is more valuable than property. Think it all over. And before you take a step of despair that can't be undone, remember that you will always find a place of refuge here. But trust! Trust our Lord with body and soul and continue along his way. He knows everything far better than we do!"

In her memoirs, where Mrs. Kahle documented this conversation, she related further, "We both knew that this would be our last time together, and we spoke for a long time about the religious and spiritual life. Before we parted, we went into his little chapel and prayed together, and he blessed me for the difficult way I was about to go."

Months later, Marie Kahle and her family succeeded in fleeing out of Nazi Germany in an adventurous way. She, her husband, and her sons traveled at different times via Belgium, the Netherlands, or Switzerland to England, where they could gradually establish a new life. The help they experienced during this time from friends but also through "heavenly interventions," as they called them, was so astonishing that in all her reports, Mrs. Kahle returned time and again to her conversation with Father Kentenich, in which he had encouraged her to take the daring step and had prophesied the good outcome of her escape.

Schoenstatt did not remain an undisturbed place of refuge for pious souls, an "island" untouched by all the turmoil. Since 1938—already before Mrs. Kahle's visit—the House of Studies had been seized by the Nazis and turned into a National Socialist teacher training institution at the beginning of the year 1939. The relief of Mary above the entrance provoked irritation among the new inhabitants and was therefore to be destroyed. The only bricklayer who would stoop low enough to do this was unemployed and usually drunk. But when in a foggy state he was about to set to work, he changed his mind without further ado and slurred, throwing the sledgehammer aside, "Nah! I won't do it!" So the only remaining solution for the Nazis was to cover the lovely stone image of Madonna and Child with a swastika flag.

Since 1938, the Austrian Father Franz Reinisch had belonged to "King Arthur's Round Table," the close circle of priests in Schoenstatt who were active in the movement. His area of responsibility was the pastoral care of men. On April 7, 1942, he received the news that he was drafted into the armed forces. He purposely delayed his arrival at the camp by one day.

"Becoming a soldier seems to be of little value to you!"

His answer: "I would value it if I were asked to serve a different regime." His frank remark and his refusal to take the oath of allegiance to Hitler would promptly lead to his incarceration.

There had already been a discussion on the question of the oath of allegiance at "King Arthur's Round Table" in 1939. One confrere chipped in, "There's probably no way to get around it. Even the bishops aren't saying anything against it."

Franz Reinisch raised the argument, "We cannot swear the soldier's oath of allegiance to the National Socialist banner, to Hitler. That is sinful! That would mean swearing an oath to a criminal."

Another objected, "God-given authority ..."

Reinisch became vehement. "Our conscience forbids us to follow an authority who only brings murder and death into the world for the sake of covetous conquest. We may not swear an oath to this criminal."

Awkward silence. All of them looked at Father Kentenich. What would he have to say about it? After a brief pause, he peacefully and calmly gave his opinion using Goethe's words, *"'There is no answer fit for all; let each one see how he shall do it!' If one's conscience says to take the oath, it is right. If one's conscience rejects the oath, one must follow this call of conscience."*

From then on, Franz Reinisch knew he had Father Kentenich's support and special guidance for the time to come. In the beginning, when they were getting to know each other, he had almost felt stifled at times by the strong and towering priestly figure of Joseph Kentenich, so exemplary in many ways. But over the years, Father Reinisch matured more and more into the priestly ideal he desired for himself. At the climax of this development, he had completely stepped into the footprints of his fatherly spiritual director as his spiritual son.

By nature, Reinisch was short-tempered and had to powerfully face his own limitations in the longing for his personal priestly ideal. It also bothered him a lot that he wasn't able to stop smoking. His personality structure didn't allow him to live halfway or with false compromises. And so he was not willing, either, to make cheap concessions to Hitler and his regime. He simply considered him diabolical. Father Kentenich seemed to understand Franz Reinisch well precisely in his clarity and uncompromising manner, even when his temperament ran away with him. At the end of an evening walk, Father Kentenich gave him the advice: *"In this way, follow step by step the signs the Blessed Mother sends you, and if it's God's will, you will die as a sacrificial lamb."* He obviously belonged to the few who supported Franz—in reverence before the voice of God in his conscience—although Father Kentenich thus had to count on losing one of his most valuable collaborators in the core leadership circle. Unlike many others, he didn't try to dissuade Father Reinisch from his decision, but he did make him aware of its weight. *"Of course, you must consider whether you also have the strength to persevere until the last moment. If you believe you have that strength, then I advise you to follow your conscience."* From then on, with prayer and vigilant attentiveness, he accompanied Franz on the path he took in 1939. In view of all possible consequences, Father Kentenich answered him in a letter, *"You are right, as you write, in abandoning yourself completely to the loving will of the Father in heaven. And if you remain faithful to the dear Blessed Mother, your final decision will turn out well, either now or at the moment of death ..."*

In 1941, just as Reinisch was kneeling in the shrine in Schoenstatt struggling for clarity, he received a message from Father

Kentenich from the Gestapo prison in Koblenz. On brown bag paper scribbled in dull pencil were the words, *"I have your card always before me. I have much extra light and warmth and could give you some of it ... If you could abandon yourself completely in the spirit of the inscriptio and give yourself to the dear Blessed Mother, your hot Tyrol blood would surely cool down a little ... Perhaps you don't even know how many gifts—intellectual gifts, deep insights, and a firm will—the dear God has given you. Give all these gifts back to him, multiplied in rich measure. What might your concrete task consist in? Here I must pose a counterquestion to you: Where does your heart urge you to go, and which possibilities still exist for you in the present conditions? You should sell your life for as high a price as possible. And your life's path shall not have crossed S(choenstatt) in vain."*

By the time Father Reinisch was arrested in April 1942 on account of his remarks about military service, his struggle to recognize what God wanted of him had already come to a certain conclusion. He had struggled through everything in advance in the spirit of the "*inscriptio*," simply inscribing himself spiritually into the heart of God. By this time, his fatherly advisor had himself already been sent to the concentration camp of Dachau. From a distance, Father Reinisch had been able to follow Father Kentenich's process of total surrender to God in the preceding months. But with his transport to Berlin as a prisoner and the transfer of his records to the Reich Court-Martial, long and difficult weeks of waiting began for Reinisch, in which his fate stood clearly before his eyes. They were weeks of human fear and great loneliness, amid which he interiorly oriented himself time and again on the faith-filled support of his parents and on all the spiritual gifts that Schoenstatt and his Pallottine community had given him along the way. And yet, in addition to the pain he had to cause his parents, there was the pressure from outside—not only that representatives of his own community tried to persuade him to take back his decision, but his prison chaplain even refused to give him Holy Communion in order to place his obligation to take the oath drastically before his eyes. For the Nazi Regime, what he was doing was a betrayal of the fatherland, which he loved—and a few of his superiors and confreres accused him of being disobedient, stubborn, and irresponsible toward the community. They feared that his refusal to take the oath would lead to the persecution of their whole community. The spiritual torments he had to pass through in those months were devastating.

In prison, Franz Reinisch lived completely from what Schoenstatt had given him. He composed his own spiritual daily order. The Bible, especially the New Testament, became his most important "consolation reading," as he called it. With joy he worked through many of the talks by Father Kentenich on the *"Marian priest,"* which his new prison chaplain, Father Heinrich Kreutzberg, who was also a Schoenstatter, had smuggled into his cell. "Ever since you have been here," he said, "I can see very clearly. You are my guardian angel. I am not afraid of death. But it was terrible before. I can't even describe for you this inner struggle with God about whether I'm doing the right thing. During this time I've only been able to orient myself on a few small hints."

His case was heard on July 7 in Berlin-Charlottenburg before the Reich Court-Martial. He courageously defended his position during the process but was frequently interrupted by the judge, who ultimately disparaged and insulted him. "Don't give any propaganda speeches here. Incidentally, we are not a Church tribunal but a court-martial. We have no respect for you at all since you know that the issue today is Bolshevism ..." Toward the end, the judge shouted at him, "I ask you once more: Will you swear the oath of allegiance or not? I demand a clear yes or no!" And as if to crown the whole thing, he referred to the Bible: "Because you are lukewarm, ... I will spit you out of my mouth. Whoever is not with me is against me!"

Father Reinisch responded with a loudly audible answer, "No!"

The prosecutor stood up and made the request for the death penalty, which was granted. In the time thereafter, the possibility for Franz Reinisch to avert this sentence still remained open; he only had to "change his mind for the better."

He admitted to his "guardian angel" that the only one who could dissuade him from his decision was Father Kentenich. He trusted this man of God more than himself, confident that he knew well how to recognize God's wish and will in his situation. On July 21, 1942, after many grueling interrogations, Father Reinisch sat in his cell in Berlin-Tegel, looking back at the weeks that lay behind him, and wrote, "Whenever I was seized by fear—before interrogations or any time during the day—I liked to think of Father Kentenich and how he praised us for preserving our inner and outer peace whenever we had to withstand difficult situations. This is the sign of heroic faith in Divine Providence."

The fear of death returned. A good three weeks before his death, Father Reinisch had to struggle hard again. All human support seemed to have been taken from him. This drove him, as he wrote, into the arms of God. He implored Mary not to permit him to be unfaithful to his decision unless this would serve the greater glory of God. Then he continued, "Perhaps this may be my dying prayer: 'Lord, you know everything, you know that I love you. My whole life has been nothing but one great proof of your mercy and love.'" As things got more serious, he said to Father Kreutzberg that Father Kentenich bore the main responsibility for his decision. His provincial superior and a few confreres had pushed him hard not to persist to the end in refusing to take the oath because otherwise he would put the whole community in danger. By his own suggestion, he was dismissed from his community—*pro forma* and only by civil law—in order to protect them. But Franz Reinisch stood by his refusal to pledge the oath of allegiance to Adolf Hitler and serve as a soldier in the German armed forces. He was the only Catholic priest under the Nazi Regime to do so.

On July 30, his death sentence became final. Father Kreutzberg, the prison chaplain, brought him the news. Franz Reinisch knelt down before the Most Blessed Sacrament, secretly hidden in his cell, and prayed, "Savior, Mother, I can never thank you enough. My every breath shall thank you. My every heartbeat shall thank you until my heart beats its last on the final day. My every thought shall thank you. There is nothing more I wish to speak but to say thank you, thank you."

A few days before his execution, he wrote a poem to Mary with chained hands: "I hear the Father's calling for heroes strong and true. O offer me, dear Mother, as loving victim, too. O Queen of Earth and Heaven, command the storms to cease. Destroy the devil's power, O Victress, grant us peace! Make me your own apostle, your knight, I ask and pray. My dying smile shall whisper: O dearest MTA!"

On the day before his execution, he asked Father Kreutzberg, "Please notify Father Kentenich that tomorrow on Thursday I will pray and surrender the sacrifice of my life for his release and that of all confreres imprisoned in Dachau." On this last day of his earthly life he also celebrated holy Mass for Father Kentenich.

Early in the morning at 5:03 on August 21, 1942, at the age of thirty-nine, Father Franz Reinisch was executed by guillotine in Berlin-Brandenburg. Shortly beforehand, he had received the message that Father Kentenich stood behind him completely. His last piece of advice had been, *"Follow your conscience!"* From then on, all his fears gave way, and he experienced himself as already living in another world, "borne by an otherworldly power." In two letters from the concentration camp immediately before and a few days after his execution, Father Kentenich emphasized that Reinisch's martyrdom was a *"blood sacrifice."*

The Net Gets Tighter

Despite all caution and prudence, Schoenstatt didn't succeed in slipping through the mesh of the ever-tightening net of control in the National Socialist State. Events had been dispersed all over Germany, but there was no way they could escape surveillance because of their sheer magnitude. In September 1935, for example, a "special report" was received by the Reich Main Security Office of the SS in Berlin. It contained not only some information on statistics and structure, as was common with other Catholic associations, but also a treatise of several pages on the dangerous "Catholic Action" which existed under the name "Schoenstatt" or "Apostolic Movement of Schoenstatt" or, more recently, "Marian Community of Prayer and Sacrifice." The information was intended for senior officials of the National Socialist German Workers' Party. In the detailed report, Schoenstatt was portrayed as an association "that is highly dangerous to the spirit and aims of the 'new Germany.'" No one in Schoenstatt knew anything about the detailed report. But one day in 1936, a member of the women's federation, fulfilling her obligatory service as a secretary of a Gestapo agent, heard him say without knowing who she was, "Schoenstatt is the greatest enemy of National Socialism!" But until this point there was one thing the spies hadn't been able to do: apprehend the head of the whole organization. Nazi leadership knew very well who it was, because a former sodalist, Ferdinand Duchêne, had lost his faith during the Nazi time and worked in Heinrich Himmler's department in Berlin. There he compiled lists of prominent priests in Germany. Father Kentenich's name was among them.

They sought evidence and first discovered it in the "Schoenstatt Apostolate of the Sick," whose members were dependent on written communication. One day, the Gestapo appeared at the leader's house, confiscated her duplicating machine and a few documents, and arrested her. Although they later released her, these were the first signs of an increasingly fierce persecution. In the fall of 1935, Father Kentenich sent six suitcases full of documents and important correspondence to a secret place in the Black Forest, where they were hidden in the attic of a house. This was fortunate, because a few weeks later, while he was staying in Speyer, the Gestapo officially appeared for the first time in Schoenstatt and searched the rooms of the Fathers who worked in the movement. Thanks to favorable circumstances, Father Kentenich's office was omitted. Quite a number of letters had piled up there again that by no means could fall into the hands of the Gestapo. When he came back, he went down by the garages and burned baskets full of important documents and incriminating letters.

From then on, his closest collaborators in the core leadership circle were followed around the clock. Father Menningen's biography about Joseph Engling, which he had consciously titled *Everyday Hero* in order to highlight an ideal of a hero that was diametrically opposed to that of the Nazis, was confiscated and added to the list of forbidden books. When he published the same book again in an abridged form and by another title, he was summoned for a lengthy interrogation. Since he was an advisor for theology students in matters of labor and military service arrangements, he had already been accused earlier of "deterring them from military service" and "making them useless for war service." The following year, he was summoned for further questioning and accused among other things of "vicious attacks against the Party." Finally, in February 1937, he received a grave warning from the Reich Ministry of Public Enlightenment and Propaganda. All his mail was controlled. In 1938, due to the publication of his book, the situation became extremely precarious. He absolutely had to go underground.

The Gestapo compiled complete dossiers about individual Schoenstatters and watched their every action, including Father Eise, who had to undergo a four-hour interrogation in 1935. In July 1939, he was summoned to another interrogation in Stuttgart after having given a series of sermons on marriage and family. Once again, Father Eise succeeded in escaping their grasp and talking his way out, even if they did accuse him of the "Jesuit art of distortion." Spies were to be counted on at every moment, so addresses and talks had to be skillfully formulated. The catchphrase "Careful! The enemy is listening!" circulated around and was sometimes written on a slip of paper and placed on the speaker's podium. But the Gestapo was far from catching the head of the whole thing. A common agreement had been made to keep Father Kentenich's person in the background as far as possible, not to mention his name, and not to carry around any notes from his talks. Once during an interrogation when Father

Muehlbeyer was asked what Kentenich's task was as the leader, he answered, "Father Kentenich's leadership consists in asking Limburg for the Fathers needed for pastoral care." Things became more dangerous for him.

A number of magazines, books, and small publications that were specifically directed against the Nazi ideology landed on the mountain of books to be burned because they unfolded a countervision to the National Socialist image of the human person and the world. Among these were Hermann Schmidt's *Organic Asceticism,* books about Joseph Engling such as *Omnibus Omnia* by Heinrich Schulte or *Everyday Hero* by Alex Menningen, Ferdinand Kastner's *Marian Formation of the World in Christ,* as well as *Everyday Sanctity* by Sister Annette Nailis—a work that summarized Schoenstatt's asceticism, religious education, and spirituality and enjoyed great acclaim by the Church.

"Sister Borromaea, the Gestapo are in the house again!" The date on the calendar page was November 27, 1940. It was already the third time that men in leather coats and with hats pulled low over their faces tramped noisily through the hallways, throwing doors open, ransacking drawers and cabinets, and asking about particular persons. Pale as a ghost, the sister on entrance duty stood before her superior, whose facial color had likewise changed. Had the moment come? Were they looking for him? Fortunately, Father Kentenich was in Kevelaer at the moment, giving a retreat for priests.

Hardly had she finished that thought when one of the Gestapo men stood before her. "Where is the office?"

"Come along; I'll show you." Father had always advised them to stay calm and not show any fear. Jesus said not to worry about what to say; he would be there.

"Where are the books?"

"What books?"

"Don't act dumber than you are! The books that have the names of all the visitors to the house!" the officer barked at her.

There was no choice. She took the books from the last two years out of the cabinet. But one of the two Gestapo men tore all of them off the shelf and packed them into a crate.

Three weeks later came the official order from the Gestapo headquarters in Koblenz that no more courses or conferences for lay people could be held in the Schoenstatt Retreat House. In order to prevent the confiscation of the house by the Gestapo, two Sisters of Mary sought out the chief medical officer in Wiesbaden, whom they knew well, and offered that he could use the Retreat House in Vallendar as a military hospital. At first, the matter didn't seem to be too promising. But when the sisters appeared in Wiesbaden a second time, they agreed, and soon afterwards they sent the first soldiers—ill with scarlet fever—and their caretakers.

The more the Nazi persecution intensified, the more the underground work blossomed. At a conference for pastors in 1940, Father Kentenich himself gave insight into the resistance work: "*The Nazis can do what they will; they will never be able to abolish us because they can't comprehend our organization. The whole system is so carefully thought out that the Gestapo cannot overcome us. We have completely suspended the outer organization, but practically, we work harder than ever before.*"

But among the ranks of the Schoenstatters, searches, interrogations, incarcerations, and ultimately deportations to concentration camps happened with increasing frequency. The first one was Deacon Karl Leisner, who had been taken prisoner on November 9, 1939. Over the course of the year 1941, Father Joseph Fischer, Father Joseph Boehr, Father Heinz Dresbach, Father Hans Rindermann, Father Heinrich Koenig, and Father Albert Eise followed him on the way into the concentration camp. In 1943, Lotte Holubars and Maria Hilfrich, members of the Institute of the Ladies of Schoenstatt, were sent to the concentration camp. That same year, Father Richard Henkes was also imprisoned. He had been one of the first Schoenstatt sodalists and had worked in the movement later on, but afterwards he went a different direction. He died of typhus in 1945 in the concentration camp of Dachau, where he had become infected through his selfless service as a nurse.

Father Kentenich had prepared himself and the Schoenstatt Movement as well as he could ...

6. Prisoner of the Gestapo

Actually, he should've counted on it, but then it suddenly happened, so suddenly that he couldn't even hide his briefcase containing the risky materials. He had already been seriously warned on numerous occasions. They had been spying on him for a long time. A young woman infiltrated by the Nazis into the Pedagogical College of Koblenz had pretended to be a devout Catholic and had mingled among the female students belonging to the movement. She was the only one who had diligently taken notes during the talks. However, she had already stood out at holy Mass because she quite obviously didn't have the faintest idea. She also hadn't gone to Holy Communion. And then she suddenly disappeared. The students had been so careful about this, lodging all over the city in private accommodations, moving the conference from Schoenstatt to the Monastery of St. Barbara in Koblenz, and holding their gatherings in the choir loft of the cloister church.

August 4, 1941, in the evening. Father Eise was in the middle of giving a talk. Four black limousines and two trucks screeched to a halt in front of the building. Within moments, the monastery was surrounded by fifteen SS and Gestapo men. Eight Gestapo officers stormed into the choir loft and arrested the speaker. All thirty students were taken along and interrogated individually that night. As the men led Father Eise away in handcuffs, he said softly to one of the students, "Now it's getting serious!"

Around midnight, the students were released with crude insults and a warning. Father Eise's interrogation lasted until 3:30 in the morning. The situation was extremely alarming. They had confiscated a whole set of his notes from talks by Father Kentenich, including the "Cross Talk," which he had given to the Ladies of Schoenstatt. Father Eise himself had expressed many daring things in his talks, meticulously jotted down by the Gestapo spy who denounced him. Moreover, he bumbled multiple times during the interrogation. He became insecure at the thought, "They already know everything anyway. Father himself once said, *'Yes, it might be all right if you avoid mentioning me during interrogations, but the Nazis know everything anyway; they also know who and what it's all about.*"

Father Eise implored the Holy Spirit. He came to realize that hiding or denying things made no sense anymore. Had he said too much? They had really given him the third degree until he finally "had" to admit that the talks were indeed given by Joseph Kentenich. One of the officers stood up in front of him. "Did he say what it says here: *'My life's task consists in undermining National Socialism in order thereby to conquer it'?*"

The other Gestapo officer, who had stood at the window with his back to him the whole time, now turned around. For hours, the desk lamp had been pointed at the captive's face so that the officer could watch him closely in the reflection of the windowpane. "Be reasonable, man! Admit it! We already know everything! You only make his and your situation worse by denying it!" His tone was friendly and benevolent. Father Eise kept quiet. It had already been going on like this for hours. The one officer constantly threatened, insulted, and roared at him, while the other stood at the window appearing to be calm and spoke to him persuasively in a friendly tone.

"You know, we can also use totally different ways to make you talk!" the first one roared again.

"Ach, Theo, leave the poor priest alone! He himself can see that it doesn't make sense anymore to deny it!"

"Did Kentenich say that or not?" The officer's fist banged on the desk. The cup of coffee fell to the ground with a loud clang.

Exhausted, Father Eise buried his face in his hands. Softly and wearily came his answer, "Yes! If you know it anyway, why do you bother to keep asking me?"

The furious Gestapo officer turned to the clerk who had been typing unremittingly. "Did you get that?"

He nodded. Then he jumped up from his chair, tore open the door, and barked at the security guard on duty, "Lead him away!"

Two SS men took Father Eise into "custody." They brought him to the prison on Karmeliterstrasse and locked him in one of the cells. Worn out, he collapsed on the plank bed. "My God, what's coming now?" He couldn't think much further. Sleep overtook him.

A few weeks later, on September 14, 1941, after having found out when Father Kentenich would be back from his trip to southern Germany, the Gestapo appeared at the Retreat House in Schoenstatt. Two officers stomped up the front steps where they immediately ran into Sister Perpetua, member of the general government of the sisters. She, of all people, was quite adept at dealing with the Gestapo. One time when they had summoned her, she arrived at the Gestapo headquarters on Vogelsang in Koblenz, completely peaceful and calm as if it were an everyday affair. The Gestapo read her a letter from a Sister of Mary that they had filtered out of the mail and opened: "What a great mission F. has for these modern times!" Upon being asked who "F." was, Sister Perpetua answered in a tone that downplayed the situation, "Oh, you shouldn't take it wrong when a young sister raves about her confessor!" With that, the matter was settled for the time being.

Sister Perpetua immediately sensed that the situation was considerably more volatile now.

"Heil Hitler! Secret State Police! Where can we find Kentenich?"

It annoyed her that the officer expressed himself so irreverently. Instead of responding with the Hitler salute, she said emphatically, "Grüss Gott! I can't tell you exactly where Father Kentenich is at the moment. It's a big house." Out of the corner of her eye, she saw a sister quickly take leave. She would warn Father. So she tried to stall for time and got the officer engaged in a conversation. After a bit of back-and-forth, she finally declared, "His office is one floor up!"

The officers looked at each other. The military hospital was on that floor. The Gestapo were not on friendly terms with the military and wouldn't be welcome there, either. So, one of the two ordered her, "You get him! He must be somewhere!"

"Yes, I can look for him!" At that moment, Father Kentenich was already coming down the stairs. Up in his office, he had been able to quickly stash away the letters and documents that had piled up there again. If they were to fall into the hands of the Gestapo, it would be fatal, and not only for him ...

The officers were just about to turn around and leave, saying they would come back tomorrow, when Father Kentenich called down the steps, "You want to speak with me? I'm Father Kentenich. Please come into our visiting room!"

They turned down the friendly offer to have a seat, but they did decide to use a more polite tone. "Heil Hitler! We don't want to cause a scene here. We only want to ask you to appear at Vogelsang tomorrow at 9:00 a.m. We have a few questions for you."

Now and then, the Pallottine Fathers belonging to "King Arthur's Round Table" had role-played how they should react in such situations—what to answer and what never to say and how to evade trick questions. By no means were they to mention names, and the most important thing was to stay completely calm. This wasn't hard for Father Kentenich at all; composed and firm, he responded, "That's not possible!"

"Why not?"

"You said you don't want to cause a scene. Tonight I am starting a retreat course for priests. If it has to be canceled, they will right away assume you have taken me, and that will quickly make the rounds all over Germany."

The officers looked at each other pensively. "Fine. When does the course end?"

"On Saturday."

"Then report at Vogelsang on Saturday morning at 8:00. And be punctual. We don't like tardiness!"

Father Kentenich nodded. But before he could accompany both of them to the door, they had already disappeared.

The talks given thereafter bore the mark of what he announced at the beginning of the retreat: *"I will now sing my swan song for you."*

Saturday, September 20. Early in the morning, Father Kentenich celebrated holy Mass once more in the shrine. After breakfast he put on his oldest habit and his oldest shoes and set out to take the train to Koblenz. He sensed that he wouldn't return. When he asked a lady how to get to the Gestapo headquarters, she looked at him with alarm, gave him directions, and sorrowfully watched him walk away.

He had been sitting on a wooden bench in the hallway already since 8:00 a.m. He pulled out his pocket watch: almost 1:00 p.m. This was the usual method for wearing down victims and making them nervous. Suddenly the door opened and he was called in for interrogation. It started with the same tactics used with Father Eise. Two Gestapo officers with various roles passed each other the ball. They read him passages from notes taken of various talks: "'Let the others adhere to their cross; we follow our cross.' Did you say that? Yes or no?"

Further quotes followed. "No, those are not my words," he replied. "The notes are not correct."

But instead of further questions and statements, they simply said, "We must detain you here."

"But that's not possible. I have to hold a course for priests in Munich." But this strategy didn't work the second time around.

"Into the basement! Bunker 3." Two guards led him away. The mere use of the word "bunker" was meant to instill fear in him. But he was interiorly prepared. That gave him strength and a peculiar tranquility.

In the Bunker

He was led away without any justification, accusation, or information as to the length and type of punishment. He first had to empty his pockets of everything that a prisoner could use to commit suicide. He was only allowed to keep his rosary, a small MTA picture, and a little crucifix. When they got to the "bunker," he only remarked, *"Now I can at least have a little bit of vacation."* The chief guard stared at him in disbelief and murmured to his colleague, "Man, he's already lost his mind! A little off his rocker, isn't he?!"

The heavy iron door was pulled open, revealing a small space, three meters (ten feet) long and about one meter (three feet) wide, and just high enough for him to stand. His eyes scrutinized the inside of the cell: a tipped-up plank bed, a stool with a washbasin, and a bucket to relieve himself. That was all. The whole space consisted only of cold, bare concrete—no heat, no window, no light, nothing. Now he realized what the space had been: one of the vaults of the former federal bank converted by the Nazis into a Gestapo prison. The door slammed shut. The keys rattled in the lock, and in an instant it became dark as night. In the evening, as someone pushed a meager meal through the hatch for him, he demanded a second interrogation. Against all expectations, it was granted to him. The next day he was led back upstairs. He proved to the Gestapo that he couldn't have said what they had read to him. The alleged notes about St. Margaret Mary Alacoque were nonsense and incorrect. He had never said anything like that. This meant that all the notes were a farce and not authentic. The reason for the accusation was thus invalid.

But all his legal objections were swept off the table. They told him that only a confession could help him and that the documents clearly substantiated his anti-state views and his acts of high treason toward the German people. With that, he was led back into the basement, two levels down. Back into the bunker.

Hour after hour, day after day passed by. Soon he could no longer tell whether it was day or night. There was absolute darkness, poor air, and a damp cold that crept under his skin. The space was so tight. He could hardly turn around. No distractions, no possibility to hear or read anything. That was how the Gestapo attempted to "wear people down," driving them either to insanity or to a blind confession. Most people couldn't endure it for more than three days. Father Kentenich tried to preserve his sense of the time of day by keeping track of the meal times or by asking what day of the week it was.

The silence was broken time and again by the prisoners' cries of despair as they were tortured and by the weeping and wailing of those who couldn't take it anymore. It sent chills down his spine. He had prepared countless priests for life in prison and concentration camps. He had motivated them to interiorly struggle their way into everything in advance so that they would be prepared in the event of an emergency and could give God their yes. He told them that the "*inscriptio attitude*" would be of great help—asking God for the things one feared the most, if he willed it. It meant literally embracing the will of God, full of trust and out of love. He had already interiorly "trained" himself for a long time toward this disposition: "*I myself also imagined all possible atrocities: What would you do if this happened or if that happened?*" In this way he had spiritually predisposed himself for cross and suffering. He was of the conviction that this was exactly where Mary—in her task as Educator—could play her special pedagogical part. "*The covenant of love obliges the Mother of God to educate me the same way the loving God educated the Savior. And the Savior had to hang on the cross. Therefore, those who seal the covenant of love must also count on being nailed to the cross.*"

Now in the bunker, as he heard the cries, the thought occurred to him, "*Holding still in the midst of the uncertainty as to whether the same thing might happen to me is the best means for me to love God.*" With that, the anxiety passed. But it hit him hard that he couldn't help his tormented fellow prisoners, that he couldn't console them or do anything for them. So he began to pray the rosary out loud in order to calm them, in order to awaken their trust in another power. He sang all the songs he knew by heart. He felt sorry that he didn't know more verses. Suddenly he could hear someone in another cell timidly beginning to sing along. Then others joined in praying along. Throughout this entire time, he was only led back upstairs once—to be photographed for the "album of criminals." But he was immediately led back downstairs afterwards.

Four weeks in darkness had already passed by. In his longing to be more deeply united with Christ and Mary, he had made use of the many lonely hours as a retreat. He sought a constant dialogue with God. Over time, he had sensed more intensely that an inner power was growing within him—the power of God's nearness. Suddenly a special experience overcame him in the early morning hours. It happened precisely on the founding day, which was to be solemnly celebrated in Schoenstatt. *"On the morning of October 18"*—as he later recorded in writing—*"I experienced myself in a peculiar state down in the bunker. It was like being half-asleep, and I thought: 'If God wanted you to sacrifice all your abilities down here, would you be ready?' ... My disposition was, 'Yes, I am completely ready.'"* But when he was once again fully conscious, he was no longer sure: "Was that just meant as a possibility? Or was it a foregone conclusion that God wants this of you ...?" He struggled his way to an unreserved, total yes. Yes, God could do with him what *he* wanted, even though he knew what that might mean. It was *"playing with life,"* a gamble as risky as with all people who "built their cities on the edge of Vesuvius."

In the midst of his meditative thoughts, an unusual image came to his mind. "Doesn't every mother prepare *'the best diapers'* for her child? Doesn't Mary do the same thing for us?" Everything that happened or didn't happen was "the best diapers" ... *"An extraordinarily deep and tender love is hidden behind them. Even if it's the biggest cross! It means that love is what dictates this or that thing that touches my life as a blow of fate."* Nothing and no one else!

His concentration became increasingly and totally directed to God. Everything around him became less important. The isolation that was meant to kill his nerves and lead to a breakdown was suddenly outshone by the experience of a completely childlike openness for the "you" of God his Father. This living relationship with God, which he had sought his whole life long, now gave him—in the midst of this dungeon experience—an inner freedom that could withstand the extreme psychological pressure. The Nazis could take his exterior freedom and everything else, even his life. But they couldn't take away his inner freedom to give God his own free yes. This made him stand above them. Even though they had all the exterior power over him, he had the inner power to define whether and how he would take all these constraints and how they would affect him. He was freer than they because he sensed God on his side. This made the darkness of the bunker turn to light.

And as if he'd had a premonition that something would happen on this October 18, the door of the old vault opened. As he followed the guard somewhat stiffly up the stairs, it took some time for his eyes to get used to the light he hadn't seen for so long. Outside in the prison courtyard, he took a few deep breaths. Fresh air! The air in the bunker had been so extremely poor that it had aggravated his damaged lung and led to bloody noses and coughing attacks. In addition, the cell was terribly cold, and he had gotten an infection. But otherwise everything was fine. Already as he was being led upstairs, he caused a great stir among the prison guards and even among the Gestapo men. This man was the first one seemingly not affected by the darkness at all ... Four weeks! Others broke down after just a short time. But this one here seemed unbroken in body and soul. From then on, they all had quite some respect for this priest with the long beard. The guards sensed that there was something special here. Something radiated from this man. He was free of fear. That impressed them.

Thrown into Prison–but Not Sidelined

The Gestapo now decided that he should first be led over to the prison on Karmeliterstrasse, a former Carmelite monastery not far from Vogelsang. The prison director gave him the order, "You must take off your habit."

"No, I will not."

"But you must. The bishops themselves don't want imprisoned priests to wear their cassocks."

"Very well. But then I would like to have my own civilian suit. Please inform Schoenstatt that someone should bring me my suit."

And so it happened. It was astonishing that the Gestapo didn't only let him get away with that. Despite the strictest prohibitions regarding contact among prisoners, his guard immediately assigned him the cell next to Father Eise. They could communicate with each other by knocking signals. Sometimes they prayed or sang together. They sang one song with particular ardor: "Protect us with your mantle, Lady of Victory! Ter Admirabilis Mater, the Tower of Ivory! ... We trust and believe in our mission, in storms we will set our sail. The ages will see you conquer. With you we shall never fail!" This "Schoenstatt Hymn" seemed to fit for this time better than any other. Whenever they could go outside for a half-hour walk in the courtyard, they tried to walk next to each other. In the chapel, Father Kentenich usually knelt next to Father Eise. By that he intended to show that he did not reproach him in any way; rather, he wanted to encourage his former student to believe that God has our lives in his hands and determines everything that happens—not human mistakes or human rulers. On November 15, Father Eise was transported to Dachau, and they had to say goodbye. One of the guards who was well-disposed to Father Kentenich ensured that Father Eise could still go to confession with his spiritual director before his departure.

The prisoners were supposed to paste paper bags. They all did that. Father Kentenich thought about it and refused. One thought governed him: "*As a free person, you go your own way, and therefore you never put up with anything beneath your dignity.*" No, it was not his task to paste paper bags, but to continue serving the Schoenstatt Work in some way. They did bring him the paper bag material, but they never came back to pick up the finished bags. Even his wish for a single cell was granted, although the guards were surprised about it. Most inmates didn't want to be alone. But Father Kentenich had been accustomed to this for decades. Before Christmas, when they put a priest in his cell who could barely stand captivity and needed reassuring company, it cost him a real effort. Now all privacy was gone.

The newly arrived priest wasn't the only one who sought conversation with him. Soon, individual prison wardens started coming with some excuse to talk to him. Most of them were Nazis. Joseph Behringer from Koblenz had been wounded in the war, and since he was of no use anymore on the front lines, he was assigned to the Koblenz prison as a warden. Father Kentenich shared the foodstuffs brought from Schoenstatt with his cellmate and the warden—apples, sometimes a cake, a hard smoked sausage, and other such things. The warden even generously permitted them to keep foodstuffs in their cell, which was actually strictly forbidden. It is said that a few wardens almost got into a fight over who could accompany him for the courtyard walk or bring him his meals since these frequently became occasions for shorter or longer conversations with Father Kentenich. They had never experienced anyone like this in the prison before—a priest who could listen like that and knew how to give such down-to-earth advice.

One time, when they came back from a walk in the courtyard, his shoes were dripping wet from the pouring rain. "I shouldn't have taken precisely my oldest ones. They have holes in them and the water gets through. Herr Behringer, do you know of the Brothers' Hospital?"

"Yes, I even live very close by!"

"Do you think it would be possible for you to ask the superior there if she could send me a different pair of shoes?"

"Sure, I can do that! Here, take this slip of paper and write a note yourself. I'll go there!"

The warden gave him a slip of paper and a pencil, and Father Kentenich wrote his own personal lines for the first time in five weeks. *"On Friday or Saturday when my laundry is brought from Schoenstatt, please also bring shoes. Water gets into the ones I have here. Sincere congratulations to all who took their exams! Read St. Paul's first letter to the Thessalonians more often: chap. 2:17-3:13 and chap. 4:9-13. Heartfelt greetings and blessings to all, and thanks for the novena. Thus it remains; we remain faithful."* He had to give the pencil back right away.

That was the second half of October 1941. The superior sent shoes and also wrote a little personal greeting. Joseph Behringer delivered everything to Father Kentenich. This was the start of an illegal letter exchange between Schoenstatt and its founder. Behringer was happy to do him this favor, even though it put the lives of both of them in danger. Father Kentenich saw this accommodation as an open door that made it possible for him to work for his followers. Behringer brought the mail while he made his rounds during night duty, and once it had been read, he picked it up again.

Joseph Kentenich wrote under difficult conditions, on paper bag material with pencil stubs. His prison cell was poorly lit because the church tower across from it absorbed a lot of light, and at this time of year it got dark early. The rough side of the paper was good for writing, but the shiny side—that was strenuous business. The pencil stub dulled more quickly and there was nothing to sharpen it with. Father Kentenich tried to push the lead forward a little bit from the other end. His eyes and hands hurt. But it was his duty to care for the Work that God had entrusted to him and commissioned him to lead.

Johannes Nattermann was a respectable prison warden who likewise had little to do with the Nazis. He, too, liked to seek opportunities for conversation with the priest in the second-to-last cell of the corridor. He gradually confided all his concerns to him. Nattermann wanted to show his gratitude in some way. Since he lived on the island of Niederwerth near Koblenz, he offered to bring greetings to Schoenstatt. In the middle of November, he headed to the Wildburg for the first time in order to meet Sister Blandina there and pass on the greetings to her. She was speechless at having heard something from Father Kentenich in this way. Naturally, she asked with great concern about how he was doing and prepared a few sandwiches for him and his warden, something very coveted during this time of war and hunger. She told him he could gladly stop by again on occasion. And he did. The second time, he brought a written greeting along. This grew as more and more mail found its way to those responsible in Schoenstatt via Mr. Nattermann. The two messengers—the "short" messenger and the "tall" messenger, as they were called in Schoenstatt because of their stature—knew nothing of each other. They proceeded very carefully, with alternating meeting points and always under the seal of absolute secrecy. Johannes Nattermann confided to Father Kentenich that he was worried about his thirteen-year-old son who was having such a hard time with Latin in school. Father Kentenich then sent a message to Sister Blandina that she should give private tutoring lessons in Latin to Mr. Nattermann's son. Every Saturday from then on, Rudi Nattermann appeared at the Wildburg for tutoring sessions with the sister who seemingly knew his father well. Everyone involved was happy with the results: He got a two in Latin on his report card.

Many risks were taken during this time. One time, Father Kentenich wrote, "*Since there will be a big inspection here on Monday, I wouldn't like to leave these things here.*" After the search was over, he commented in a further letter, "*If you saw me here, you would quickly notice how my life and all my actions are one great, bold, dangerous game from morning to night.*" Nattermann also brought all the items—in miniature—that Father Kentenich needed to celebrate holy Mass. The sisters had given him a tiny stole, a small missal, a little Emser pillbox containing hosts, little glasses for wine and water, and a small silver cup. Actually the cup had originally come from a shop in Koblenz and served as a valuable little schnapps glass. Father Kentenich used the pocket watch cover bearing the image of Christ crowned with thorns as a paten. Priests were forbidden under penalty of death to celebrate Mass, but Father Joseph Kentenich considered the sacrifice of the Mass to be the center of his life and he didn't want to renounce it. "*I will celebrate the first holy Mass for you,"* he gratefully told Johannes Nattermann, who right away objected and said, "No, that you must offer for your sisters." But Father Kentenich couldn't be dissuaded from his Mass intention. Each morning, when the noise and yelling were the loudest, when doors were thrown open and buckets brought in for cleaning the floors, Joseph Kentenich knelt silently. With his back to the peephole, and facing the stool on which he had laid everything out, he celebrated holy Mass—short, concentrated, and with inner recollection. His cellmate silently and inconspicuously celebrated with him; he didn't dare to celebrate on his own. He admired Father Kentenich for his courage, but also for his convincing priestly personality. Time and again, he would suggest that they pray together, hold spiritual conversations, and present theological topics to each other. And his cellmate was impressed by Father Kentenich's deep relationship with God. Not long after he had arrived in their shared cell, he had woken up one night to find Father Kentenich kneeling motionless on the floor, immersed in prayer. And that wasn't the only time. Father Kentenich would pray during the night for hours on end on the cold stone floor of the damp cell. That must have been the secret of his inner strength.

The illegal letters facilitated communication between the founder and his Schoenstatt Family, making their close relationship increasingly clear. Ten days after his transfer from the bunker to the Carmel Prison, he wrote to the sisters, *"Good thing the soul is a spirit and not dependent on exterior nearness; good thing God maintains direct access to the human heart and himself determines the climate in which it can fulfill its main vocation most quickly and surely; finally, good thing we can speak not only to people about God but also to God about people. I make ample use of this opportunity—just like St. Paul did (Gal. 4:19)."*

Father Kentenich could hardly believe his eyes! While meditating, he happened to look over toward the Carmelite Church tower and suddenly discovered the head of a Sister of Mary in the dormer window. It was Sister Annette, who had written *Everyday Sanctity* with him and was active in the formation of the young sisters. And then—another head! It was Sister Laurentia, the procurator of the community. Incredible! They had even been able to track him down here! Naturally, the joy was great—on both sides. He couldn't help but laugh about the situation. The heads appeared and disappeared like a puppet show! But he was happy about the faithful bond that always led them to find possibilities. Both sides tried to make themselves understood by way of signs and gestures. But this could also be seen by other prison inmates who had their cells on that side. Perhaps this was too dangerous. Plus, the prisoners might make all kinds of comments about the sisters. After this visit from the tower, he wrote to Schoenstatt, asking them please to refrain from returning, as nice as the visit was.

Now they looked for new possibilities. Perhaps there was a better way. While they were scouting things out, the two sisters ran into the sexton of the Carmelite Church. He identified himself as a former student of Father Kentenich in Vallendar. Happy to be of service, he went ahead of them and showed them a tower window that could only be seen from Father Kentenich's cell and the cell above it. It couldn't be a more favorable spot. From then on, Father Kentenich received visitors from Schoenstatt more often: priests, Pallottine Fathers, and sisters. The Jewish prisoner occupying the cell above Father Kentenich would knock to make him aware of his "visitors." It was simply an incomprehensible joy at least to be able to see each other again in this way! Shortly before Christmas, he answered on brown paper, *"That was a surprise! I had just written my Christmas letter and given it to X., when I looked out and there—that was my first great Christmas joy. ... You surely would have liked me to open the window. Well, if only I could have! Freedom is restricted here down to the smallest details. 'Peter, the time is coming when someone else will gird you!' That time has come. But it's not hard for me because all of that is secondary. The main thing is God in your souls. And they are maturing to the measure of the full stature of Christ. That is my greatest joy of all. Were you able to see me through the window as well as I could see you? Then you could tell how well I'm doing. I also have a better idea of how you look. Now stick together faithfully, too—each one at her place—and serve the sisters in love and sincere goodness of heart. You must do in my stead what I am not able to do. Heartfelt Christmas wishes."* For security reasons, he never wrote a date or a name.

Living in a Different World

Christmas Eve 1941. His fellow prisoner missed the warm atmosphere of home he usually experienced in the parish rectory at Christmas. Tremendous homesickness overcame him whenever he thought of it. The tears fell as he poured his heart out to Father Kentenich. Soon afterwards, feeling a bit relieved, he lay down on the plank bed and fell fast asleep. Joseph Kentenich's thoughts circled around his spiritual family. He thought of the priests and sisters and all their sacrifices and prayers for his release. Shortly before midnight, he heard something outside the door of his cell. He sat up and paid close attention. A little letter was pushed under his door. He got up quietly. The moon was shining brightly into the room, enabling him to read the message immediately on his plank bed. It was an anonymous letter to the Christ Child, the kind children sometimes wrote before Christmas. But the handwriting was not unfamiliar to him. In spirit he saw the young Sister Mariengard before his eyes. She and 54 other sisters worked hard at the hospital in Koblenz. What he now read was so refreshing to the heart and at the same time so deep and tender that it seemed to him *"like a fairy tale from the Arabian Nights"*:

"Dear Christ Child! Soon you will come down to earth again this Holy Night, and I haven't even written my wish list to you. Each year you bring many nice things to all good children. I shall gladly go without them if only Father comes back. This is my one very big petition for you this year. Our beloved father has been away from us now for so long, and we are all homesick for him. Couldn't you arrange it that you send an angel to Father when you come down to earth this Holy Night? Then his cell would suddenly be filled with light. The angel would say, 'Fear not, for behold, I proclaim to you good news of great joy. Today the Savior has been born to you in

Schoenstatt. Go in haste to the shrine. There you will find the Child in the arms of his Mother!' And then many angels would come and prepare Father's way to the little shrine. There he would see the 'Miracle of the Holy Night.' The Child would say, 'Now you may always stay close to me and tell your children much about me, so that hand-in-hand with my Mother, they will find their way to me, too.' And all Schoenstatt children would be blissfully happy and spend the whole night praising you and your Mother. And ever after, future generations would speak of the 'Miracle of the Holy Night.'"

The letter ended with a self-composed prayer in poetic form. As it later became apparent, the writer had never thought these innocent lines could end up reaching "Father"—as he was referred to in the letter—in his prison cell. She had simply dropped the Christ Child letter into the superior's mailbox shortly before Christmas Eve so that she could read it to the community. She had hoped it would inspire them all to pray for their founder even more. But the superior made use of the opportunity to smuggle the letter into the prison via the "short messenger," Mr. Behringer.

Father Kentenich straightened up and looked into the starry night through the window in his cell. The childlike trust and tender love revealed in these lines touched him most deeply. But there was something more he could perceive in the childlike style of the Christ Child letter. There was a genuine readiness to give everything out of responsibility for one another, for him and for their common Work. He had to reply. Right away! He quietly pulled the stool over, sat on his plank bed, took a pencil and paper, and began to respond in the name of the Christ Child with the same tender and childlike language. He addressed the writer directly and allowed her name—Mariengard—to inspire him. Yes, the Christ Child would free "Father" when her heart and the heart of the entire sisters' family had become a *"blossoming Garden of Mary."* That meant that the fulfillment of her wish was placed into her hands *"and the hands of all Schoenstatt children."*

It wasn't just nice, flowery poetry. The situation was much too serious for that. Behind the beautiful imagery was the hidden petition that they grow with him toward a greater love and inner freedom in mutual responsibility for one another.

Sister Mariengard received his reply from prison still during the Christmas days. She hurried to her superior with it right away. In the end, the whole community at the Koblenz hospital listened carefully and full of excitement to the little letter. They understood the request of the "Christ Child"! The inspiration to keep their "*garden in fine trim*" met with an enthusiastic reaction. The letter—written by the founder's own hand—sparked something new. It awakened a flood of ideas regarding how to make use of everyday life to give God more joy. The small, closed community guarded everything as their secret for the time being. Now, in the midst of hard daily life in the military hospital, they were filled with one thought alone: The loving services they rendered to God in a thousand little ways through their patients, doctors, and fellow sisters could help free their father and founder from imprisonment and enable him to work for Schoenstatt once again unhindered. It was no usual "rescue operation." It was borne by faith in the reality of God and in their communion in God: Whatever each individual did had an effect on others. It was this representative, co-redemptive activity as disciples of Jesus that appealed to them.

The mail Father Kentenich received afterwards made it ever more clear how important he had become for his "family." They knew they were known and appreciated by him, and they appreciated him. He led them on the ways of God. This mutual attachment had grown in depth over the course of many years. His incarceration had initiated an extraordinary maturation process on the human and spiritual levels. He understood the responsibility God had given him in this regard. Their fates had become "*interwoven*" with his, so to speak, and his with theirs.

His life had anyway never been an end in itself. Through his vocation to the priesthood, he had been designated for a life given to others. But now there was something more. He recognized how much he had really become a father for his Schoenstatt Family. They followed him, believed in him and his mission, and oriented their lives on his inspirations and guidance in the Holy Spirit. Again and again, he read holy Scripture and discovered references, especially in St. Paul's letters, that confirmed his responsibility for them. In his letters he repeatedly referred to St. Paul's letter to the Philippians: "I give thanks to my God at every remembrance of you, praying always with joy in my every prayer for all of you, because of your partnership for the gospel from the first day until now. I am confident of this, that the one who began a good work in you will continue to complete it until the day of Christ Jesus. It is right that I should think this way about all of you, because I hold you in my heart, you who are all partners with me in grace, both in my imprisonment and in the defense and confirmation of the gospel ..." (Philippians 1:3ff). He wrote to Schoenstatt on Christmas, *"I sincerely and gladly surrender this loss (of freedom) to the loving God and am ready to bear it in every imaginable way until the end of my life—if I can thereby 'ransom' the continued existence, fruitfulness, and holiness of the whole family and each one of you until the end of times ... The most valuable thing the human being possesses is his freedom. With sincere, glowing love, I sacrifice this freedom so that the loving God may lavishly give to the family for all times the spirit of the freedom of God's children which I desire so much for you. ... Before entering into his Passion, the Savior prayed: No one takes my life from me ... I give it myself because I so will it. I do the same. No one takes my freedom from me; I give it voluntarily ... that is, because I so will it, or more precisely, because God wishes it so ... And my food is to do the will of the one who sent me."*

"That must sure be some impressive man if you're willing to put us all in such danger! But if you think it's the right thing, we'll make it through together!" Mrs. Behringer put the rice pudding on the table, sweetened with a little bit of sugar and cinnamon, together with a few cookies, apples, and nuts. She lit the candles. More than that, she wasn't able to offer today.

Joseph Behringer had just pressed a pouch into his eldest daughter's hand and asked her to take it to the Brothers' Hospital. "But watch out, it's very important. And be careful!" Her father normally spoke little, but now he replied to his wife, "You have no idea what kind of man he is, how he came out of that darkness, and how much the people in Schoenstatt are attached to him—priests, sisters, men, women, youth. He means something to so many people! And I can understand why. We've never had anyone like this there, and the Gestapo either."

They had already opened gifts together early on that Christmas Eve 1941 because Behringer was on night duty again. Now he pulled a piece of ham out of his briefcase. He had received it from the sisters at the hospital for Christmas. His wife's eyes got bigger and bigger and began to shine. She quickly grabbed some bread and a knife.

Her husband had no way of knowing the significance of the little piece of mail he would slip under Joseph Kentenich's cell door this Holy Night. He had volunteered again for night duty, so he was able to do many favors for this priest he esteemed so much. For example, he could permit him to open his window at night to get some better air. This made it possible for Father Kentenich also to open the window secretly during the day when visitors came to the tower window so they could speak to each other.

All of this had to be done with extreme caution and prudence. One day, Father Kentenich had the inner inspiration to stash a few things away before their walk, especially the latest letters. His intuition had not deceived him. When he returned, he found his cell ransacked. Out of jealousy, the chief guard had ordered a search of his cell; he found foodstuffs, but no letters. As a result, he pressured Father Kentenich to admit that he had gotten those things from one of the wardens. Fortunately, he'd had a visitor a few days earlier. His cousin Henriette had brought him some good things. The chief guard knew that. With that, the prisoner was able to convince him. By the time the grand search took place on the next day, everything suspicious had disappeared. Nothing else was to be found.

The Decision

In the meantime, he had drafted a long, precise defense statement proving the legal errors of the Gestapo and demanding his immediate release. On a human level, he hadn't wanted to leave any stone unturned to oppose the restrictions on his activity. On January 13, he was called to another interrogation. When he didn't give the answers the Gestapo wanted to hear, they threatened him with the concentration camp. That didn't faze him, which irritated the officers. Three days later, Kentenich was brought to the prison doctor. The results: "Fit for camp, although limited due to age!" Now, after a four-month imprisonment, he finally received an official red slip stating that he'd been taken into custody. With that it was clear that he would soon be sent to the concentration camp. When the news reached Schoenstatt, it hit them like a bomb. Now they sought possibilities to keep the founder from going to the concentration camp—presumably Dachau.

Still that same day in the afternoon, Sister Laurentia sought out a certain Mr. Johannes Schmitz, a man she knew well. As a municipal official, he had been responsible since the beginning of the war for the administration of the city hospitals as well as new auxiliary hospitals for the civilian population. He had a lot of contact with Church institutions. Since he was an opponent of the Regime, and especially because of his position, he could secretly avert or mitigate many calamities. Sister Laurentia now told him about Father Kentenich's case and asked him to exert influence on the prison doctor, a convinced Nazi. "Can't you somehow move the doctor to examine Father Kentenich once more and declare him 'unfit for camp'?"

Looking skeptical, Johannes Schmitz turned up the corners of his mouth. "All right, I'll try it at least. There is a ray of hope—I often work with him at the Kemperhof Hospital and run into him almost every day."

A few days later, he joyfully reported to his older daughter what he had in fact managed to do: "First, with my clever but seemingly casual questions, I got the doctor to confirm that he had indeed declared Father Kentenich fit for camp. By pretending to be astonished that a 'deathly ill man' was supposed to go to Dachau, I lured him into admitting that the examination was merely a formality. Then I acted surprised again: 'How can a man who is anyway as good as dead and won't live much longer be considered dangerous? That's unnecessary brutality, and besides, it's a proof of ineptitude that will be more harmful to the Regime than helpful.' You won't believe this, but after a while he was actually willing to re-examine the 'deathly ill old man' and declare him unfit for camp, provided the latter would report sick. What do you think of that?" His daughter returned his expectant look with a proud, approving smile. The news was immediately passed via Schoenstatt into the prison—with the beseeching plea to Father Kentenich to report sick and so initiate a new examination.

Sister Laurentia climbed hurriedly up to the tower window. He had to sign it! Both she and others from the leadership circles in Schoenstatt had already taken up contact with him multiple times through letters and visits to the tower window. She feared for him but also for the community. What would happen if the founder had to go to the concentration camp? That was a sure death sentence. After all, she knew how many things still had to be settled and how insecure the leadership of the community was in the hands of Sister Anna! Whenever Father Kentenich was there, he could complement and compensate for whatever the general superior wasn't able to give. He had almost become both father and mother for the sisters. If he as the complementary influence and "father of the family" were now to be taken out of the picture, it would be a perfect catastrophe ... She herself had given the founder examples of how the general superior had "often terrified the whole house" during his absence and created chaos and confusion. "In council meetings or individual encounters it sometimes seems to me as if there were two people inside her. Sometimes she'll be friendly, empathetic, religious, and ready for action, and then suddenly, from one moment to the next, she becomes violent, impulsive, and uncontrollable, asserting her own importance. Goethe's words fit her well: 'Two souls live in my breast.'"

"But—the one soul knows nothing of the other. She is not conscious of it." He didn't give her more of an answer than this, but his face couldn't help but show concern.

Sister Laurentia had no way of knowing that the founder had already taken precautions. He had told one of the council sisters that he had decided to accommodate Sister Anna's repeated request to be relieved of her office. Should he not survive the Nazi imprisonment, Sister Anna would be required to resign. He had also communicated this with Sister Anna herself as well as with two of the Pallottine Fathers. It was a kind of final provision by the founder, which, however, was known by no one but those four persons.

Joseph Kentenich stood at the little barred window of his prison cell with the official report and all the letters still in his hands. A struggle now began within him which he would later refer to as *"mein Freiheitskampf [my struggle for freedom]."* Should he accept the offer of a new doctor's examination, grasping at this straw? Should he, the shepherd, try to get his head out of the noose while his flock—those entrusted to him, like Father Eise, Father Fischer, and many other priests—were already in the concentration camp? Should he leave them all to their fate without carrying the cross with them? He had prepared so many people for the concentration camp. And now he was supposed to do all he could to escape it? Moreover, it wasn't even certain that he wouldn't go to Dachau anyway, even if he would now be declared unfit for camp. Ultimately this medical certificate was of no decisive significance. And hadn't his inner inspirations gone in a totally different direction up until now? To trust entirely in the reality of God for his release? To stake everything on this one truth? After all, for him it had always been a matter of the *"supernatural person."* Wasn't the striving for a disposition and attitude of faith ultimately the key to conquering such a diabolical regime?

Humanly speaking, it now became incredibly difficult for him to make the right decision. Could he really disappoint those who had already worked so hard for his freedom in faith and trust? Could he really leave them behind with a Work still in its founding process? In all probability, Dachau would mean *"eternal separation"* from his own; it would mean his death. Who ever came back from there? And what would become of the sisters? Would Sister Anna keep his directive if he didn't return? Although she had already distanced herself from him back in 1931, he had tried everything to help her. Yes, for the first time in years he had even *"treated her with harsh strictness,"* openly telling her how uncontrolled and power-hungry she was and how much the sisters and the council suffered under her. Breaking out in tears, she had then asked to be relieved of her office. But he had always believed in the good in her and that it would prevail. But he might have been wrong. The larger the sisters' family became and the more the demands and burdens of governing such a community grew, the more strongly her inability and her incapacity for the office came to light. And still, he couldn't make the decision to relieve her. For him, it was ultimately a matter of a new type of religious family. Parents weren't simply relieved of their task. God would have to give him a clear sign.

He paused and looked out the window, pondering: But wasn't all of this God's work? Schoenstatt and all its life and communities were not built on human abilities. He himself knew that best of all. He actually owed everything to God who had given him life. If he now staked everything on this one card, God, wouldn't it be even more possible to lead his spiritual sons and daughters on the same way of surrender? He wanted to give them something so much greater than his own active involvement—namely, growth into the deep conviction of the reality of God. *"God is an indispensable reality!"* He could vouch for that with his whole person, his whole life. And everything was possible for God! If only they would all take their discipleship of Christ seriously and learn to love the cross, even to the point of readiness to renounce his person if God so willed it! But that would mean declining purely human means and heroically relying only on faith, hope, and love ... Was it stubbornness or an inspiration of the Holy Spirit that made him hesitate to accept the offer? He wrote to Schoenstatt, *"And now visitor after visitor is coming and making the decision hard for me ... Now even letters are coming, too ... They torment me."* His eyes welled up with tears. He suffered so much with those who appeared at the tower window pleading and begging. What was he to do?

During the night of January 19-20, 1942, he had to make his way to a decision. By 5:00 p.m. the following day he was supposed to have signed the application for a new examination. His natural feeling urged him to do it—after all, he had hoped for so long that he would be freed. But now? All night long, hour after hour, he paced those few steps back and forth in his prison cell, occupied with nothing else but the one question: What did God want? Morning dawned. He celebrated the sacrifice of the Mass by himself at daybreak. And then it was clear to him. He wrote to Father Menningen, *"Just now during holy Mass I received the answer to the question left open yesterday. Our priests should take the inscriptio seriously ... especially some of the older ones. Then I'll be set free. Please understand my answer in the light of faith in the reality of supernature and of the interwovenness of destiny of the members of our family."*

The decision had been made. The deadline passed; he had not signed the application. During the following weeks, he went back and forth between hoping for his release and preparing for Dachau. Sometimes as he prayed he had the almost certain impression that he would be "ransomed" by all the sacrifices and prayers of his spiritual children. But then it really did turn out differently. In the middle of his personal retreat, one of the guards whispered to him that he was slated for transport to Dachau on March 11. The news reached Schoenstatt two days before this date.

When Mrs. Behringer's husband returned from night duty and gave her this news, she spontaneously said, "But then I must see him right now!"

Joseph Behringer put on his civilian clothing and did indeed go with his wife to Platform 1 in Koblenz, where the prisoners were to depart for Dachau in cattle cars. As Father Kentenich stepped onto the platform with the other prisoners, closely watched by armed SS men and fierce guard dogs, Mr. Behringer ran up to him and introduced his wife. Their daughter later related, "My mother had no idea how to describe this encounter to me, so impressed had she been by Father Kentenich. But then she was better able to understand my father's dangerous mission."

In a matter of moments, amid loud yelling and brutal blows with rifle butts and batons, all drowned out by the wild barking of the dogs, the inmates were driven into the cattle cars with the other prisoners. A young communist with a face full of fear latched on to Father Kentenich and from that moment never left his side. Carls, too, the director of Caritas from Wuppertal who knew him well, also pushed his way through the crowd over to Father Kentenich, and the two of them stayed together from then on. In Frankfurt and Wuerzburg, they were driven out again under the supervision of armed SS men and barking dogs. They stayed overnight in underground vaults. The transport took two days and two nights. The prisoners were herded closely together without any rest. Only twice were they given a stingy meal, but never anything to drink. The requests of individual prisoners for something to eat or even just for water were met with scornful laughter and blows with rifle butts. *"Wherever possible, one's sense of honor and one's human sensitivity were deliberately violated."*

7. In the Dachau Concentration Camp

One hundred seventy-eight prisoners arrived at the train station in the small town of Dachau on the afternoon of March 13. A cool wind was blowing. They could already hear the dogs barking even before the locomotive rolled in. Hardly had they stumbled out of the cattle cars when SS men herded them into covered cargo trucks with loud screams, beatings, and kicks. They stood closely packed together in the cargo space; only the SS men, armed with machine guns, had reserved two wooden benches for themselves in front. The tarps were drawn; sudden pitch-black darkness enveloped them. Not a word was spoken. Although it was cold, the air was stale with the suffocating smell of dust and sweat. An eerie, fear-laden silence pervaded the inside of the truck and slowly crept through the prisoners' bodies, pulsating through their veins all the way to the tips of their toes.

No sooner had the prisoners arrived at the concentration camp when commands and insults were shouted at them. "Go on, move! Faster! Get out! We're sure going to make you run, you filthy, gluttonous swine. You'd better get moving, you lazy scum! Line up and march!"

"It's all a strategy of intimidation!" he thought. Now he saw where they had ended up. A huge complex: Along the access road, the beautiful villas of the SS leadership and their families displayed their splendor. Further back was the SS training camp for future commanders of other concentration camps as well as the headquarters and barracks of the Totenkopfverbände [Death's Head Units] and the Waffen-SS [Armed SS]. Next to it was the penal camp for SS men who had gone astray and the SS payroll center for all of Germany. And finally, the prison camp proper. It consisted of a spacious roll-call area in front of the horseshoe-shaped economic and administrative wing, the "honorary bunkers" for prominent prisoners behind it, and the infamous punishment bunker—a place of horror where people were subjected to unspeakable tortures and torments and where thousands were hung or shot to death at the execution wall.

"Arbeit macht frei [Work will make you free]" ... Behind the iron gate with this cynical inscription, thirty-four barracks extended on the left side in two rows for almost a kilometer (about half a mile), each of them one hundred meters (330 feet) long and ten meters (thirty-three feet) wide with four dormitories and four living rooms connected by an anteroom and two washrooms. Three-tier primitive wooden bunkbeds with rough straw sacks filled the dormitory up to the ceiling. The washroom, which consisted of one large washbasin in the middle with seven water faucets on each side, was used by up to 300 inmates. Next to it was the restroom with ten free-standing toilet bowls. Between the two rows of buildings was the broad camp street; the block streets ran perpendicular to it. Everything was arranged so that from the side doors of the barracks, the prisoners could march in step in rows of ten from both sides in a well-ordered manner to the roll-call square. After all, even in "hell" there had to be order ... The camp was originally built for 5,000 prisoners. One block was supposed to hold a maximum of 200 inmates. Since then, 600 to 800 prisoners were housed in each block. From 1934 until the end of the war, some 230,000 prisoners passed through the Dachau concentration camp; over 41,000 died there.

At the time when Joseph Kentenich came into the camp, it held more than 14,000 prisoners from various nations. Those who in some way didn't conform to the reigning ideology and government were gradually removed from the "national body" and brought into concentration camps: Jews, gypsies, vagabonds, felons, and political opponents, as well as homosexuals, Jehovah's witnesses, and priests. Almost 3,000 clerics, mostly Catholic priests, had been sent to Dachau from all over Germany and occupied regions such as Austria and Poland. There were thirteen sickbays and the priests' block 26 containing the camp chapel in which the German priests were allowed to celebrate Mass. In blocks 28 and 30, almost 1,700 Polish

Photo 10: On the day of his internment in Dachau, March 13, 1942

priests had to live packed together in unbearably overcrowded conditions. The plantation and camp nursery were among the many on-site work detachments. Everything was strictly guarded and secured. The property was illumined by floodlights and monitored day and night by SS men armed with machine guns in seven watchtowers. A high wall, a moat with flowing water, electric barbed-wire fences, a two-meter (seven-foot) wide ditch, and a "no-man's land" ensured that there would be no escape. Those who ran onto the neutral zone in despair or were purposely driven there were immediately shot without warning. Some miserable figures were always made to stand on the roll-call square as a punishment. A nauseating smell from the burning of corpses hung day and night over the camp. Rabbit hutches? Yes, angora rabbits were bred there, well-fed and carefully cultivated for their beautiful wool ... It was a *"city of slaves, of fools, of heathens, and of death,"* as Father Kentenich rightly characterized this whole panorama in his first letter to Schoenstatt.

The Life of the Miserable Ones

Hardly had they set foot on the square in front of the administration building when the SS began their harassments again. They strode up and down the rows in their heavy boots and asked individuals why they were there, insulting them and violently striking them in the face. They were to learn fear in order to be made compliant from the beginning. The whole strategy of the camp leadership was built on this principle. Priests were especially taunted and insulted: "You filthy, gluttonous swine!"

"Hey, you there!" an SS man snapped at Father Kentenich. "Are you a Jew?"

"No!"

"What are you?"

"A Catholic priest."

"Then why do you wear a beard?" To this he got no answer.

As another SS squad leader challenged him with questions, Joseph Kentenich remained silent again and smiled. "Does this one want to provoke me, by chance?" The SS man drew back his hand to strike him. But the prisoner simply stood there motionless and looked at him with calm eyes. Slowly he let down his arm.

The new arrivals were driven to the main office of the Gestapo where they were registered. Each one received a number, and priests received a red triangle standing for "political opponent." From then on, Father Kentenich was number 29392.

"Hand over all your things! Undress completely!" They threw him a white drill suit—used prison clothes, rather thin, torn, and shabby. Then a pair of socks and some wooden clogs. No consideration was given as to whether the things fit or not. The prisoners were supposed to worry about that themselves and exchange with each other. "Off to the disinfection baths!" They were all hustled into the showers, which were either much too hot or much too cold. Then their heads were shaved bare. Everything was taken from them: their clothes, their hair, their home, their family and friends, their name and rights, and with all that, their dignity. "The German people have expelled you. Scum is what you are! Nothing more! You yourselves have forfeited all rights," they explained to them. The next order: to line up on the roll-call square where they would be picked up by the corresponding block elder.

Within the camp, the SS had roped prisoners into supervisory duties: a "camp elder" with representatives, a "block elder" for each row of barracks, and a "room elder" in each room. The word "elder" was appropriate in as far as they usually selected those who had already been in the camp for a long time, who knew the camp order, and who had learned over the course of the years "to bow toward above and to kick toward below." They were usually communists or social democrats; these had been in the camp the longest because they were among the first ones taken into Nazi custody in 1933. After having lived so long in the camp, many of them had become interiorly brutalized. They were supposed to have "organizational capabilities," but by this the SS meant the ability to be brutal and ruthless. However, the camp commandant's office was mistaken about some of the prisoners. There were good and benevolent ones among them who only faked their fits of yelling when SS men were present.

Hugo Gutmann, leader of the admission block (for new arrivals), was a baptized Catholic but had distanced himself from the faith; as a Swiss journalist he had committed himself to communism. The prisoners considered him volatile. Already at the first encounter it was possible to ruin everything by saying the wrong thing. But with Father Kentenich, things happened differently, perhaps because he showed no fear. Immediately upon receiving the prisoners, Hugo Gutmann couldn't resist provoking the priests: "You preachers talk about the Lord God! I've never come across him in this place!" He challenged Father Kentenich, looking him directly in the face, "Maybe you have?"

"If you still haven't come across the Lord God in this place, then surely you must have seen the devil." He looked Gutmann directly in the eye, unimpressed.

The block elder was so stunned that on his return he went straight to the priests' block. He liked to go there from time to time to have a little spiritual discussion "with the preachers." "These days the Gestapo aren't bringing anything intelligent into the camp anymore! It was different back in our day! But today we had two admissions: a Carls and a Kentemich." And then he shared the news about the latter, hot off the press. He hadn't remembered his name correctly. Later he was also impressed by the practical sense this Kentenich displayed in his room and "how quickly he found his way around in everything." But above all, he liked how sociably he interacted with others.

The next day, the new arrivals had to return to the administration office to write their life story and be photographed. There, the SS squad leader met Father Kentenich again, the object of his fierce rage the day before. Now was his chance to show that "Jewish" preacher who was in charge! His sharp orders echoed through the cold room: "That missionary there can clean my bike!"

"Yes, I can gladly do that, but not because I have to, but in order to offer you a service as a free man."

The SS officer was so stunned that later, he unobtrusively pushed his way close to this priest again in order to look over his shoulder, curious to see what he was writing. But at that moment the prisoner calmly turned around to face him and said amiably, *"Why did you actually shout at me like that yesterday?"*

And a conversation developed between the two of them. The SS squad leader inconspicuously gave him a sign to follow him into a side room and began to tell him his life story, ending with the words, "If you ever get out of here, don't say where you met me!"

Upon higher orders from Berlin, the camp headquarters of the SS ordered that Father Kentenich was to remain in the isolated admission block. He was considered a "night and fog prisoner"—"NF prisoner," in code—who was not officially condemned to death but who under strict surveillance had to "disappear" permanently without a splash or a trace—in other words, to be killed. Such a thing was much easier to accomplish in the admission block since there was a constant coming and going. He owed the fact that he wasn't silently eliminated to the special protection of the block elder Gutmann.

Normally, the new arrivals only stayed in the admission block for three or four weeks in order to be introduced into the order of the camp and then assigned to the other blocks. The admission block was extremely loud and restless, with a frequent change of assigned lockers and beds. Joseph Kentenich stayed there for seven months. He was not allowed to join the other priests nor to take part in any Mass in the camp chapel which had been obtained for the priests by the efforts of the German bishops.

But right away on the first day, to his great joy, a fellow prisoner and priest secretly handed him a tiny particle of a host. "Father, this is the Most Blessed Sacrament." His confrere cast a furtive glance at a small piece of paper in his hand. Full of joy, Father Kentenich received Communion. He saw it as a tender, thoughtful gift from heaven. The Lord had personally received him in this place of horror.

The way the SS leadership had orchestrated camp life was no accident. Joseph Kentenich quickly saw through the underlying strategy. They tried to rob human beings—who in the eyes of the Nazis were actually "subhuman beings" and "traitors of the nation"—of all the values and ideals they had always believed in.

They were to have no name, no rights, no honor. It was imperative to enslave this "unworthy life," or even better, to exterminate it completely. *"In Dachau the human being was an outlaw,"* as Joseph Kentenich described the lack of rights. *"The prisoners had fewer rights than a herd of cattle."* From the very beginning of their time in the camp they were to experience that they were "nothing." After the Jews, who were treated the worst, they zeroed in on the priests, especially the priests from foreign countries. They crammed the clerics together in the tightest spaces so that they would soon get on each other's nerves and quarrel with one another. By this they wanted to mock their ideals of love of neighbor and trust in God, especially by depriving them of things that were necessary to live. Contact with other prisoners was not permitted so that they wouldn't have any pastoral influence on others. The Nazis fueled the hatred of the other prisoners by derisively flaunting the temporarily effective privileges for priests; they were made to chug the allotment of cocoa and wine in front of others. They were released from work duty for a time, but in exchange, they had to carry the 150-liter (forty-gallon) food containers in pairs from the kitchen to the barracks, or they had to take charge of the revolting task of cleaning the latrines. In 1942, all "privileges" were rescinded. Like everyone else, the priests had to join work crews, and those who were not capable of doing so ended up on the transport of invalids, a ride to death. In the long run, an atmosphere of hatred developed in the camp—a hatred systematically "trained" by the Nazis throughout the Reich, a climate of mutual resentment and hostility where envy and jealousy, intrigues and denunciations were able to flourish. This was precisely the intention of SS leadership. No solidarity or community among them should be able to form. Prisoners who couldn't stand their fellow inmates "stabbed them in the back." Precisely because the oppressive measures they experienced from without had no natural outlet—they were all powerless before the SS—they directed their built-up aggression, hiddenly or openly, toward each other.

The concentration camp was truly a pool of evil, inhumanity, and hatred of human beings—"hell." It was with sadness that Father Kentenich observed this seemingly "successfully orchestrated" situation in the camp. Instead of forging a bond between them, the suffering the prisoners experienced drove them against each other. *"How little communion of hearts, how little sincere mutual benevolence there was in Dachau. ... People hardly supported each other in the camp; they hardly found their way to each other. By and large there wasn't much true communion,"* he commented about the situation.

The course of the day hardly left space for any kind of personal thoughts. The prisoners were so constantly pushed around that not a minute of reflection was possible. The permanent living together in close-packed quarters made it impossible to come to inner peace. The day began at 4:30 a.m. (and even earlier for the priests because of Mass). The prisoners awakened to the unpleasant, hollow blare of sirens. Then came the mad rush of washing, dressing, and making the straw-sack beds. The sacks had to be straightened as exactly *"as if made of cement."* Right after that, the blow of whistles began again. The prisoners of the admission block and the punishment block—both "isolation blocks" fenced off from the others by wire netting—gathered on their block street, while all the others were ordered onto the large camp street in rows of ten. They had to take their assigned places on the roll-call square amid singing that was more like raucous shouting. Upon the command, "Work detachments, form!" the individual crews assembled and marched off in step toward hardest physical labor. They returned only in the evening, completely exhausted.

"When people get into a certain situation, most of them stop leading a humanly dignified life, and that's also why there was the consciously targeted aim: Throw the human being into primitive conditions; then you will make even the most astute into primitive human beings," as Father Kentenich stated, summarizing the intention of the SS and their camp regulations. He often had to watch as prisoners were chased around on the roll-call square like slaves, made to pull heavy carts *"as in the days of old paganism. Chains were wrapped around them, and*

finally the SS men climbed into the cart and struck the prisoners, often throwing things at them."

There were no flowers in the camp, nothing green, nothing that brought anything beautiful and good to mind—just a row of dead poplars. The prisoners were tormented and made to endure cruel punishments. One of the "usual" tortures for these weakened and exhausted prisoners was the often hours-long standing punishment in scorching heat or ice-cold weather. The most barbarous punishments were imposed for the smallest trivialities. Sadistic SS men, but also "capos" and elders, often looked for just one reason to torment human beings. *"I wouldn't have been able to imagine back then that animals could exist like that,"* acknowledged Father Kentenich later. The most distressing thing which took away his sleep for several nights was the report by Dr. Eduard Pesendorfer, a friend who was the head orderly at the sickbay. On that day he had to "empty out" train cars that terrified even the SS men themselves—a transport that had started out with 200 men but arrived with only 150 living prisoners. The prisoners had been locked up for five whole days without receiving anything to eat or drink.

"The rabbits," said Father Kentenich, *"were treated much better in Dachau than the people. They had utility value. Today, the human person is in many regards no longer valued as a personality. When people get old and become a burden for their surroundings, then 'Away with them!' The human person is nothing more than a piece of a machine. The useless piece gets thrown away and a new one replaces it ... This is how human beings have been treated in the last decades. Indeed, when God is no longer acknowledged, that's the end of the dignity of the human personality. Once ideas hostile to God have become a common possession, the genuine image of the human person is on its way out."*

There was a group of doctors who didn't shy away from conducting horrific experiments on people. And lastly, the inexpressible hunger. Precisely in the year 1942, due to the overcrowding of the camp and the bad war situation, a great period of hunger set in. The daily rations weren't enough to survive, and it wasn't permitted to receive food packages from outside. In the morning there was a liter (two pints) of coffee actually consisting of brown water, at noon a watery vegetable soup, and in the evening a third to a fifth of a sourdough loaf that had to last also for the following morning. Due to undernourishment, many prisoners developed phlegmons, festering wounds that wouldn't heal. Thousands contracted dysentery. Epidemics spread quickly throughout the whole camp.

"Sometimes transports also arrived with prisoners who were completely miserable and close to death because of hunger. When SS men noticed that there was still life in the starving, they approached them with their heavy boots and murdered them before the eyes of the others. It was horrible in 1942; you saw nothing else but 'walking corpses' and staggering figures. In 1944, a famine broke out again. People were walking around—nothing but skin and bones. They were lying on the streets. And what's more, it was the cold of winter, the many epidemics! Prisoners died by the masses. Besides abdominal typhus, spotted fever was especially devastating. Miserable figures were lying and walking around by the masses. To eke out an existence amid this lack of bread ... while really remaining close to God—how hard that was! How should such people remain spiritually alert and alive if they don't have enough to eat? How can people in such need still somehow live a dignified life? I wasn't spared these things; to constantly see this screaming affliction, this maltreatment! ... Ultimately I, too, was nothing but a skeleton," Father Kentenich recalled. Father Joseph Fischer, the Schoenstatt priest who had been temporarily assigned to carrying the heavy food containers, later recorded, "The most frequent daily conversation was the conversation about the food. Each one wanted his food first and was suspiciously intent on getting the most. It was a picture of pity."

And then there was the "transport of invalids." *"It worked like a cattle market. The prisoners they wanted to get rid of, who had no work at the moment, were simply gathered together. They were scrutinized; they usually had to walk by naked while the SS men sat at the tables and looked at the 'swine.' The ones that were still useful they labeled 'swine'; all the rest were murdered."* Since Father Kentenich was not assigned to any work detachment in the admission block, he, too, was in great danger.

June 24, 1942. Once again a commission from Berlin had appeared to round up prisoners unable to work for an invalid transport. Panic immediately broke out in the camp. All "unassigned" prisoners were to report on the roll-call square immediately. Hugo Gutmann hurried into the admission block, looked for Father Kentenich—who anyway was already fifty-six years old—and brought him to Jacob Koch. He had been imprisoned as a separatist and made capo of the disinfection detachment. "Take this priest into your straw sack detachment. Please! Do it for me!"

Father Eise and Father Fischer were also assigned to mending straw sacks. "Fischer is working today in the camp office, so that works well. Kentenich can quickly state Fischer's name and number as soon as the SS come in."

By doing this, both the block elder of the admission block and the capo of the work detachment for mending straw sacks risked their lives. But everything went well. The commission passed by uninterested. Joseph Kentenich was saved. Three days later he was officially taken into the straw sack mending detachment.

When later invalid transports were set to take place, Father Kentenich succeeded in getting individuals crossed off the list due to his influence on prisoners charged with compiling the transport lists. This, too, was extremely dangerous for all involved. When it failed one time due to a mishap in the case of the Belgian professor De Kuning, he was shaken, and tears came to his eyes—tears of compassion, but also of powerlessness and anger. *"I can still see today how the prisoners were rounded up for the 'transport.' There they stood; ... strong figures who had once accomplished great things in life were mercilessly delivered up to death here in the most gruesome way. How much it offended one's sense of justice! The Lord God later took care that nothing was left of the SS regime."*

Ark and Beacon in the Midst of Hell

From the very first day, Father Kentenich did the opposite of what the SS wanted to accomplish by their strategy with the prisoners. He had no intention of adapting blindly to everything and fulfilling the inhuman expectations of the SS. He was convinced that *"the greatness of the modern person"* consists in *"resisting the dictatorship of his or her surroundings."* No, they could not be proven right. In matters of the human person they had to be proven wrong. Therefore he made every effort not to give up his own dignity and to strengthen others in their human dignity. He didn't adapt to the customary leveling and therefore devaluing "Du" [informal form of address], but out of respect for the personality used the formal "Sie" with everyone, with the exception of his closest confreres. *"From the beginning it was my conviction that Dachau was meant to put the rule to the test for me personally. It was imperative not only to proclaim the gospel of the interiorly free and animated person but also to model it in practice."* He wanted to prove that the Nazi image of the human person was heretical and that there was something great and good in every human person. He wanted to show that the human person could live out of ideals on a spiritually and morally high level in contrast to surroundings and even react nobly amid forced primitivity. He thus especially encouraged the priests time and again, *"As priests in the concentration camp of Dachau, we don't want to become primitive in the most primitive conditions, but to react naively* (that is, in a childlike way), *and if God wills it, to die a hero's death in the camp as strong, priestly personalities or to continue to work zealously and fruitfully for the Kingdom of God sometime later as matured priests. ... As priests, we don't want to waste our time concentrating on whether we have enough to eat, or how we will survive and get out of here unharmed, but rather on trying to be an ark and a beacon for the other prisoners."*

As soon as they had arrived, Father Eise and Father Fischer had started to form "small cells," groups of about eight to ten imprisoned priests who oriented themselves toward an ideal. In this way they worked in opposition to the climate in the camp. The number of such groups had grown. When Father Kentenich came into the camp, he could only cooperate by giving inspirations from a distance. After seven months in the admission block, he was placed in the Polish priests' block—a new chess move on the part of the SS intended to sideline him and with the hope that Polish hatred of Germans would blow off some steam at him. But it came to naught. He gave talks every evening in Latin to the Polish priests. When Father Francis Cegielka from East Prussia saw him, he immediately ran up to him. "Father Kentenich—my greatest joy is that you are here!" Later he explained, "Father Kentenich saved my life in Dachau." Two months later, Joseph Kentenich was finally transferred to the German priests' block. Now he organized evening talks on certain topics. Sometimes a Jesuit gave the talk, sometimes a Franciscan, sometimes a Benedictine, and sometimes he himself. His concern was that the speakers would give their confreres spiritual impulses from the wealth of their spirituality. At least during these hours, they were distracted from the primitivity of camp life and the camp dictatorship.

From the very first day, Joseph Kentenich always saved a bit of his meager bread rations to give to another prisoner who seemed especially hungry. Or he didn't eat everything in his bowl and inconspicuously passed it to someone else. Hugo Gutmann observed this a few times and his respect for this priest increased even more. As soon as he tried to slip him something, he would refuse it, asking Gutmann instead to give it to someone else who was in worse shape than he. That's why Hugo Gutmann also silently tolerated the increasing number of "visitors" who sought advice from this priest or came to him for confession. Father Kentenich quickly established good contact with communists and social democrats. He saw them as people who followed a false ideology but who recognized high ideals and were ready to die for them. To Joseph Fischer he expressed the hope that perhaps one or the other could be won over for the Church if they were given a good example of genuinely Christian social behavior. At his release, he actually made one socialist—to whom he had listened for hours on many evenings—

promise to read the New Testament from beginning to end if he was now freed. The prisoners that sought him increasingly included communists and socialists, causing the camp leadership to suspect that he was cooperating with socialist enemies even outside the camp.

Whenever it was at all possible, Father Kentenich tried to establish contacts. When the Schoenstatt priests lamented the fact that he still was not with them in the priests' block, he expressed the opinion that it was surely *"God's providence."* In this way he could hold conversations with lay people to whom he otherwise would have had no access. This led Fischer to a resourceful idea. Very early in the morning, he crept into the camp chapel and secretly took a few not-yet-consecrated hosts from the prepared paten, wrapped them in paper, and hid them in his pocket. During holy Mass, he consecrated them and brought them unseen to the admission block. There he gave the Eucharistic bread to Father Kentenich, who didn't only receive Communion himself but could also give Communion in this way to many others who had asked for it. For a long time this went well, until at some point it seeped through and the camp chaplain forbade the matter out of fear. From then on, the paten of hosts was kept under lock and key.

The first person Joseph Joos met—full of joy—when he arrived in the admission block just happened to be Father Kentenich. Joos was one of the most well-known politicians of the German Center Party from the Weimar Period and had held numerous offices. He had vehemently resisted in 1933 when his party wanted to give their consent to Hitler's Enabling Act, but he ultimately had to bow to the parliamentary majority in the Reichstag. While serving on the board of the Central Committee of German Catholics, he was denounced and arrested in 1940 for his contacts with the resistance. In 1941 he was deported to Dachau. In his books, Joos wrote about Joseph Kentenich, "For years, this unusually gifted priest unfolded an amazingly manifold and dangerous apostolic activity in the camp of Dachau." Indeed, through conversations, evening spiritual meditations, and talks about the truths of the faith, Father Kentenich gained the attention of others at least temporarily and oriented them to the world of God. He himself had experienced how much it could help master the hunger. But he, too, increasingly lost weight week by week. Not everyone could be won over, but many prisoners later reported that they owed their survival to these inspirations.

One day, as 120 Jewish children were driven into "the showers," they screamed in horror for fear they would be gassed, something they had heard about from Auschwitz. The Pallottine Father Wilhelm Poiess reported that he found out later that the children were transported further to a neighboring camp at Kaufbeuren and murdered by lethal injection. "It was easy to become numb, even raw, in the face of such horrors of death. And we thank Father Kentenich for inspiring us time and again to reflect and meditate and for admonishing us not to lose our soul's fine feeling toward things and people. He showed us the camp as a demonstration of the de-divinized and thus demonized human person. By his daily care, he preserved our souls from becoming tired and impoverished through the demoralizing atmosphere of the camp. He helped us to really make use of the camp as a test of holiness and a training for what was to come." Since Hugo Gutmann was well disposed toward him, those seeking advice only needed to tell the watchman at the door of the admission block that they were a friend of Father Kentenich's and they would be allowed in without a problem. Steiner, a communist and the dormitory capo, also protected the priest, to whom he confessed one day, "I esteem you like my father!"

"Danger awakens initiative!" It seemingly didn't trigger fear in Father Kentenich, but daring.

"Father, I am terribly afraid of all that the SS can do to a person here in the camp!" admitted Father Dresbach, a young Schoenstatt priest, in one of their first conversations.

Father Kentenich took him by the arm, looked calmly into his eyes, and said with a firm voice, *"Heinz, there is nothing at all that can happen to us that hasn't been foreseen for us by God!"* This question could be discussed endlessly. But the peculiar thing was that the security with which he stressed this reality abruptly took away Heinz Dresbach's fears. Father Kentenich animated the Schoenstatters toward friendliness, benevolence, and mutual help, thus creating a climate of solidarity that overcame all conflict. A family-like community grew around him, a "refuge for humanity," like "a bit of shelter in the heart of another amid the hell of Dachau," an ark that sought to house many others in an ocean of hatred and contempt.

"Sometimes I used the little free time I had to walk through the camp alone, and I had only this one thought: 'That is the first human being you have ever met in your life.' By that I meant that he is so human, such a naturally genuine human being from head to toe, so familiar with all things human, and able to come so interiorly close to another person—a human being like I had never known or experienced before and who at the same time was so supernaturally oriented that God and his world were more real to him than everything he could take in with his senses." That's how Heinz Dresbach experienced his first encounters with Father Kentenich in the camp.

He wasn't the only one to whom he seemed like a father. Father Poiess still distinctly remembered: "It was the morning of my second day in the admission block. A small, stocky figure made his way through the hustle and bustle. I looked into a smiling face and almost flung my arms around him for joy and jubilation. There was Father Kentenich standing before me. I can't even express how happy this reunion made me. But I have to say that during that time and later, too, he always cared for us like a father and mother in one."

Dachau brought Joseph Kentenich together with *"almost all nations and intellectual trends."* His contacts with priests from Poland, France, and other countries, who also showed interest in Schoenstatt, inspired him to expressly broaden the radius of his foundation into the international dimension. For many of his confreres, the fact that Schoenstatt was located in Germany tended to be an obstacle that made it hard for them to open themselves to this movement. When it became known in Dachau that an exact replica of the Schoenstatt Shrine had been built in South America in 1943, this helped them overcome their inhibitions and understand Schoenstatt as a supranational initiative.

Father Kentenich also got to know married Protestant pastors more closely in the camp. With keen interest he listened to them talk about their family life, their marriage, and the task they had in their communities to be examples in this regard. Afterwards he declared to Father Fischer, "The Catholic Church is lacking that!" By that he didn't mean a rejection of celibacy, but rather the idea that had been swimming around in his head for a long time already—to found a community of families who sought to model the vocation of a Christian family. Already early on, he had commissioned Father Eise with the task to lead such a family movement. It would be something totally new for the Church—married couples who, similar to the religious orders, would live Christian discipleship through their marriage and family life and so represent a model case.

New Life in the Shadow of Death

Another idea had occupied him already since 1920. Schoenstatt was lacking a community of brothers, men who would "be like leaven" in the midst of society. Since then he had already made several failed attempts at a founding. As a community, the brothers were intended to cooperate in the formation of boys and men in Schoenstatt. He had wholeheartedly entrusted this second "favorite idea" to Father Menningen's care. He wrote letters to him from Dachau referring to this concern in disguised language. Alex was supposed to take over the special responsibility for the future "Schoenstatt Brothers of Mary." Now Joseph Kentenich waited for a sign from God that would point to *"an open door."*

In April 1942, Joseph Joos introduced him to his acquaintance Dr. Fritz Kuehr. Both men had been very socially and politically active in the Weimar Republic. Kuehr was of Jewish descent and had converted to the Catholic faith. He had been awarded a doctorate in the social sciences and belonged to the "Koenigswinter Circle," a group made up of Catholic scholars who worked closely with the resistance. Due to his political views, he and his wife left Germany for South Africa in 1933, where he was able to take up a teaching position. Five years later they returned to Europe, where he became an Austrian citizen. Starting in 1938, he became the general secretary of the Austrian Chamber of Labor in Vienna. Shortly after the "annexation" of Austria, a political friend offered him the chance to flee at night to Switzerland. After making one last effort to secure a suitcase full of dangerous documents before he left, he was awaited by the Gestapo already at the door of his house and from there deported to the concentration camp of Dachau.

Fritz Kuehr had heard about Schoenstatt from Richard Schmitz, the mayor of Vienna, and it had made him curious. One day in April 1942, he approached his good friend Dr. Eduard Pesendorfer about it. "Have you ever heard anything about Schoenstatt? They work in small cells so that the Gestapo can't catch them. The head of the movement is supposedly here in Dachau, I heard. Couldn't you take me to him once?"

"I don't know ..." Pesendorfer hesitated, but as he saw his disappointed face, he finally responded, "Well, all right, if you really want it that much. I'll take you to him."

Soon thereafter, both of them appeared in the admission block and kept watch for Father Kentenich. Fritz Kuehr immediately assailed him with all kinds of questions. There was nothing Father Kentenich was happier to do than to give the two of them a personal introduction into the history and spirituality of the movement. Maybe this Dr. Kuehr would actually be the instrument God had sent him for the future Family Institute. Father Kentenich's concern in the service of a new pastoral care of families struck a note with Fritz Kuehr; as an active Catholic he had borne this heart's desire within him for a long time. "For this we would need an organized community!" explained Father Kentenich. From then on they met every evening to exchange ideas and continue training. However, Kuehr's wife had emigrated to Brazil already before her husband's imprisonment to prepare a common future for themselves there. The matter was not easy to decide without her.

His friend, Dr. Eduard Pesendorfer, a lawyer, had been taken into custody in 1938 due to his anti-Nazi sentiments and transported to the concentration camp of Dachau. Pesendorfer, whose name was camouflaged with "Edi" in letters, had established his reputation in the camp as the head orderly on account of his medical knowledge and human empathy. Actually he had never thought of entering a brothers' community, much less of co-founding one.

"What did you talk about? Can you share anything?" Heinz Dresbach was curious—and Pesendorfer was proud to give a report.

"About a spiritual daily order, about 'everyday sanctity,' and of course about Mary as Queen. Father explained, *'We who have been robbed of our freedom have a Queen who is more powerful than those who have the last word here in the camp.'* I asked him how to achieve intimacy with God. *'Look at God often, speak to him, and make sacrifices for him,'* was his answer. And since then we have prayed for intimacy with God and for being gripped by God. We also prayed a novena together for Father Eise and implored the *'Mother of Bread'* to help the prisoners here. The months of May and June were an amazing time. Father Kentenich came down with a serious ear inflammation and Fritz was able to order him to come here. He just told the doctor, 'The priest urgently needs infrared light.'"

"I still remember that. Fritz was jumping around the room like crazy. 'The priest needs infrared light. Hurray, the priest needs infrared light!'"

"Those were simply wonderful weeks with him. He could come every evening and give training to Franz Zuber and me for the founding of our community. Father Kentenich even snuck over here sometimes in the evening and secretly climbed in through the window." Dr. Pesendorfer became ever more expressive. "One time I asked him, 'What do you think about your future brothers smoking?' He responded, *'Is it necessary?'* I said, 'Yes, it is one of my great passions!' To that he replied, *'What shall we do about that? All right, you may smoke! But there is one thing you can do. If you want to break the habit of smoking, bring the Blessed Mother this sacrifice as a gift with the petition that she may give the future brothers' community the grace that this passion may never find its way in.'*"

"And how's it going with the smoking?"

"Well, you won't believe it. On October 4, I was madder than a hornet. So many things had happened. Then I got an idea. I went to Father Kentenich and suggested to him that Joseph Engling—his death day was the fourth—could be something like the patron of our community. He immediately responded, *'That's right, let's do that! But if you take him as a patron, he should also give you a gift now. Ask him for many brothers or some other great gift!'* I went straight to my barracks still a passionate smoker and went to bed rather early. I thought, 'Actually, you thought of Joseph Engling far too little today, shamefully little! Your suggestion to make him patron was just a matter of embarrassment, to feel like you were doing something for him.' Then I thought of Joseph Engling in a special way and asked him now to do something for me. At that moment I felt a very strong aversion toward smoking that has lasted until now. I even have a real disgust toward it. That's a great miracle!"

"Yes, that's really a miracle! Now, aren't your meetings in the nurse's room quite dangerous?"

"Yes, indeed—we keep the Most Blessed Sacrament in a drawer inside the locked medicine cabinet. What do you think would happen to us if we were discovered?!"

"And Father walks through the camp as if it were no big deal."

"He knows no fear and claims that this is a fruit of the inscriptio. He recently explained this, quoting a memo from Goebbels in the 'National Observer': Build your cities on the edge of Vesuvius! And he said, *'This article is wonderful! It applies perfectly to us.'*"

"Because of the inscriptio?"

"Exactly!"

"Franz and Bernhard now belong to your circle, too?"

"Yes, but there's no jealousy among us at all. Each one considers himself the preferred one."

"That's what it's like with him."

"A person who esteems and treats each one as an original and yet loves us all the same."

Heinz Dresbach gave a confirming nod. His father had fallen during World War I when he was still a young boy. Heinz had never called anybody "Father." But after he had gotten to know Father more closely here in the camp, a deep longing suddenly arose in him: "I would like to call him Father."

Pesendorfer interrupted his thoughts. "He has fatherly empathy. He suffered terribly when the block elder gave Fischer a beating in July on the camp street."

July 16, 1942. Pesendorfer and Kuehr were ready to call the two new communities to life together with Father Kentenich. Around 4:00 p.m., they joined the straw sack mending crew—Fathers Fischer, Eise, and Kentenich—in Block 14, Room 3. A little "altar" with the Most Blessed Sacrament, candles, and a tiny MTA picture had been hidden between two wedge pillows. In a simple but deep celebration, the two first founding members sealed their consecration (with the founding of the Brothers of Mary around 6:00 p.m.). This day marked the beginning of their novitiate and the building of two new arks. In the midst of the *"hell of Dachau"*—in this *"city of death"*—new religious life had come into being without the SS having even the slightest clue. The risk was great, but Joseph Kentenich continued to pursue his strategy unperturbed. *"Once it became clear that something was God's will, we always took it up without hesitation."*

A further highpoint was the secret priestly ordination of the Schoenstatt deacon Karl Leisner, carried out amid danger of death for all involved. He had been imprisoned toward the end of his theology studies due to his courageous commitment as the diocesan leader of the Catholic Youth community and on account of a hasty comment he had made after the assassination attempt on Hitler. He had become familiar with Schoenstatt as a high school student and later reminded a friend of their common experience there—the "glorious high school retreat in Schoenstatt, to which I owe my vocation and so many graces." After that, he joined the Schoenstatt circle of seminarians. In September 1944, when the French bishop of Clermont-Ferrand, Gabriel Piguet, arrived in the camp, Karl's deepest desire could be fulfilled. The bishop was willing to ordain the young but seriously ill deacon to the priesthood in the concentration camp. After the written permission of Bishop Clemens August von Galen of Muenster had arrived, Karl received the sacrament of holy orders on December 17, 1944, in the Dachau camp chapel. "Victor in Chains" was the original ideal of Christian discipleship that his Schoenstatt group in the concentration camp had chosen. Already soon after his release from the camp, Leisner died at age 30 due to the consequences of the harsh living conditions in the camp. He would also become the first Schoenstatter to be beatified as a martyr—about fifty years later, on June 23, 1996, by Pope John Paul II.

As they walked past each other on the camp street, Joseph Fischer whispered to Heinz Dresbach, "It's been clear to him since March 25 that God doesn't want him to spend his time just mending straw sacks. He says he bears the responsibility for the Schoenstatt Family, his foundation. Therefore he resolved to 'break through' and make contact with the outside. You know, when he's sure something is God's will, he can't be stopped."

"But that's much too dangerous! How do you intend to go about it?"

"Via the plantation! People go there to shop for flowers and vegetables. We'll smuggle the mail out through them. And there's also another possibility via the camp office." Since the legal mail route was no longer possible for Joseph Kentenich as an NF prisoner, he used every possibility to assist his movement and its growing branch communities from a distance.

"That will surely mean his death if he gets caught."

"He himself won't write anything; he'll dictate to you and me. Then if he's interrogated he'll always be able to say, 'I have not written anything!'"

"Clever!"

"And are you willing?"

"Yes. Whenever he's convinced of something, all my fears evaporate. It's strange!"

"He wants to dictate in coded verse form. If it's discovered, it will look like a compilation of harmless, pious little prayers." Heinz nodded.

And thus began a lively exchange of letters. Father Kentenich composed 5,870 four-line stanzas, the so-called Shepherd's Mirror, on the government, formation, structure, and spirit of the Sisters of Mary alone, as an orientation for the leaders of the community. He formulated treatises that filled entire books. In doing so, he followed his very own daily rhythm, determining his own life even in Dachau and letting nothing simply be forced upon him. Early in the morning, before the others awakened, he got up, got himself ready alone in the washroom, and surprised the others with his freshness and intellectual creative power. What they admired about him, or what some jealously observed, was this constant inner equanimity and the calm he radiated. But hunger affected him considerably. Almost everyone got sick with dysentery. Father Eise was hit the hardest; he was hardly able to survive on such little nourishment. In the end, the stately man weighed less than 110 pounds. Whenever Father Kentenich asked him, "Albert, are you hungry?" he would answer from the depths of his soul, "And how!"

But now Albert was in such poor condition that Dr. Pesendorfer finally succeeded in bringing him to the sickbay. But the admission block was restricted, so Joseph Kentenich couldn't visit the younger co-worker he had guided already back at the House of Studies. That was painful and hard for both of them. News traveled back and forth daily via Pesendorfer and Fischer. "On August 22, Father Kentenich commissioned me to tell Eise that he should think back to the beginning of his time in the military and give his reclaimed life to the Blessed Mother once more in a renewed inscriptio." Eduard Pesendorfer informed Heinz Dresbach about the last weeks. "During the First World War, Albert must have had to experience a state of soul similar to the one he's in now. He ravenously absorbs everything I pass on to him from Father Kentenich, and he told me, 'Yes, I want to make my spiritual testament now.' I was able to sit with him for half an hour, and afterwards I repeated everything to Father, down to the smallest detail. He wrote down word-for-word what Albert had given of himself and then read it back to me out loud. 'Is that right? I don't want to write anything incorrect. Quite evidently, it's a matter of an especially intimate type of surrender on the part of Eise to the Blessed Mother.' 'Yes, you have it right,' I answered." Pesendorfer paused and swallowed. "At times Fritz couldn't go there anymore because Father Eise's condition depressed him too strongly. But Father Eise is now so gripped by the words Father Kentenich often quoted to us from the Bible—'Your citizenship is in heaven!'—and by the way he interpreted it for us."

Once Pesendorfer had taken Father Eise under his medical supervision, his condition seemed to improve. But one night, when a mishap occurred due to Father Eise's dysentery, one of the brutal caregivers on night duty took the deathly ill man naked into the washroom and sprayed him with ice-cold water, taunting him all the while. His feverish condition worsened. That became the starting point of his early death. It wasn't easy for him to say yes to his dying. Father Kentenich knew this. But on September 2—the day before his death—Pesendorfer found him happy and cheerful. "I would like to ask you to tell Father that I actually have only three wishes. I would like so much to be with him again, and then I would like to really be a child before him once again, and lastly, I would still like to give him my spiritual testament."

"But," Pesendorfer sadly told Father Dresbach, "we weren't able to arrange it. It was impossible. He still said, 'Whatever the Blessed

Mother wants; whether I live or die, it's the same to me.' During the last night he sang Schoenstatt songs out loud, called out ejaculatory prayers, and then peacefully continued sleeping. Early in the morning of September 3, he shook violently as he often did, and right after that he was dead."

Heinz stared down sadly. "So young! What will Father have to say about it?"

Father Kentenich was deeply moved by the reality that Father Eise had found the strength to surrender his young life. Two days after his death, and after Father Reinisch, too, had surrendered his life, he wrote in a letter, *"What Nietzsche expects of a secularized inscriptio when he writes, 'Build your cities on the edge of Vesuvius! For believe me! The greatest fruitfulness and the greatest enjoyment of human existence consists in living dangerously,' applies in the fullest sense of the word to religious total surrender."*

"Father Kentenich won't make it much longer! Two weeks more at the most! He has the same thing Albert had." Eduard Pesendorfer stormed into the sickbay and approached Father Fischer, who was just beginning to recuperate from his dysentery on account of Eduard's good care.

"Edi, none of us Schoenstatters here are counting on experiencing Christmas anymore—but for him you must do everything so that he makes it!" Joseph Fischer gasped for air. "Heinz told me that already on October 13, when he finally arrived at the priests' block, he told him, 'Father, how much weight you have lost! You won't endure that much longer!' To this he had responded with complete calm, *'Just a couple weeks more and it will be the end.'* And the way he said it, so weakened and totally surrendered. He himself is counting on the worst! You have to do something! Get him over here to the sickbay! Think of something! He can't die!"

Pesendorfer shook his head. "If we can't get him to eat more, he'll perish from our midst. Hunger can't be stilled only by *'faith in the reality of supernature'*!"

Fischer nodded. "He's worn himself out completely."

"As long as I've known Father Kentenich, I've only noticed one single time that he even has any human needs at all. He came to me with various physical ailments and was quite thirsty."

"This illness makes you terribly thirsty. I feel that way constantly. Everything just passes through you."

"I then made him a peppermint tea and he drank it. I warned him, 'But this is the only time you may have something to drink; you absolutely may not drink anything else!' He said plainly, 'Yes, Edi, but I already drank some of that strange sweet soda water you can buy in the canteen.' To that I said, 'But you may not do that! That is not good for your health!' He replied, 'You know, Edi, I was just so incredibly thirsty.' In September he came to me: 'Edi, I'll be back a little later, I'm on room-cleaning duty.' He was so weak that he could hardly walk, and he himself noticed it. He soaked up a cloth with water in the anteroom, tottering for sheer weakness. Then he knelt down to mop and almost couldn't stand up again. I had to watch the scene from a distance for a quarter of an hour and could not help him. He is too weak, and hunger is the main problem, also for him."

Shivering, Joseph Fischer pulled the blanket up higher. "Of all people, it was our good Albert who was horrified that Father wanted to appoint the Blessed Mother as 'Mother of Bread.' His thought was that she is the Educator, but not the 'Mother of Bread.' But Father stuck to it! At the beginning of July, we solemnly exalted her as 'Queen of the Camp' and 'Mother of Bread.' Today is October 22! Just four days after the 18th, 'covenant day.' We could pray that Mary will do something for him."

"You won't believe it!" Franz stood breathless at the sickbay door and clapped his hands for joy. "Precisely on October 18, the SS camp leadership lifted the package restriction! Father received a little package of foodstuffs! We're all supposed to go to him. He wants to share it with us. Can you stand up, Joseph?"

"I can indeed!"

They hurried to the priests' block, where Father Kentenich had spread out the few precious treasures behind a wedge pillow: two boiled eggs, a half-pound of butter, and a few apples. He welcomed them with a smile on his pale, gaunt face. Right away he called upon Pesendorfer: "Now you have to tell us how to proceed. We want to divide everything fairly."

"With the butter, just lick some at first and see if your stomach can still handle it." They did so, carefully, gratefully, and with exuberant happiness.

From then on, things took a turn upward. With time, more and more food packages arrived—even a cake with a bunch of letters baked inside. Packages were delivered to him despite the mail restrictions. However, the distribution of goods was not so simple, for there were too many hungry eyes and stomachs. Joseph Fischer knew "how Father pondered the right way to distribute the gifts received, and how this responsibility led him to formulate a prayer he often spoke: '*I gratefully place these gifts of love back into your gentle mother hands and warmly ask you: Tell me how to distribute them to your honor and joy.*'" He squatted down by the barracks window and inconspicuously handed out hundreds of butter sandwiches—prepared by his co-workers as soon as foodstuffs arrived—to those who passed by.

One day, the SS discovered piles of letters in a fruit basket with a double bottom. These were all sent to the Gestapo in Koblenz. Joseph Kentenich immediately smuggled out a camouflaged message asking the senders to be especially careful with packages from now on. Soon thereafter, searches were conducted in the priests' block and in Kentenich's work block. As if by a miracle, nothing of the mail hidden in a window casing was found. Each little slip of paper a prisoner possessed had to be stamped. If that wasn't the case, even a small scrap of paper became a life-threatening danger.

March 9, 1944. Father Dresbach intercepted Joseph Fischer on his way back from the plantation. "Joseph, Father is sitting in the bunker. They took a whole bunch of mail along! We have to brace ourselves for the worst! The horrible thing is that they were there already yesterday and searched my locker. Fortunately, I don't know how, but the SS section leader took the whole bundle I had hidden there, and as he sensed the leading SS officer wasn't watching him, he discreetly stashed it all away again in my box. That was a close call!" Heinz could hardly get the words out and gasped for air, so quickly had he run in his excitement. "And if they now still discover the hiding place Father just showed me yesterday ..." His voice failed.

Joseph carefully looked around and pulled him closer by his sleeve. "Come on, let's go see!" Fortunately, Fischer always stayed level-headed in such situations. They hurried to the dormitory. Joseph Kentenich had hidden a cloth folder in a certain place. When they entered the dormitory, they found his bed in complete disarray and things lying all over.

"All the prisoners had to stand outside in punishment until they had searched through everything," one of the prisoners told them grumpily.

They hurried to the hiding place. "Impossible. It's all still there, the whole folder!"

"Quickly throw it into the stove!" Dresbach opened the stove door and put the whole bundle into the fire.

Already early the next morning, someone from the political department appeared and said, "They just took Kentenich for an interrogation and the dorm capo and the block elder, too. This is going to be fun!"

Both looked at each other distraught. Neither of them knew what the SS had found or what had already fallen into their hands during the past months. Joseph Kentenich didn't know, either.

Father Kentenich sat across from three officers from the Main Security Office in Berlin who had started a blitz campaign in the camp in order to track down illegal letter writers and reporters. "What are we accusing you of? You supply foreign broadcasters with news from the camp. You meet with communists every evening. You have tremendous influence here—don't try to fool us! You make pacts with leftists! What do you talk about there every evening? What do you report to the outside? Atrocities in the camp?"

"I give religious talks. I don't even mention the conditions here!"

"We'll see about that. Stand up! Hands behind your back! Face to the wall!"

The official ordered the SS noncommissioned officer on duty, "Bring in the block elder and the capo of the dormitory!" Pale-faced, the two entered. "What things does the priest speak about to the prisoners in the dormitory every evening?"

"About the suffering of Christ and about the Holy Father. He thinks we need a Holy Father."

"What nonsense! We have a Fuehrer! Step out!"

Now Kentenich was told to sit down again so that they could observe him closely. "You write illegal mail! Will you at least admit that?"

"I write neither illegal nor legal mail. I am under a mail prohibition." Upon further questioning, he simply remained silent. Father Kentenich was brought back to the isolation cell of the punishment block.

"What did you find?" asked one of the lawyers who had arrived from Berlin.

"Nothing but worthless, pious stuff! The man is harmless!"

"Then let him go, but we have to keep an eye on the priests. Permit none of them to enter the post office, camp office, or payroll office by any means. And one more thing: Keep the German priests absolutely separated from the foreign ones!"

"What about Carls?"

"Let him go! We'll get the right ones yet!"

Hardly did Father Kentenich appear in his barracks when he was welcomed with loud jubilation by his confreres. Others grumbled behind their back, saying he was putting their lives in danger, too. He whispered into Heinz's ear, "This afternoon we'll pick up where we left off!" He looked at him incredulously. Who could believe this?

At the beginning of the year 1944, the provincial of the Pallottines in Limburg, Father Heinrich Schulte, was deported to the camp. He told Father Kentenich that the archbishop of Freiburg had also raised complaints against Schoenstatt in a twelve-page document. He had passed this document on to the clergy of his diocese, "to the Most Reverend Greater German Episcopate," and to the "Holy Office" in Rome. Heinrich Schulte was still outraged about it. "What does that even mean—'Greater German Episcopate'? In my answer I simply wrote, 'German Episcopate.'" Father Kentenich calmly waved it aside. Father Schulte continued, "The bishop has gotten worked up about newer circles that have cultivated an 'obvious spiritual division within the Greater German clergy.' He says these circles look down upon the 'eternal adherents to yesterday' and make harsh criticisms of what is traditional. He also says that on the part of the liturgical movement, the episcopate is accused of 'not having enough humility to be guided by experts in liturgy and pastoral care or scholars in the area of religious education of youth.' In this context the bishop also seemingly mentioned Schoenstatt—and just now, while the founder is in the concentration camp." Schulte's face turned purple with anger. Joseph Kentenich lightly stroked his drill suit and remained silent with a motionless expression. "He said that the pastorally zealous 'Schoenstatters' have formed a type of state within the state in his diocese, with a separate core leadership circle and organization and their own 'organic asceticism and dogmatic teaching.'" Father Schulte said that in this regard the bishop had referred to two books, *Organische Aszese [Organic Asceticism]* by Dr. Hermann Schmidt and *Marianische Christusgestaltung [Marian Formation in Christ]* by Dr. Ferdinand Kastner. The bishop reportedly stated, "The Viennese activists condemn what is old as if it had only been something external, following a template." For him, the contrast between the "old" and the "young" had "unfortunately sometimes become so gaping" that "the young ones speak of abysses that separate them from the old ones," since the latter, in the eyes of the young ones, "are still living in the baroque era." To his criticism of the youth, the bishop reportedly added the misgiving that he sees it as "an incomprehensible disaster" "that such a profound rupture in the hitherto existing life of faith and in the conventional religious tradition within our dioceses would take place precisely now, in the midst of a double war."

Father Kentenich remained standing and looked calmly at Father Schulte. "Heinrich, you have to understand that! We are moving towards a new time. A change has been initiated in the Church and the bishop considers it questionable."

Father Schulte turned around to see if anyone might overhear their conversation. "I answered him reverently but clearly and thoroughly: 'You disapprove of our terminology. You think we earnestly promote the belief that Mary appeared in Schoenstatt as at other pilgrimage places, for example, Lourdes or Fatima. Therefore here and there you speak of mysticism.' I explained first of all that 'as the Catholic Apostolate of Schoenstatt we are under the Society of the Pallottines' and so 'in complete harmony with current canon law,' not just a wild growth! Moreover, I wrote, 'I most especially regret the fact that Father Kentenich, whom these accusations mainly concern, is unfortunately not in a position today to be able to defend his own personal honor and the ecclesial spirit of his teaching and his work.'"

"All right. But we must explain our view in principle and in detail. You have experienced our history and its development from the beginning, how God has led us. But whoever doesn't know the whole thing can't understand it at first glance and has to voice his doubts. Besides Pompei, I don't know of any other pilgrimage place in the Church that has come into being like ours has. I'll draft something."

Joseph Kentenich sat on a stool between the straw sacks and began his dictation *"Fatima and Schoenstatt."* He was in the concentration camp because of his commitment to the Church. He had to help the Church understand how much Schoenstatt and its ideas are a *movement of renewal* grounded in the Catholic faith and that it doesn't simply want to break with the tradition of the Church nor circumvent the hierarchy. In his illegal mail he encouraged the Schoenstatters to seek more contact with Church hierarchy, to inform them and to correct false impressions. Kentenich dictated and dictated. Entire books about his institutes' original spirituality and pedagogy came into being. Time thus passed in the midst of dreadful camp life all the way up to the spring of 1945 ...

Liberation

In spite of all danger, individual prisoners had gotten news reports from foreign broadcasters and found out how badly things were going for the German army in the meantime. The Allies advanced on all fronts. American and British low-flying planes flew over the camp, but no bomb ever fell. So it could be assumed that the Allies knew what place they were dealing with. But what would the SS camp leadership do? What would happen with them, the prisoners? What was subliminally feared had long since been decided in Berlin: Himmler had ordered the release of a few clergymen in order to ingratiate himself with the Vatican at the last minute. But at the same time, he had decided that none of the remaining concentration camp prisoners were to fall into the hands of the enemy alive and so be able to tell "horror stories" about the Third Reich. They were to be eliminated as quickly as possible. But the former camp commander Martin Weiss, who had been the inspector for all concentration camps since 1944, prevented this mass murder. On March 24, as seven Danish and Norwegian clergymen were called up by name and led away, a real panic broke out among the prisoners. Where were the allegedly "released" prisoners going to end up? Were they secretly shot somewhere, or set free?

March 29, 1945, 11:00 a.m. "Quickly, put everything in order! The SS are around! They're already at Room 2! Watch out, they're coming!"

The SS passed by the window. Everyone jumped up. One of the block leaders held a slip of paper in his hand and read eight names. "All those whose names were called, pack up your things and get ready!"

Tremendous excitement immediately ensued. What was the meaning of this? ... A Salvatorian priest became pale as a ghost and began to shake. Now anything could happen. An hour later, the block elder brought news: "The eight prisoners were given a complete change of clothes and released!"

Then the block clerk also appeared. "Tomorrow about fifty clergymen will be released!" New rumors constantly sprang up.

Fischer related, "Then came Holy Week and the Easter days. The releases continued on Easter Tuesday. On Wednesday, April 4, 1945, they began with the second list. Now the prisoners were released in alphabetical order. On the sixth we went out onto the roll-call square as usual. 'Attention! Caps off!' The block elder counted the rows. It was correct. 'Caps on! At ease!' Spellbound tension reigned over all. Was the camp clerk coming? Yes, he was coming! He dictated the names of those released to the block clerk ... A couple of times I was tempted to step out of the row and ask the block clerk. Finally I dared it. What a joy when he told me, 'Yes, Father Kentenich is among them! But please don't say it too loud!' I quickly made my way to Father, who was standing there peacefully as usual. 'Father, you are released!' 'Joseph, is that really true?' 'The block clerk told me.' 'All right, then come right away to pack.'"

He stood there very calmly and thought about what he had always wished for: "If I am freed, then by the Americans, not by the Nazis." But now it had happened otherwise. Since the middle of March, Schoenstatt had already been freed and cleared of danger as the Western Front came through. He set out with a spring in his step. In the administration wing, he received his few belongings and a little bit of money. Then he was led into the basement, where fresh laundry and socks were prepared. It was possible to fish out something that fit from the abundance of clothing and shoes. Then there were a few modest provisions for the march. Around 9:00 a.m. they stood outside before the iron gate, he and Father Kostron. Incomprehensible. "We're free!"

April 17, 1945. Still completely dazed by what he had experienced the day before, he stood in the parish garden and cleaned out the berry hedge. He couldn't forget the picture of the twenty-two-year-old man, a certain Walter from Oldenburg. They had picked him up at 4:00 in the morning. Two young people—one a Protestant and the other, Walter, a Catholic—were to be executed because they had deserted. "How he clung to me saying he didn't want to die so young and under such dreadful circumstances. How I tried to console him, powerless against this regime of violence. How they chained the two of them to the beech trees and I prayed with him, 'Jesus, I live for you, Jesus, I die for you, I am yours in death and in life; Jesus, Mary, Joseph, I give you my heart and my soul. May my soul depart with you in peace.' And how the officer then read the death sentence, their eyes were blindfolded, he raised his sword, and gave the command to load. 'Fire!' Both of them went to their death so bravely. I think everyone was shaken to the core. And then right after that I celebrated the Holy Sacrifice on the MTA altar as I had promised Walter as a consolation. I will probably never forget this experience. I think I will never in my life be able to laugh again." Joseph Kulmus, pastor of Ennabeuren, was completely lost in these thoughts and continued to pick berries. Suddenly he heard his visitors coming—the Russian prince and scholar from Kiev, who was also an icon painter, and his friend. They had arrived in the little town a few days earlier as immigrants. He went with them into the sacristy. Just as he was showing them the MTA picture and telling them about Father Kentenich, the founder of the Schoenstatt Movement who was now in the concentration camp of Dachau, his sister, that faithful soul, the housekeeper of the rectory, called to him from the parish lawn that two chaplains had come. "Oh, new asylum-seekers!" he thought. Since the end of 1944, he had given lodging to thirteen persons in his rectory, including a Ukrainian refugee family. He asked his Russian visitors to excuse him, went back into the sanctuary of the church, and stopped cold as he suddenly almost ran into Father Kentenich. In "shabby Dachau garb, beardless, and with a clean-shaven head," he could at first only recognize him by his eyes and his voice. Father Kulmus was beside himself with amazement, joy, and gratitude. "It all seemed like a dream!"

One of the sisters saw the unfamiliar car coming from a distance just as she was bringing the milk from the farm. A young priest was sitting on the hood in his priestly garb to signal to low-flying planes that the inhabitants were harmless and should not be bombed. It was a daring undertaking if one considers that everything that moved was shot at, even civilian populations who were fleeing. The little towns were heavily bombed again and again, and the air raid warning frequently sounded in the Swabian Alps, chasing those nearby into cellars and roadside ditches. War was still raging!

A gentleman with a gray leather coat got out of the car, his hat low on his face. "So, do you still know me?"

The sister replied in bewilderment, "No!—Oh, yes, Father! What a joy!" She had recognized him only by his voice.

Now there were indescribably happy greetings all over. Shortly after that, Father Dresbach, who had already been able to leave the concentration camp on April 5, arrived. He had first traveled to Pallottine Father Quirmbach in Freising. Hardly had he heard that Father Kentenich was free and on the way to Ennabeuren when he immediately set out by train and by foot. They all found shelter. Joseph Kentenich moved into a tiny hermitage with its own entrance under the sacristy next to the church. It was simply but nicely arranged. From then on it was given the name "the Father Hermitage." Now both of them had to tell their stories:

After his release, Father Kostron—like Father Dresbach the day before—had likewise set out for Freising, to Father Quirmbach's. Father Kentenich, on the other hand—as long as his train to Schönbrunn wasn't traveling—had marched to Father Pfanzelt, the pastor of the Dachau parish, to thank him for the help he gave the prisoners. In a conversation it occurred to both of them how important it would be after the war to erect a memorial in Dachau to the victims, together with a contemplative cloister in which prayer and reparation would be offered day and night for the horrors that had happened at this place.

He had actually thought of spending a few days of retreat at the cloister in Schönbrunn. It was close by and offered a place of silence where he could once more bring his experiences of the past years to God and process them interiorly. But the peace didn't last long. Hardly had Father Kostron appeared in Freising and reported that Father Kentenich had been released and was in Schönbrunn, when Father Dresbach immediately set out to make his way there. Some days later, as he took him along to Freising, it got to be late in the evening before they arrived at Father Quirmbach's. By the dim light, Father Quirmbach saw another figure behind Father Dresbach and grumbled, "Who's this old pastor you've brought along here?"

At that moment Father Kentenich stepped out of the hallway and into the light, and mischievously smiling, said, "What do you mean, 'old pastor'?"

Father Quirmbach greeted him most warmly. Father Kentenich now got invitations everywhere; he visited the rector of the seminary, the rector of the cathedral, the general vicar, the Pallottine Fathers, and on April 14, the archbishop of Munich-Freising, Cardinal Michael von Faulhaber, in an audience. He spoke in great detail with him about the concentration camp of Dachau and pastoral care in future postwar Germany. The bishop had publicly defended Schoenstatt, since here and there questions had arisen time and again regarding the new movement.

As soon as it was known that Father Kentenich was free, Schoenstatters asked him to come to Ulm and Ehrenstein to give talks. When due to the war situation only some of the youth arrived at the set time, he said that whenever the rest of the youth had arrived, they should call him, and he would give the talk again for those who had been delayed.

Soon after they were done telling their stories in Father Kulmus' rectory, Father Kentenich hurried to the small filiation of sisters in Ennabeuren and rang the doorbell. The sister who answered the door stood there transfixed and could "not believe the miracle": The founder was truly free. After all, they had heard that he was ill with typhus and that they had to count on the worst. "We were all speechless," as the chronicle states, "as Father now stood before us. It was like when a father returns home to his children after many long years. His first words were, *'The first Sisters of Mary in four years!'*"

But the dangers of war were not yet averted. In particular, the neighboring town of Westerheim was being heavily bombed. Father Kentenich tried to offer words of consolation to the inhabitants of the town. He preached in their parish church "in a Rhineland singsong tone," warm and engaged, "in his Dachau garb: heavy, iron-studded army boots and a large pocket watch in his waistcoat pocket that was secured around his neck by a black band. Day by day, his beard grew longer and our joy grew greater," as Father Kulmus recalled. "His longing for Schoenstatt grew so much that he wanted to tackle the 400-kilometer (250-mile) trip on foot. But we were gradually able to talk him out of that." Meanwhile, the front was moving closer and closer. He planned to let the front "roll past him" and then to follow the Allied troops quickly to Schoenstatt.

April 22, 1945. That day, Joseph Kentenich was wearing priestly attire again for the first time. Suddenly, two Americans stood at the door to search the house. Father Kentenich immediately greeted them with "a few fatherly words in English" and accompanied them into the house. They were both quite friendly, stepping curiously into the sisters' constricted dining room and looking at the pious "little altar." One of them asked, "Catholic?" since the sisters' clothing seemed modern to him and didn't look as "Catholic" as what he had been familiar with. They all nodded. Some time later, the American soldier rang the doorbell again. "He had been moved by the little altar," the chronicle reported. The report then abruptly continued, "When we asked Father if he wasn't worried that something might happen to him on the street, he only said that he wanted to consciously make himself visible on the street in order to calm the inhabitants of the town and take away their fear."

Every day, Joseph Kentenich celebrated holy Mass in the parish church and looked for ways to help the listeners in their suffering. Many had lost sons, fathers, and brothers in the war and ultimately had to be moved out because their houses and farms had been so badly damaged that it was no longer possible to live there. The topic of his sermon was, *"Take the Child and his Mother and go to the house of your neighbor!"* In the language of the people, he interpreted the past twelve years of Nazi rule. Now it was imperative *"to help"* Mary *"build a new world."* He thus began to hold a real parish mission.

On May 7, late in the evening, American soldiers stormed into the parish rectory and announced the German capitulation. They wanted to celebrate with wine and the ringing of bells. Everything happened as they wished. Father Dresbach recalled, "All those who were in the parish rectory went along to the church. The bell rang loudly into the nighttime silence of the Upper Alps and proclaimed the end of the war, and in the little church, with overflowing hearts, we sang the 'Te Deum,' 'Holy God, We Praise Thy Name.'"

Right away the next day, freedom was the topic of Joseph Kentenich's sermon. *"What do the bells of freedom say to us? … That the murdering has been put to an end. Bells of peace are bells of thanksgiving. The murdering has now come to an end."* But he immediately also spoke of the *"penance our nation now has to do for the great guilt it has taken upon its shoulders."* He hadn't simply left behind all the happenings in Dachau and all the atrocities of the war Germany had started. In another sermon on May 11, he explained, *"Whoever wants to profit from the world has to enter into the depths of truth. Today's system is a hodgepodge of all the false teachings that have ever existed. Nothing like this has ever happened before. What an onslaught against truth! It's impossible for the imagination to come up with any false teaching that isn't already contained in this system here. There is no false teaching that could still come that hasn't already been taught by National Socialism, just as there is no atrocity that hasn't already happened here. You're familiar with taverns and their smoke and fumes. Even if we ourselves don't smoke and drink, our clothes are full of fumes and smoke. We all have to go into quarantine and conduct a disinfection. We have to change our views. We*

Photo 11: With former prisoners after being released from the concentration camp, second from right

want to bow before Christ and what he tells us. Never before ... has the devil attacked the human personality as he does today. God is the greatest protection for the image of the human person."

In the afternoon, Joseph Kentenich gave his nineteenth talk in the cycle of his "parish mission." His concern was a fundamental reappraisal of the past. He wanted his listeners to penetrate the whole Nazi system more deeply and to be awakened from their naive and often blind credulity. *"Isn't it the summit of immorality to rob the human person of the foundation of morality, of his deeply personal freedom and dignity? ... The Christian teaching of the endless significance of the personality and of the dignity of the individual was contrasted with the redemptive teaching of the endless insignificance of the personality and the endless significance of the nation and of being completely absorbed in and for the nation. The crime of our modern times is the suffocation of the personality. We were well on the way to transforming all of Europe into a concentration camp. Depersonalization is the summit of a lack of culture."*

On a carriage ride in the neighboring town of Westerheim, Father Kentenich first got the idea that perhaps he could go to Schoenstatt with such "little horses." That same evening someone rang the doorbell. As a sister opened the door, six men stood there and asked for a night's lodging in the parish rectory. Two Dutch prisoners from the concentration camp of Dachau were among them. "When they found out," as the chronicle reports, "that Father and Father Dresbach were here, they were like happy children. They immediately wanted to see both of them. People who witnessed the greeting related how warm and sincere it was. That evening we ourselves could experience that Father had been a father for these men in Dachau in the truest sense of the word."

Right away the next day, Joseph Kentenich took the two emaciated men with him into the church and explained to the assembled faithful, "*You are astonished at our visitors, the two whose sweaters are full of holes and who wear the mighty red letters K and L on their backs, with the white cross painted on. They are foreign fellow Catholics, Dutch priests. We warmly welcome them. May they leave with the conviction that they were received with open hearts and hands by brothers and sisters who have shared with them both their suffering in Dachau as well as their great joy and speedy return home. 'Today salvation has come to this house!' (Luke 19:9). ... Both priests have been led by God's guidance through Munich, Augsburg, and Ulm precisely to us here in Ennabeuren, to us of all people. I have been reunited with my confreres here. For years we bore suffering and joy together in the concentration camp. We who have experienced such hard days together and savored so many bitter things may now shake hands again.*" In his sermon he passionately advocated international unification and international understanding as a way to overcome all enemy images and resentment. "*There is so much that unites us. ... We have the same life's task. Here, too, we give our hands to one another. Each one should and wants to help that in his or her own nation, hatred among people and nations will gradually disappear.*"

Meanwhile, his longing for Schoenstatt grew. He made trial runs to see how he could manage a horse-drawn carriage and to

Photo 12: Planned return to Schoenstatt with steppe horses and carriage

practice steering the two Russian steppe horses Father Kulmus had bought him to use for his trip home. One of the trial runs led him one afternoon to the parish rectory in Westerheim. While he was there, a car suddenly honked outside the door. Unbelievable: Father Alexander Menningen was standing at the door with a car and its owner, his brother Hermann. Following their intuition, the two of them had not driven to Ennabeuren, but to Westerheim, in order to bring Father Kentenich to Schoenstatt. It couldn't have happened in a better way. After the initial outburst of joy, and after lots of story-telling and planning, Father Kentenich could no longer be held back. On May 18, after a heartfelt farewell, they set out on the trip home, and on May 20, 1945, Pentecost Sunday, amid ringing bells, they were solemnly and festively welcomed home. It was an unforgettable festival of joy, a welcome fit for a statesman. Father Kentenich stood straight and tall in the open car while they drove from Vallendar into Schoenstatt. He was deeply moved to see Schoenstatt again and all the familiar faces as well as the "new" ones. Home again! At first, those waiting on the edges of the street were rather timid. The impression was too deep. But then joy broke through. His first path through the crowd of people led him to the founding place, the shrine. Now it was called the "Original Shrine," because in the meantime an exact replica of this first shrine had been built in Uruguay.

"It was all like a dream," a Sister of Mary related, "to have Father back in our midst, healthy and spiritually unbroken, after an imprisonment of three years and eight months and despite the danger of death. He himself radiated so much fatherly goodness, so much concern for us all. He gave many talks, visited all the houses in Schoenstatt, and took part in everything we had experienced and all that was in our hearts."

8. Target of Church Accusations

Recuperation Is out of the Question

From the moment Joseph Kentenich arrived in Schoenstatt, there was no talk of taking a break after his time in the concentration camp. In any case, it never occurred to him. Late in the evening of May 19, 1945, when he arrived at the hospital filiation in Koblenz, he candidly explained to the sisters, *"I haven't come to rest. I have great plans ..."*

Right after the war, Germany was caught in an extremely difficult predicament. The country was hated by the whole world and destroyed both exteriorly and interiorly. Many cities lay in ruins and the survivors suffered greatly—and not only economically. Shaken by the happenings of the war and surrounded by the dying still present everywhere, hundreds of thousands waited for missing soldiers. Almost every family mourned a relative or welcomed home husbands, fathers, and brothers completely changed by captivity as prisoners of war. In many cases, those returning home had been deeply wounded, not only physically but also emotionally. Many Germans had lost their home and been driven from their homeland. What's more, they lost the ideals they had steadfastly believed in. For more than a few, life had become meaningless. People went to their churches to seek a stronghold and orientation, consolation and encouragement, and answers to many open questions. But many had lost their faith entirely. "Where was God in Auschwitz?" wasn't the only question that pressed upon their embittered hearts.

Father Kentenich saw immense tasks for the Church and especially for Schoenstatt. At the October Convention for leaders of the movement in 1945, he pointed to the complex problems: *"You sense the distress of our modern time. How many people are losing their faith in the Church and in Church representatives!"* He stressed the importance of a renewed, credibly modeled Christianity. Whether at the newly revived pedagogical conferences or in seminars, talks, sermons, or individual conversations, he brought the various afflictions of the people into conscious awareness everywhere. "*One of the great tasks of our educators will be to look after the returning soldiers who aren't acknowledged and are filled with bitterness.*" Joseph Kentenich didn't belong to those who suppressed German guilt or glossed it over. It was still urgently necessary to process the past. "*What does the lost war tell us? It means freedom from an unbearable yoke of slavery. Yes, the occupation is a new slavery for us. ... But the occupation has freed us in the first place from the chains of slavery of the past years which became tighter and tighter and which we wouldn't have been able to break anymore of our own strength. ... Many voices are already speaking out who have forgotten what we've experienced. That's why it's important to emphasize this. ... The greater majority of the soldiers and the people have been completely infected by the times, including some of our army priests. Some of them might even say, 'The war was just; we are a poor people—the others are rich!' But is that a legal basis for justifying the war? Not in the least! We have to bear in mind that we've taken a heavy guilt upon ourselves!*" He characterized the Second World War as an "*international war of slaves, war of religion, and cultural battle*" of incomparable dimensions. "*Diseased ideas have made humanity still more ill!*" he emphasized at the 1945 October Convention concerning National Socialism. At a conference for men at the end of September, he encouraged them to make a fresh start: "*We don't want to remain in the background. The time of the catacombs has passed.*" He saw Eastern Bolshevism as a new, real danger rolling toward Europe that needed to be faced with spiritual forces. The Allied Powers couldn't be expected to bring about such an inner renewal. "*People like the Allies who've won so many victories are hardly capable of correctly interpreting those victories. But if we interpret our defeat correctly in order to become truly free persons, then we'll be well on the way to finally achieving political and economic victory. Our task is to ensure that our German people become freedom fighters, freedom apostles, and freedom heralds. That's our task as priests.*" In this and similar ways, he corrected a number of views held by the people, who couldn't come to terms with the outcome of the war. He motivated the Sisters of Mary to be there for the people in every way. *"Breadless—homeless—rightless—honorless—defenseless. All these 'lessnesses' have to be overcome! How can I now help the people to overcome breadlessness?"*

His educational work was devoted above all to the deeper causes of the diseased ideologies: *"A mechanistic image of the human person! The masses exist; the individual is nothing. Examine, if you will, how they consciously formed this type of person in the concentration camp, how a person had to give up his entire personality. ... We must counteract this ideology. Whoever wants to serve people today must struggle for the image of the human person marked by God and willed by God."* Participants at a pedagogical conference in Schwäbisch Gmünd in November 1945 looked at each other in amazement and listened spellbound. *"Ever since we heard about the atomic bomb, pessimism has increased. Falling away (from God) means falling into ruin! ... Wouldn't it be terrible if tomorrow or the next day we stood on the brink of nihilism? Whose hand can safely isolate and control the atomic bomb? The meaning of my life: Down into the pit!"* It was one of his main concerns to give life in today's world a new and deeper meaning. In doing so, Father Kentenich didn't limit himself to religious consolation; he addressed the unspeakable suffering in concrete terms. In his view, pastors and educators needed to see the insecurity and uncertainty of today's people and understand what was making them tired and driving them to resignation.

For Joseph Kentenich, the rebuilding of Germany was closely bound up with the reawakening of Christian values so urgently needed on an international level. He saw this as the only way human dignity could be lastingly safeguarded. A change in mentality was also necessary within the Church to enable it to contribute to the renewal of society. He directed people's attention to the many destroyed families and above all to the *"crisis of the father figure."* Like most leadership authorities, fathers had lost their credibility. They had returned from the lost war or from a life of deprivation in prison hardened and embittered. They had become strangers to their children, and the worldview for which they had apparently fought had been declared "reprehensible." Adolescents eyed their fathers with distrust: "How could you fight for such an ideology? What did you give yourselves for?" People were insecure; family relationships lay shattered on the floor. Many women had carried their families through the war years and so gained independence and self-confidence. Father Kentenich sought to work against this tendency toward a *"fatherless society"* through the ideal of *"renewed, genuine fatherliness."*

The growing East-West conflict of ideologies strengthened in him the necessity to promote the *"inner armament of the individual"* and to support societal and ecclesial community life through a new mutual trust. New sustainable family bonds had to be created—genuine community. This was also true of religious communities. Church and society now urgently needed successful models of human working and living together. That's why Father Kentenich was so concerned about demonstrating the ideal of *"a new order of society"* in his own communities—not so much in a theoretical way, but much more through *"lived examples."* He wanted to give his *"new communities"* now more than ever to the Catholic Church and present what had matured in them over the decades. This was still very foreign to Church representatives; they were accustomed to an old type of asceticism and religious formation more like that of the orders. The meaning of *"attachment"* and the *"organism of attachments"* in Schoenstatt was especially new. At the end of May 1945, Father Kentenich—just back from Dachau—described one fundamental concern of *"the new community"* at the occasion of a solemn clothing celebration of the Schoenstatt Sisters of Mary: *"The organ of love wants to be awakened within us. Therefore, this great thought, this great idea, prevails in our family: We may love one another also in a human way and should love one another in a human way. If nothing but an absolute love of God is supposed to hold us, we know it won't be sustainable for life. The heart must be enkindled for human love, too. Then we'll have an organ prepared to embrace Eternal Love."*

Late one evening, Joseph Kentenich sat by himself in the back right corner of the *"Original Shrine"* and reflected on all that had happened since Dachau. Due to his long imprisonment, many things had been postponed that he'd now courageously begun to tackle. The Institute of the Ladies of Schoenstatt had adopted their "constitutions." The word "constitutions" was consciously borrowed from the associations. It was meant to replace the customary term "rules" used in the religious orders and emphasize the lay character of his communities. Each Schoenstatt community and its original mission had come into being over the years by way of life, through the original people God had sent him along the way. He had tried to discern the voice of God through these *"inclinations of souls"* in every individual vocation. Each community was to develop autonomously and arrive at a certain self-containment in order to fulfill its special mission. *"Autonomy awakens strengths that otherwise never become effective,"* he underlined at the constitution of the Institute of the Ladies of Schoenstatt. As for the community of the *"Federation Priests,"* who worked individually in parishes, he had written to "King Arthur's Round Table" already from Dachau, *"If I'm correct in understanding and interpreting God's purposes with our family as a whole, our federation priests may and should strive for an autonomy and independence from the Pallottines that's as pronounced as possible. The partially common origin, the common spirit, and the common tasks urge us of themselves to moderately build bridges so that both communities remain closely united with each other despite their juridical autonomy and so that they protect and support each other outwardly to the greatest possible extent."* The federation priests should choose a leader *"from among their own ranks"* and take care *"that he can be released as far as possible for his tasks. He stands beside the general superior of the Pallottines with full and independent authority, maintaining friendly contact with him and periodically meeting with him in the manner of a working group."* He had thoroughly discussed these questions with the Pallottine government and come to an agreement with them.

The same was true for the Institute of Diocesan Priests, which had now begun to work out their first constitutions. So incredibly much had been done in just a few years. The Schoenstatt community of married couples had taken shape—yet another novelty in the Church! The "Brothers of Mary" were still in their infancy. But with time they would surely develop. Time would tell. "In any case," he continued reflecting, "there are now distinct leadership entities everywhere." He considered it important to expand democratic elements and safeguard the growth and variety of original life. Schoenstatt, with its many communities, was meant to be neither a "hodgepodge" nor a "multiplication of the same." "*Self-government*" and a "*decentralization of power*" were crucial for stimulating life. But it was clear to him that by far not everyone would understand his way of thinking. The community of the Ladies of Schoenstatt had asked him in 1946 to appoint their first government. He could still clearly recall how it happened. "*You have placed the burden on me personally to undertake the appointments. It would've been easier for me if you had made use of your right of election, but now it's all right like this. Such a step is invariably an incision and a turning point and won't be possible without the sacrifices of many ... General superior: Gertrud Gramlich; family father: Father Muehlbeyer ... Now perhaps you will say that I'm going to withdraw now, since that seems reasonable. No, in the future my entire goodwill will be devoted to your family even more than before. I will carry the family in my heart the same as always, and even more than before, helping to ensure that the whole Work is completed. ... It won't take long before I also give up the Sisters of Mary so that the family can freely unfold more and more.*"

At the moment, many communities were fearing that he would now pull back or that the unity of the movement could be lost. But there was no need to worry. Far too many common religious and pedagogical experiences and increased attachments had united them as one large family: the attachment to the shrine and to Mary, the experience of her special nearness and power of transformation, and of course the attachment of all the communities to him as the father and founder. Since Dachau they had gathered around him even more closely. "I want to follow you wherever you go." He spontaneously recalled the words of the apostle to Jesus. How often in Christian discipleship had such a "followership commitment" repeated itself and become concrete in people! He wanted to follow Christ with all its consequences, and they followed him on the way to Christ. They had symbolically expressed their followership commitment—each in their original way and independent of each other—also toward him as the founder. They gave different names to this followership communion, but the process was the same. "It's peculiar," he observed, "how the Holy Spirit sometimes initiates similar things in souls without them knowing of each other." Such life processes were a clear sign to him that God stood behind them.

Since Dachau it had been clear to him that he could no longer stay in the background if he wanted to unite the large *community* and preserve it from the danger of fragmentation while maintaining all growth toward independence. He had to accept their readiness to follow him. It was precisely the leaders, who, under the burden of their new responsibility, pushed toward a stronger unity with him. He could not suppress this "father trend" that had broken forth with respect to him, particularly since the father figure in the Church and society was the very thing that had come into a serious and profound crisis. A new beginning in the Church and society required a new, vital faith. But people can only believe when they love. And really, people can only genuinely love when they have experienced it and learned it on the natural level. *"Most people no longer have any idea what love is,"* he concluded, *"because they have experienced it too little."* Yes, they knew about physical attraction, but what about genuine, deep, true love?

Ever since his decision of January 20, 1942, in the Koblenz prison, the various communities had grown in their readiness to surrender to God. Many of them had grown to extraordinary depths. He could only be grateful for such a breakthrough of life. He sensed that God was using him for it. They intuitively transferred to God the love they felt for him as the father and founder. Whereas he used to resist this, tending to be more reserved, he now supported these trends because he could see the impact they had on their inner growth and their faith.

He looked at the MTA picture, lost in thought. How long had this picture already accompanied Schoenstatt's development! No one had liked it at first. But love for this picture—no, for Mary—had quickly grown. "Love simply needs forms of expression, symbols, pictures, not only in the interpersonal sphere but also in the religious realm." He thought once more of the Ladies of Schoenstatt. With Gertrud Gramlich as the general superior and Father Muehlbeyer as the spiritual director, both as *"spiritual parents"* in the highest position, he had actually made a really good choice. In that case he would be able to confidently withdraw a little. But with the Sisters of Mary it wasn't so simple. At the moment he couldn't think of withdrawing from the government of the institute. Precisely during the years of his long imprisonment, it had become even clearer that the general superior, Sister Anna, was unable to manage her office. The general council had borne the matter with admirable closedness. Due to her strong drive for recognition, the general superior had increasingly disregarded other leadership entities. But when she herself felt disregarded, she reacted hurt. She had *"organic thinking"* clear in her mind, but in reality it wasn't her strength. Father Kentenich sensed already early on what a doctor would later confirm about her: her unhealthy self-centeredness that bordered on "autism" and her "schizophrenic disposition" with a tendency toward "hallucinations disconnected from reality and delusions" she firmly believed. Because of this absolutely self-centered disposition, she was ultimately incapable of sisterly and childlike attachments and true, selfless motherliness. But what was there to do? He knelt down, burying his head in his hands for a moment. Then his eyes involuntarily searched for the cross above the tabernacle. God still hadn't given him a sign that he should deviate from the principle oriented on the life of a natural family. After all, that was exactly the characteristic of the new community he wanted to give to the Church! "Parents remain parents—for life! Moreover, every person can begin each day anew and learn something new—including her!" Due to the growing number of sisters, he had resolved already in Dachau to divide the community into "provinces" with their own provincial superior and provincial government. They would be more manageable and able to adapt on regional and national levels. A province could give the individual sisters a home in a much different way. In addition, such a division supported the decentralization of governing power. When he proposed his suggestion to the general council, Sister Anna was not impressed—as could be expected. She interpreted the suggestion as a personal attack on her person ... Father Kentenich was so tired he couldn't keep his eyes open. In fact, he dozed off on his chair in the shrine.

Threatening Storms on the Horizon

Ever since he had returned from the concentration camp, Father Kentenich counted on a new dictatorship in Germany, this time from the East. He was convinced that Siberia would become the next Dachau. The *internationality* of the movement, which had been founded in Dachau, increased in significance. The time came for him to visit the sisters and Pallottines abroad. He couldn't let the young sisters—with whom hardly any contact was possible in all those years—wait any longer. They had traveled to South Africa and to countries in South America to do pioneer missionary work there, fending for themselves in the face of great risks, without knowing the language, and with minimal financial means. Many questions and problems had piled up, also because they were Germans, and they wanted and needed to speak with the founder about them.

Still in the summer of 1945, Joseph Kentenich traveled to Switzerland to apply for a foreign travel permit, passport, and visa. In between the subsequent trips to Brazil, Argentina, Chile, Uruguay, Africa, and to confreres in the USA, he went to Rome in 1947. His purpose was to start the process of obtaining ecclesial recognition for the Sisters of Mary. Even as he was trying to schedule

Photo 13: On his world travels—at the airport in Chile, 1947

a private audience with Pope Pius XII, the Vatican published the document *Provida Mater Ecclesia,* which created a juridical basis in the Church for the so-called secular institutes. This event, and the fact that it occurred during his stay in Rome, became for the founder a *"sign of the special love of God and his providence."* The new communities, which were similar to the religious orders, were given the name "secular institutes," as they had chosen a form of life directed toward the world. Now, after twenty years had passed without a juridical place in the Church for his communities, a decisive door opened. There was hardly any other topic of conversation at the papal audience. He thanked the Holy Father for the document and promised to help take care that this new community form would become a blessing for the Church.

With the new framework in place, an application could soon be made for the ecclesial recognition of the Sisters of Mary. Things were successfully set in motion—so successfully that just one year later, on February 1, 1948, Rome declared that all obstacles for the official juridical establishment of the Institute of the Schoenstatt Sisters of Mary had been cleared. In May, the diocese of Trier decreed the solemn "canonical erection of the community." A thorough review of the statutes had raised fundamental debates in Rome about the original form and structure of the bond. In the Schoenstatt institutes there was no obligatory vow for a life of poverty, chastity, and obedience, as was customary in the orders. There were no vows that only Rome had the power to dissolve. For Church authorities, this was something unusual—a women's community without vows! It was also something really new to have two authorities in the highest position, the general superior and the general director. Questions about the family character and the position of the general director as the bearer of the "father principle" were discussed in depth; Father Kentenich could personally give his perspective on them.

Ultimately, the constitutions were passed and the community became an "institute of papal right" on account of its international expansion. The "prodecretum laudis," a first preliminary commendation and approbation of the community by canon law, was rapidly issued. The news from Rome arrived in Schoenstatt precisely on October 18 of the same year. The joy this triggered everywhere was indescribable. Father Kentenich himself could hardly contain his happiness. Rome had spoken. In Trier, not everyone was so enthused about this swift development. They felt they had been passed over.

Meanwhile, skepticism against Schoenstatt had spread further. In any case, at the plenary assembly of the German Bishops'

Conference in August 1948, the criticism against Schoenstatt had not fallen silent. One of the bishops present identified a series of points. He said that more and more priests of the dioceses were orienting themselves on the core leadership circle in Schoenstatt and the movement was growing without the control of the bishops. Another cause of annoyance was the peculiar terminology that Schoenstatt didn't back away from, such as "covenant of love," "contributions to the capital of grace," "Schoenstatt secret," or "inscriptio act." Already in 1935, this terminology had been described as "unusual," "tasteless," and too "modern." Another point was the publication of the booklet *Heavenwards*, a collection of prayers composed in Dachau whose "rhyming couplets," he said, lacked any aesthetical sense. In his opinion, the strong emphasis on the "*unity of Jesus and Mary*" would need to undergo a thorough theological and dogmatic examination. The bishop criticized the designation of Schoenstatt as a "place of grace," saying that after all, there had been no Marian apparition there. He also stated that the peculiar "closedness" toward the outside gave the impression of a "sect" and caused particular mistrust. And lastly, he mentioned the influential position Father Kentenich occupied even though he held no office in the Church! Everyone streamed to him.

Father Kentenich was in no way shaken or offended by all the criticism that reached his ears. On the contrary, he was pleased. Finally, after decades of a "catacomb existence," Schoenstatt was a topic of discussion in the German Bishops' Conference. The questions finally offered a chance to present Schoenstatt and its mission to the official Church and enter into dialogue with the relevant authorities. He longed for nothing more than to have a "study commission" from Trier take a closer look at what had come about in Schoenstatt over the years from the standpoint of theology and pedagogy. To this end, he invited Auxiliary Bishop Bernhard Stein of Trier, with whom he kept friendly contact, to come to Schoenstatt. Their conversations had given him hope that he had found someone who could understand the originality and the spiritual world of Schoenstatt and represent it before the official Church.

But what Joseph Kentenich didn't know was this: The German Bishops' Conference hadn't even considered a scholarly discourse with and about Schoenstatt. Instead, they had decided that Trier should conduct a "visitation" in Schoenstatt. Hidden behind this was the unspoken accusation that something "wasn't right" that required a visitation. Schoenstatt was to be examined as to whether it was even in the spirit of the Church at all.

A Visitation instead of a Visit

It couldn't be determined with certainty afterwards whether that was now the reason why Auxiliary Bishop Stein didn't accept the invitation to come to Schoenstatt for a scholarly examination, or whether the decisive factor came through the secret accusations a former Sister of Mary brought to the auxiliary bishop. In any case, he pressed Father Kentenich to make an official application to the bishop of Trier, Franz Rudolf Bornewasser. But on February 14, 1949, before the invitation to the bishop had arrived, the Schoenstatt leadership circles received the notification through the general vicariate of Trier that a diocesan visitation would be conducted in five days in Schoenstatt and that the visitator would be Auxiliary Bishop Bernhard Stein.

The news hit Schoenstatt like a lightning bolt while the founder was overseas. Until then, no one had the slightest idea that there could be something in their ranks that was not in harmony with the Church, its teachings, or its laws. Overnight, the planned visit had become a visitation. The news reached Father Kentenich in Argentina via members of "King Arthur's Round Table," not via the episcopal authorities. By the time the telegram reached the founder, the visitation—scheduled for February 19-28—was already well underway.

Right away in his opening talk, the auxiliary bishop struck notes that sounded foreign to most of them. First, he unfolded the biblical image of the "Visitation," Mary's visit to Elizabeth, in an appealing way. But then came paragraphs from canon law that were meant to justify the visitation. There was in fact a juridical problem which he addressed, namely, the question of the legitimacy of the diocesan visitation. "The constitution *Provida Mater Ecclesia,* which you all know so well, says in general that the prescriptions relating to religious orders in the Church, to the state of religious orders, do not apply as such to secular institutes, and that the entire legislation regarding religious orders is not to be applied to secular institutes. However, there can be no doubt that the visitation is justified, because the responsible diocesan representative has complete supervisory rights also over such pious associations that have no vows."

Then came instructions that left the attentive, somewhat frightened listeners with a strange aftertaste. The auxiliary bishop demanded unconditional openness and consulted canon law once again: "A visitator has the right and duty to question those religious whom he deems necessary to question. And all religious are bound in conscience to answer according to the truth, and the superiors may in no way prevent them from this obligation or otherwise impede the objective of the visitation." Superiors who "induce" the sisters "to keep silent ... should be declared unsuitable for the assumption of offices." The strong emphasis on openness toward him took an ever broader scope in the course of the talk and finally escalated to the threat, "Don't think I won't notice a lack of openness in the course of the discussion." At the same time, he mentioned that "thanks to Father's obligingness," he had had "the opportunity to gain insight into the reports, papers, and letters that as such are intended only for the closest family circle." The words of the auxiliary bishop sparked great confusion.

"But why doesn't he wait with the visitation until Father is back from overseas? I don't understand the whole thing! I mean, we haven't done anything wrong and don't have anything to hide! Just like every community, we have our internal family life that one doesn't talk about all over the place, but that has nothing to do with 'being secretive'! Why is the bishop so mistrustful?" One of the young sisters laid it on the line like she usually did. She cast a side glance at her superior with a questioning look. The superior shook her head helplessly and shrugged her shoulders.

What no one knew was the fact that two from their own ranks, a former Sister of Mary and a friend of hers who was still in the community, had brought accusations to the auxiliary bishop against the community and its founder. This was the reason he had appeared in Schoenstatt with a certain skepticism. Only rather casually did he give his attention to the Schoenstatt Work as a whole—in table conversations with Father Menningen and the assistant movement director Father Muehlbeyer as well as with other Fathers of "King Arthur's Round Table." His visitation was noticeably focused on the community of the Sisters of Mary, from whose ranks he summoned and questioned a few individual sisters.

Still during the visitation, Schoenstatters in leadership positions reported anxiously about the auxiliary bishop's questions. He thought the Fathers would know about all the internal matters of the sisters, as Father Menningen wrote in a letter to Father Kentenich. "Some things, the auxiliary bishop can understand, but other things, not at all, because he doesn't clearly see the principles standing behind them." The result was irritation, feelings of uncertainty, agitation, and anxiety because the bishop "didn't always proceed too skillfully in a pedagogical and psychological sense." This prompted Father Kentenich to write personally to the auxiliary bishop during the weeks following the visitation, which he did for the first time on March 4. In a total of ten letters, which he usually dictated at night during the period from March 4-19, 1949, he tried to give an answer to the questions in principle. During the day, he gave a four-week retreat to the community of the Missionaries of the Holy Family in Buenos Aires. Each of the three- to seven-page letters reflected his attempt to elucidate important points of Schoenstatt's spirituality and the original community structure of the Sisters of Mary and to place them into the larger framework of Church and society in the modern time. The founder thus wrote in a letter, "*We live in an epoch in which all structures of life are completely uprooted. Our Catholic way of thinking and speaking comes from a time that wasn't familiar with this process. It therefore created an ideology and terminology that suppose prerequisites that no longer exist today and that will be swept away entirely tomorrow and the day after tomorrow. Our language is already no longer understood by people of today, not even in all Church circles, much less in the world. And still, the Church has the task to absorb the coming time with its elemental dissolution process and to baptize it. Today's generation must find its way to this new shore as quickly and safely as possible despite distressing crises. We must first of all inquire much more, and much more profoundly, into the ultimate roots and principles behind these life processes. In this regard we must go much further than the accomplishments of scholasticism, which had to struggle with the problems of its own time. Thomas (Aquinas) had a tremendous mission in this regard. He saved Christian spirituality and thus Christianity itself from the subversive influences of the all-encompassing floodwaters of Arabian philosophy. He did it by integrating the Aristotelian teaching on secondary causes into Western philosophical and theological thinking. Today, our task is a different one. Today, life in its entirety is in danger everywhere. Therefore, today we must penetrate all expressions of life—both natural and supernatural—to the ultimate depths, separating the supratemporal, absolute elements from the temporal ones and proclaiming the former with great warmth and security, in order then to see which new forms of life develop and prevail in the hard struggle.*"

As an essential answer to the needs of the time, he unfolded the spirituality of *childlikeness*, falling back on St. Thérèse of Lisieux, the Indian philosopher Tagore, St. Francis de Sales, Pestalozzi, and even Nietzsche: "Today there are no more children's lands because there are no more fatherlands or motherlands." It was a rewording of Jesus' statement: "Unless you turn and become like children, you will not enter the kingdom of heaven. Whoever humbles himself like this child is the greatest in the kingdom of heaven" (Matthew 18:3-4)—

so trusting, so open, so capable of surrender, so uncomplicated, genuine, original and pure, flexible and able to learn, happy from within on account of being sustained by a healthy inner attachment. This was his idea of a healthy "organism of attachments," an entire cosmos of humanly successful relationships.

In this connection, Father Kentenich explained the relationship between the founder and his followers: *"The masses wash away the core of the personality. True love does give of itself, but as a return gift it receives not only complementation and enrichment by a personal 'you,' but also the secured and increased possession of one's originality. ... Perhaps you know, your Excellency, how great is the number of people whose power of love has not yet broken forth and who therefore arrive so little at a true love of God because they haven't received any healthy human love or because they cast themselves away in blind passion, and who furthermore no longer have an organ for Christian doctrine, which at the most penetrates the mind, but cannot find the way to the heart."*

Joseph Kentenich called *"mechanistic thinking"* the *"illness of Western thinking and above all of German thinking."* He stated that the German Church was in danger of propagating a too *"overly intellectual theology,"* of *"separating the idea of Christianity from life,"* and of withdrawing in pastoral practice into a Sunday piety instead of forming everyday life and putting *"everyday sanctity"* into the forefront. He wrote that human and divine love were being *"mechanistically"* separated like two parts of a machine and placed into competition with each other. Night after night, Joseph Kentenich persistently dictated his positions on the auxiliary bishop's individual points of criticism, including the original style of obedience, to Sister Ursula, provincial superior of the sisters in Uruguay and Argentina. Concerning "blind obedience," which he argued was anchored in faith, he cited the Church Fathers, St. Ignatius of Loyola, and the teaching of St. Thomas Aquinas. God worked *"through secondary causes,"* that is, through people. Obedience, as his institutes understood it, was based on *"love and trust"* and included *"a high degree of co-responsibility"* and *"frankness."*

He argued that obedience, if separated from faith and love, made no sense and was unworthy of a human being.

Above all, he referred to misunderstandings connected with the parent principle and the father principle. He stated that Rome had occupied itself intensively with these things and confirmed them. In his letters, Joseph Kentenich addressed the inner connections between *"freedom, human attachment, and love."* Human affection and mutual trust, he argued, in no way contradicted the virginal way of life; rather, they supported, protected, and strengthened it.

And even more misunderstandings came up. Since the auxiliary bishop, like many Church representatives, was only familiar with traditional religious orders and their long-standing practice of penance within a public chapter of faults, he was wary of a practice of penance that did away with the public character. And because the visitator—influenced by the background accusations of a mere handful of sisters—misinterpreted the attachment to the founder as unhealthy dependence, Father Kentenich saw it as his duty toward the community to resolutely take up a position on this. Bit by bit, he worked through the points in dispute and placed them into larger connections, on the background of the development of the times and the Church. He called good human relationships and attachments a *"healthy organism of attachments."* He argued that this was decisive for the psychological structure of the human person and his religiosity. He stated that no aspect of the attachment to him took the form of a juridical obligation; rather, it was a free gift of mutual trust. *"Your Excellency is also mistaken if you think I am the general spiritual director of the whole community of sisters. I would see that as an unnecessary mutual burden."*

He tried to elucidate and rectify accusations against his leadership behavior and that of the governments by means of his pedagogical insights. *"The task of any healthy and enlightened leadership consists of making oneself as superfluous as possible."* Therefore he had not appointed a "representative" during his absence, so that the sisters would gain autonomy. By this he wanted to underline his conviction regarding a *"woman's ability to govern."* But his intentions were turned into the exact opposite. Concerning closedness, for which the visitator had criticized the sisters and Schoenstatt members, Father Kentenich replied, "The background is the *special lay character of the institutes.*" The Schoenstatt institutes had no cloister walls and no cloister spaces. *"Our modern times make such an exterior cloister impossible. This is especially true of communities that live as secular institutes, like flying islands in the midst of the world, in order to penetrate the world with leaven. Like the individual, so also must the new community renounce exterior cloister walls, replacing these, however, with the safeguard of inner cloister walls, inner closedness, and so also at the same time with a corresponding seclusion from the spirit of the world."*

Father Kentenich argued, *"Everything is just still so new."* The juridical position of secular institutes and the competent jurisdictions had not yet been clarified. He explained that he had also therefore written to Rome. But the auxiliary bishop and his archbishop in Trier held precisely this point strongly against him. The letters the auxiliary bishop received within a month contained many things that remained alien to him. Father Kentenich actually must have had this clear amid all efforts, since at one point he wrote, *"If I see rightly, we are many decades ahead with our desires."* He could not sense how right he was and how precisely that would seal his fate.

On March 19, he received a first reaction from the auxiliary bishop, possibly answering his first letter due to the long mail route. It said that Father Kentenich should wait with his responses until the official visitation report arrived. The auxiliary bishop thereby broke off all further communication with the founder—without knowing that more letters were already on the way. Father Kentenich had indicated or directly formulated multiple times that the auxiliary bishop *"had been falsely informed"* or was *"completely mistaken,"* possibly because things had been brought forward to him in a way that could be misunderstood, as the writer apologetically added. After the first reaction, which had reached him on his nameday, he undertook one last effort to explain symbolic actions and customs from the standpoint of ultimate principles. He stated that a lay institute had to follow different educational and ascetical principles than a religious order. "*After all, they are a lay institute and should have greater spiritual autonomy than has been customary until now.*" Then he wrote nothing more.

February 27, 1949. In his closing talk, the visitator expressed his conviction that Schoenstatt was "a work of God" in conformity with the theological teaching of the Catholic Church and that the community of the Sisters of Mary was praiseworthy. But in practice he also saw "deficits" and "dangers." The closing report made it clear that precisely in the realm of pedagogy and psychology, many essential things remained unclear to him or had been passed on to him in a way that could be misunderstood. But that actually wouldn't have been a problem. They could work it out together. But ...

Did the problem have to do with individual points of criticism by the German Church? Or was it the honesty with which Father Kentenich devoted himself to the pertinent questions—without wanting to attack the person, as he had emphasized? Or were they simply not used to "debates" with higher Church authorities at that time? Was it ultimately the exertion of influence by certain forces within Schoenstatt's own ranks that were actually few in number but that had evidently worked effectively? Or was it simply the newness of the whole structure of ideas and life that was bound to trigger skepticism? At the end of April 1949, Father Kentenich received a letter from the auxiliary bishop that completely surprised him. In it, he said he had "fundamentally changed" his positive orientation toward Schoenstatt as he had expressed it in his closing talk. Father Kentenich wrote an alarming letter to Father Hoffmann about this: "*On April 29, he* [the auxiliary bishop] *wrote to me that the information given at that time is no longer valid. His impression, he said, is now essentially worse, for three reasons: 1. Because I wrote to him before he had sent the official report. 2. Because Father Menningen deceived him by omitting a text. 3. Because I turned to Rome.*" The matter regarding the alleged deception by Father Menningen was peculiar. In a longer letter defining principles, Father Kentenich had mentioned to his long-time co-worker in mid-February 1949 that he had not yet told the auxiliary bishop anything about the "follower trend" that had just recently awakened. He had explained that it was all simply too new and first had to prove itself in life. Moreover, he had written that it would seem strange to an outsider who knew nothing of the whole development. For this reason Father Menningen had omitted this passage of the letter when he sent the auxiliary bishop a copy on account of the other important explanations. Toward the end of the letter, Father Kentenich had asked Father Menningen to give it to Sister Anna so that she would be kept up-to-date. The general superior had passed on this letter in its complete form—without the knowledge of Father Menningen—to the auxiliary bishop, causing the latter to feel deceived and hurt.

May 14, 1949. The long-awaited official closing report of the visitator had finally reached him. The hair of all those who had a deeper insight stood on end. Although individual passages made very positive statements about Schoenstatt as a work of God, affirming that Schoenstatt was entirely faithful to the Catholic Church both dogmatically and theologically, the report as a whole had a very negative tone. It stated that there were considerable complaints especially in the pedagogical sphere. The report pronounced a scathing judgment on the community of the Sisters of Mary, closer co-workers in the movement, and the founder himself and his pedagogical practices. Joseph Kentenich was characterized as a "despot," and the sisters—even those on the general government—as "immature children," "dependent slaves" among whom there was "basically not one single independent personality." What was claimed here was completely contrary to reality. The visitator, as he himself admitted, had been able to meet with only a few sisters and had only spent time in Schoenstatt itself—and yet in the report he had spoken of "most of them" or "many Sisters of Mary."

In stunned silence, Father Kentenich held the closing report and the accompanying letter from Archbishop Bornewasser in his hands. The bishop was asking him to give a response. Now he broke his silence, turned to Sister Ursula, and said calmly but with a serious face, *"Now I must act!"* He didn't attribute the accusations and misunderstandings to personal aversions on the part of the auxiliary bishop. For him, the entire false interpretation was based on a much more fundamental problem. In his opinion, the closing report of the auxiliary bishop clearly reflected an intellectualistic, separatistic thinking that had strongly influenced the German Church. He attempted to fight against the danger this thinking posed to the faith. For him, Schoenstatt's mission consisted precisely in this, and he felt obliged to it in conscience. He immediately began his response. It became a long written reply which extended more and more into a study. He completed it in several sections during his trips to South America and sent the individual parts to "His Excellency, Most Reverend Archbishop Bornewasser." The content of the study essentially unfolded the points Father Kentenich had already addressed in his letters to the auxiliary bishop, but more thoroughly and fundamentally, as he explained: *"Because in my opinion it is a matter of the most fundamental educational question of Western civilization, I would also like to answer so thoroughly and so clearly that my views will become understandable. I regret the fact that I must contradict the Most Reverend Visitator. On account of your personal connection with him, I must fear that I will also offend Your Excellency, but I ask you to see it not as an insult but solely as an expression of love for the Church."* All of that was an extraordinarily risky undertaking in the context of the strongly hierarchically oriented Church of that time. But because the conviction had matured in him that God willed this of him, and out of responsibility for his mission, he dared to move to the edge of a volcano that had meanwhile begun to spew fire.

His response turned out to be unmistakably clear. He didn't even shrink back from criticizing the intellectual approach of the visitator. In order not to cause offense and to defuse the criticism, he referred to his own personal development and education during the years of his studies and his novitiate. He wrote that during this time, he, too, had fallen victim to similar idealistic, mechanistic thinking patterns. He stated that the claims put forward in the visitation report were based on a fundamental evil of the time which hadn't left the German Church untouched: *"the illness of mechanistic thinking, which mechanistically separates ideas from life, First Cause from secondary causes, and so nature from supernature, and human love from love of God."*

Father Kentenich was fully aware of the consequences of his long study, the *"Epistola perlonga,"* as Trier called it. He expressed to his co-workers that he could now no longer keep quiet. There were much more important things at stake than his own honor. Therefore he wanted to place the document with all its consequences entirely into the hands of God and the Blessed Mother. He wanted to dare this *"death leap"*—similar to January 20, 1942—trusting that God would continue to guide the matter. As he placed the first part of his study on the altar of the newly built shrine of the Chilean sisters in Bellavista, Santiago on May 31, 1949, he was so clearly aware of the great risk that he didn't only ask the sisters to pray, but also invited them to dare this step interiorly with him. The small community gathered in the shrine in the evening, each with a burning candle in her hand as a symbol of her total surrender to God and of her readiness to go this difficult way with the founder.

During these months, Joseph Kentenich fostered intensive written contact with his general superior, with "King Arthur's Round Table," and with the government of the sisters, including Sister Anna. He wrote to a member of the Pallottine government that he preferred to take the conflict with Church authorities upon himself so that the Society of the Pallottines would remain largely undisturbed. But would that be possible? At any rate, he kept his general superior informed about all important happenings, including all correspondence with the visitator and Archbishop Bornewasser. In one of his letters to his general superior at the end of July 1949, he expressed his conviction: *"Future times will show how important this conflict is.*" And on August 20, 1949, he wrote to one of his closer co-workers, "*My struggle will still last a long, long time. It has only just begun.*"

In response to his long study letter of May 31, he received the first answer from the archbishop of Trier on July 5, 1949: "Given the unusually large amount of activity you are engaged in, I think you could easily write the third part in a condensed form." But just fourteen days later, the tone was already less friendly. They viewed the entire study as a lecture and an accusation against the office-bearers. The archbishop ultimately responded with a list of eight episcopal demands that Schoenstatt was to fulfill. These had already been formulated in a similar way at the German Bishops' Conference one year earlier. The leadership in Schoenstatt was to commit itself to avoiding "terminology like 'increase of the capital of grace,' Schoenstatt as a 'chosen instrument,' or 'favorite occupation of God.'" "All materials, manuscripts, and newsletters printed by Schoenstatt's leadership must be submitted to the local Ordinary." The prayer book *Heavenwards* was to be recalled, and any further publications of the Dachau prayers were forbidden. "The establishment and development of Schoenstatt groups in the dioceses may only take place with the permission of the local Ordinary. The Schoenstatt priests are to give a complete account of their work in the Schoenstatt Movement to their local Ordinary. Without the express permission of the latter, Schoenstatt songs and prayers may be used neither at church nor in school." Upon the request of the leadership in Schoenstatt, Father Kentenich sent a telegram from abroad: "*Accept demands, because disciplinary regulations. May God justify himself.*" Accordingly, Father Muehlbeyer answered the bishop of Trier, saying that the leadership of the movement accepted "with reverence the episcopal demands on Schoenstatt and declared itself willing to carry them out loyally in the spirit of ecclesial obedience." The bishop directed a letter to Father Turowski, the general superior of the Pallottines, requesting that he take a stand to Father Kentenich's study of May 31. To ease their minds, Father General acknowledged that many formulations were perhaps poorly chosen, but that he had known Father Kentenich for a long time already and well enough to say with certainty that his attitude toward the Church and its authority was borne by reverence and love.

Over time, the clarification of pertinent questions and the dogmatic, theological debates stood less and less in the foreground. Ever since the German Bishops' Conference of 1948, the weight had shifted. The desired scholarly dispute the founder had hoped for had failed to materialize. Instead it increasingly became a question of influence, authority, and subordination, and ultimately of power. This stood all the more clearly before his eyes the more sharply the demands by certain Church representatives were formulated. In a letter of August 20, 1949, to "King Arthur's Round Table," he had to regretfully state, *"You immediately sense that the struggle for the truth has now become a power struggle. At any rate it is prudent to give way to this power for the time being. Time will tell."* He later explained to his general superior the burdensome responsibility that had moved him to write the study of May 31: *"Personally I am of the opinion that without that daring initiative, the movement would have become a child of death."*

Father General Turowski stood at the window holding one of the many letters in his hand and took a deep breath. Although his secretary was standing close by, he mumbled almost inaudibly, "Wouldn't it have been better if he had let the matter rest with a few friendly words? Peaceable, conciliatory, simply overlooking misunderstandings?"

His secretary came up next to him at the window and also looked out. "His confounded fanaticism for the truth will become his downfall yet!"

"Joseph Kentenich is no man of lazy compromises, and the step he took with the letter of May 31 was very hard for him."

"Of course," replied the secretary. "For him it's a matter of the honor of the Sisters of Mary and the future of the Work."

"Certainly, that too—but the crucial factor is that he is so firmly convinced of Schoenstatt's mission for the Church. I have never found such mission consciousness in anybody else. He has a glowing love for the Church—one can sense that—and he considers all the questions and tests a matter of course. He always tells me that the Church has the right to test the Work."

"But still, it would have been more prudent to stay quiet and not explain so much, or at least not to criticize the bishops' way of thinking."

"Yes, by and large, keeping quiet and proceeding diplomatically for the sake of peace would have been so much more comfortable and more pleasant for all of us!" Father Turowski offered a somewhat forced smile.

The secretary looked at him seriously. "Father Kentenich is putting his whole honor as a priest and as a person at stake! Does he actually realize that?"

"He knows! It simply fits to him! He has prepared himself for anything. Father Menningen recently showed me a letter from him. It said, '*Ultimately the time will come for all of us when we must renounce everything, even the last little bit of personal honor. None of us will likely be spared of this.*' He knows exactly how difficult the situation is, particularly for him."

"Where is he now?"

"Right now in Argentina again, giving retreats to priests of other communities and talks to the sisters, as if nothing were amiss, although he is informed about every detail of the struggles in Schoenstatt."

The secretary shook his head, baffled. "Incredible ..."

During the last days of December 1949, Sister Diemut found herself sitting in the house chapel of Villa Ballester, thinking of how often Father Kentenich had already mentioned her name in his talks. As a young nurse, she hadn't been in Argentina very long yet, and naturally she was homesick. Everything was new, just beginning; they were all young and inexperienced. There were many tensions.

"I know exactly why he mentioned me by name," she thought. "He wants to make me aware that I am the *'favorite child of God the Father.'* He likes to use those words a lot." She leafed through her shorthand notes of the talks. She had collected a lot of material since February. More than a thousand pages could easily be filled. How was he able to take in all their concerns about the new foundation, community life, and even the trivialities of their everyday life? Didn't he have enough other concerns? Writing to the archbishop, giving retreats for priests, traveling to other countries in the meantime, establishing contacts, visiting priests and bishops, and talking with people who might be able to sell them land for their province house, a shrine, and a house for the movement work? How much he liked to speak about *"Schoenstatt as God's favorite creation"*! Maybe because precisely this was being especially attacked. It was *"not meant exclusively"*—it doesn't intend to exclude others, as he had explained in his letter of May 31. Every human person was a *"favorite creation of God."* That was precisely what had appealed to her so much. *"We are a favorite occupation of the Triune God!"* When a person deeply experienced this truth, it had consequences for the soul: *"The loving God then becomes my favorite occupation."* The next day he had continued to develop the idea: *"I am just in the process of responding to the bishop. There are ascetical trends that teach us always to say, 'I am a slave of God, a little dog.' And what do we say? 'I am God's princess, God's child.' Therefore we don't tire of saying, 'He loves me!' Imagine if we had to say like most people of Western civilization, 'He looks at me to see if he needs to use the cane …' Then we would be mutts of God and would quickly try to get away from him. That's why it's such an experience of grace. We savor the mercies of God and never come to an end. … We are God's favorites. God looks with favor upon all."* She searched for the next spot where the thought appeared again. "Aha, there!" *"God can treat millions as if he had nothing else to do but care for the one child. How happy it makes us to know: 'He loves me. And even more when I haven't been good.'"* That was new for her. She hadn't been educated in this way, not at all! That God loved a person especially when that person had done something wrong and came before him with it. *"The Father can no longer resist the recognized and acknowledged weakness of his child. Therefore, childlikeness is the powerlessness of God and the omnipotence of the child."* She hadn't heard such things from any other priest but him. *"With God, it's like this: He can always pursue his favorite inclination. He thus always occupies himself with the object of his love. Who is that? Me. If we believed this entirely, if this became second nature to us, we would be the happiest people on earth. We do believe it a little. After all, that's the reason we're so happy to be together."* That was true! Whenever Father was there and spoke to them in this way, they forgot all differences of opinion among them. He always connected love of God with human love. *"God so willed it that we belong not only to him but also to each other. ... It wouldn't be a warm love of God if, for example, we were at the highest levels of love of God while here below we parted from each other saying, 'Now I belong to the loving God; away therefore with human love.' That's how we often imagine piety to be. ... That's a fundamentally wrong conception!"*

Whenever he spoke, new worlds opened up before her. *"Remember, seeing yourself and others in their weaknesses leads to such deep love. ... Whoever begins to love in God senses that it reaches into infinity. Every created love always cries out for infinity. ... That's why it's also so good that you are so good to each other. That allows a person to understand the loving God so easily!"* He had said that when a person loves deeply, he or she is no longer really capable of sinning. What a thought! *"God the Father does this; he gives us the strength. He even binds our subconscious soul life. He gives us pleasure and joy in being good."*—*"Pleasure in being good."* She had underlined this with thick lines. From childhood on she had been taught that a person had to be good, that for a Christian it was a duty, a commandment of God, and that a person would get punished for acting against it. But of *"pleasure in being good,"* like one takes pleasure in good food, never a word was spoken. Nothing seemed more important to him than that this reality of God would grip them all down to the last fibers of their souls. *"I have the deep longing within me to lead you to God the Father. That is the goal I pray for as a May grace for you and for me."*

While the waves rose ever higher in Schoenstatt, he spoke to them for hours at a time, day by day, week by week, as if there were nothing else to do. Many things that were disputed he explained so simply and plainly that sometimes they weren't even sure whether all these hard struggles really existed in Schoenstatt. "*You will notice how calm the soul becomes when it is searching for God. ... The soul doesn't need to pray God-knows-what kind of prayers, but this interiorly being with God, also in the very smallest situations, is true religiosity. I can imagine that when one prays official prayers, a religious attitude is assumed. That is not yet religiosity for me. True religiosity is found in the person who immediately establishes a connection with supernature. That doesn't happen by the etiquette book. ... Only if the whole inner person speaks.*"

Sister Diemut put the notes down for a moment. The way he unfolded the New Testament, the Passion of Christ during Holy Week, the Eucharist, and the way he spoke about Mary—as if he had just come from an encounter with her. His whole thinking circled around the One he himself had also never seen. "*The Eucharist should be a protection, but also the expression of unity. If you remain with this thought, you can also understand why a mysterious sympathy for the Savior must awaken in us.*"—*A mysterious sympathy for God!* What an expression! "*Childlikeness*" was for him nothing more than "*the way of constantly walking with God.*" Schoenstatt, he said, had "*only come about through this simple childlikeness.*"

He was awakening all the truths of the faith she had memorized from the Catechism in school and allowing them to become a genuine inner experience! "And this," she thought, "the application, is probably the problem, the reason why the Most Reverend Auxiliary Bishop can't understand our father." Father had recently explained, "*We can't hold it against the bishop that he didn't understand it.*"

Sister Diemut set the notepad aside. How much she had enjoyed these hours! Earlier, when she was thinking of becoming a sister, she would've never thought that doing so could make a person so happy. And now? That happiness was part of her calling, and he had explained to them, *"If your heart is unhappy, it's not capable of anything. ... There are very few people in the world who are as happy as we are."*

From all sides, he tried to define the structure of the *new community* they were supposed to represent. *"It was always like this within me: You must create a community that does what's right from an inner conviction. ... To be good from within, whether someone sees me or not. I must always be the same personality. If I can't, I can't be a Sister of Mary. This is something so new. ... Every superior must seek her greatness in allowing the sisters to make autonomous decisions. ... Our modern times need such persons who are good from within and bind themselves to the ideal, who don't always have to be pushed. That is also the spirit of the constitution* Provida Mater Ecclesia. *You must become aware that it is possible to live our type. People think it's not possible if a person isn't always handled with iron discipline. Others think it will only be possible as long as I am with you. It must be your pride and joy to practice everything this way, even after I'm long dead."*

Concerning the purchase of land, a miracle had happened. Father had encouraged them, although the Pallottine Fathers had given them very little hope saying that everything was very expensive and they had no money. Contrary to all reality, he was full of hope and had encouraged them *"that God and the Blessed Mother will take the matter in hand. ... It seems to be a generally valid law that God only places his riches at the disposal of those who have a very unrestrained trust in Providence and who always follow his inspirations."* And he had proved to be right! They had received land as a gift from a Protestant totally by surprise—a large piece of land, several hectares (acres) valued at two million pesos, and in addition, $40,000 for the flights of eleven urgently needed German sisters. Father had said that they couldn't speak of "miracles," but that it was indeed *"wondrous."*

He actually hardly spoke about the visitation; he only mentioned something here and there. *"We go our way. We go with the Savior, and in the Savior to the Father. I thank you for telling me so simply yesterday what your image of the Savior is like ... Hadn't his sense of justice been offended? How had he been mistreated? He wants to suffer in us ... God has given me the gift that I am able to endure tremendously much suffering. I always think that through his suffering in the Garden of Gethsemane, the Savior has obtained for me the grace that I am able to endure so much."* He said it was now important to remain interiorly free. *"I would like to urgently ask you to make yourselves independent of human judgment. ... If I hadn't been so totally independent of people, everything would have died ... I only thought, 'That corresponds to the wishes of God.' If I now see how Providence has led us, it is indisputably clear to me that God has something special in store for us. If it were my Work, I could retract it; if it's God's Work, I must accept it."* Indeed, one hardly noticed how much he suffered. Only once were they able to sense it a little. *"When inveterate enemies of the Church persecute us, we bear it, and might even see it as an honor—but when those for whom we have sacrificed ourselves suddenly turn around and thrust the arrow into our own heart, how much that must hurt."* During Holy Week, he disclosed more: *"If I would reveal to you the effect the visitation has had—one is almost afraid to speak about me."* He spoke about *"dark storm clouds"* at Jesus' arrest and over Schoenstatt. *"How people can get lost in the crowd in hours of darkness. ... Now the hour of darkness has come. ... In everything we've heard about Schoenstatt and what's connected to the visitation, here, too, we must maintain: The hour of darkness has come. There are hours of darkness for the person, for the community ... Now the Father wills that I be treated in this way. A plan also guides our life; all the current struggles about Schoenstatt are also included in this plan. ... It really is true that since what we want is all so new, people may be of different opinions, and many things can't be immediately understood. ... As I know you, and as you have opened your soul to me, I admire you for the way you have overcome public opinion. ... After all, it takes intense courage to swim against the stream and say your opinion with frankness. We have to try to please God and not people."* Even if individual Church representatives were now causing him difficulties, his love for the Church remained untarnished. *"Since we have received papal right, we've also become more strongly aware that we must also make the interests of the papacy our own. After all, we are ...*

members of the universal Church. Therefore, the longing of the whole Church for redemption, for the ideal kingdom, must also grow in our hearts. I'll go still further. If I take a look into our modern world: We should amass the whole modern world's longing for the ideal state in our small hearts."

He discussed many topics with them, including the problem of workers and their "*longing for economic independence.*" Workers, he said, were "*unjustly treated ... A worker would have to earn enough to be able to feed himself and his children without worry and to build a home of his own. What kind of background does the entire Bolshevist movement have as such? They want to build a new kingdom. ... I consider it part of my personal task to elevate the worker. So you also understand why I have the courage to powerfully come forward in the Church. In principle the Church always needs time before it can see and solve such a problem. ... That's precisely how I wrote it in the letter about the visitation. ... If something new is to come about in the world, it usually comes from the 'opponent' first! We also see that it cannot be that some just have their capital and live the high life on interest and compound interest while the worker suffers want. Within the Church we should also be much more honest. In principle, our modern times would need to create an entirely new economic system. ... The Church would need to let itself be made aware—not by its opponents—of what is necessary for reform.*"

Sister Diemut closed her notebook. She read from it more often and always gained new insights. Now she would simply need more time to reflect ...

On his return trip to Germany, Father Kentenich made a stop in Rome. The beatification of Vincent Pallotti took place there on January 22, 1950. A great event. It was a good opportunity to make connections, accompanied by two Schoenstatt priests, Joseph Schmitz and Anton Engel. Conversations at the Congregation of Religious were especially important. There he was able to present his notion of secular institutes to Don Salvator Canals from the standpoint of the philosophy of law. After a conversation with the prefect of the congregation, Cardinal Luigi Lavitrano, whom he personally thanked for the establishment of the Sisters of Mary, he was also able to bring up his intention to found a secular institute for the Schoenstatt priests. After that, he confidently sought out Don Salvator Canals once more and dared to ask about the possibilities for establishing a secular institute for couples. Naturally, this led them to speak about Schoenstatt's pedagogy and the special community structure of the Sisters of Mary.

Father Kentenich had many meetings during these eight days of his stay in Rome, including one with the general superior of the Franciscans and one with the general superior of the Steyler Sisters. He wanted to negotiate with the latter about purchasing the "Marienau" in Vallendar as a possible house of formation for the Schoenstatt priests. They met more often with Father General Turowski and Father Hoffmann at the generalate of the Pallottines for common deliberations about the current situation regarding Schoenstatt. In a conversation with Father Leiber, the private secretary of the Holy Father, they spoke about sending Sisters of Mary to Venezuela. On this occasion the papal secretary advised him to wait with the request for an audience with the pope. So they didn't take advantage of this opportunity—and in the future, the Holy Father would be dependent on what others reported to him.

From Rome, Father Kentenich set out to give his scheduled talks in Switzerland. In order to tackle important questions of government peacefully, he invited the general government of the Sisters of Mary to a business meeting at the provincial house in Quarten, in eastern Switzerland. The sisters' first general chapter was set to take place the following year, and many important questions were pending after his almost three-year absence, particularly since the visitation had raised new problems. The six general council sisters considered it appropriate that the founder would redefine important and urgent governing issues. In the midst of the community's difficult situation, the general council sisters placed their offices at the founder's disposal for a new appointment. Father Kentenich accepted this. Those who had meanwhile become provincial superiors were not reappointed and stepped down from the general government. The rest remained. Now, after having wanted to resign from office several times previously, Sister Anna handed the founder a letter with the request to be relieved of her office as general superior. Father Kentenich now accepted her offer and appointed her provincial superior of the Swiss province. He had a general vicar administer the office of general superior until it could be newly filled by election at the general chapter.

The year 1950 was filled to the brim with activities: large pedagogical conferences, a vast number of talks, addresses to the various Schoenstatt communities, extensive correspondence, conversations, and travels—primarily through Germany. Naturally, he had gotten wind of the fact that the authorities in Trier were upset about him and his letter of May 31. Therefore, he had already written to the archbishop from Rome, *"I sincerely regret that the fight against ideas might be seen as synonymous to the fight against the bearer of those ideas. In any case, the last thing I want and wanted to do was to offend the personality of the Most Reverend Auxiliary Bishop, who is worthy of esteem by the very dignity of his office."*

All further attempts at clarification, as prudently as they had been formulated and as detailed as they turned out to be, were evidently not able to reduce the resentment. But the disgruntlement reached a dramatic highpoint only when Sister Anna complained to the auxiliary bishop that Father Kentenich had put moral pressure on her and simply removed her from office. These words and complaints of the general superior carried weight. "I'm going to do something about this!" the auxiliary bishop angrily thundered at Father General Turowski in Rome, calling the events in Quarten "unlawful."

"It's highest time," the archbishop of Trier also said in a conversation with Sister Edmunda weeks later, taking the same position, "for Father Kentenich to get away from your community." And almost like a side comment, one of his main reasons slipped out: "Father Kentenich has seriously offended me by his letters." The situation became noticeably worse. When Joseph Kentenich informed the bishop of his intention to clarify pending questions before the German bishops, the ordinariate in Trier preempted the plan. They sent all the German bishops a circular letter with information and statements against Schoenstatt as well as the indication that no concessions of any kind were to be made for Father Kentenich. It said that the Congregation for Religious would take a new stand, although at this point that had only been requested by Trier but not yet confirmed. When the founder then had various audiences with the German bishops (Cologne, Muenster, Aachen, Paderborn, Wuerzburg, Bamberg, Eichstätt, Augsburg, and Speyer) and shared the main intention of his visit—to constitute the Institute of Diocesan Priests' as a secular institute—it was categorically refused by all of them, with the exception of the bishop of Wuerzburg, Julius Doepfner. Joseph Kentenich knew nothing of the background of their refusals. All diocesan measures taken in Trier concerning the Schoenstatt Movement were henceforth shared with the German bishops and unquestioningly adopted by them. But it got even worse. During a stay in Rome, Auxiliary Bishop Stein went to the Congregation for Religious to orally obtain an apostolic visitation of Schoenstatt and especially of its founder. Such requests for a visitation by Rome were inevitably forwarded to the Holy Office.

April 18, 1950. Auxiliary Bishop Stein submitted a "paper for consideration," a "Promemoria" against Schoenstatt and its founder, to the Congregation for Religious. In order to successfully attain his goal of a visitation by Rome, he stressed in it, "Both the dogmatic as well as the pastoral pedagogical principles of the Schoenstatt Work have been disputed among German theologians from the very beginning." Based on his visitation, he stated, he had reached a conclusion: "Even though these principles in themselves are good, the way they are applied in practice entails significant dangers that are obviously to be attributed above all to the fascinating personality of Father Kentenich."

During a stay of several weeks in the Soviet zone, where Father Kentenich held retreat courses for priests and Sisters of Mary, gave talks for pilgrims, and pursued a number of pastoral activities, the fateful news overtook him on May 25, 1950: He had been accused at the Holy Office. This was really alarming, because to be accused there already implied a kind of pre-judgment. Upon his return, the Pallottine general government, who stood united behind him, gave Father Kentenich the complete "Promemoria," sent to them by the Congregation for Religious. He was thus able to provide a critical response to it. In sixteen pages he demonstrated the untenability of the allegations. But that only led to further accusations against him, which reached the Holy Office in November 1950. It came to light only much later that these had originated almost verbatim from Sister Anna's pen and had evidently been accepted without critical evaluation. In the second submission, the auxiliary bishop made an official application for the envisaged Roman visitation of Schoenstatt, especially of the Sisters of Mary. He directed the addressee's attention to the points that should be especially observed during a visitation: "1. the particular circumstances under which Sr. Anna was removed from her office as general superior; 2. the inner attachment of the members to the person of Father Kentenich ...; and 3. Father Kentenich's conduct toward the Church." Having been one-sidedly informed, German bishops unquestioningly joined the demand for a visitation. Despite further attempts to clear up misunderstandings and refer to fundamental underlying causes, the accusations against the person of the founder intensified.

The archbishop of Trier asked the Congregation for Religious "to choose a prudent man, very well versed in dogmatics and canon law, as the apostolic visitator, someone who will stubbornly persist in the matter, and commission him to visit not only the various houses at the Schoenstatt locality but also a few other larger and smaller communities, even very small ones, and to oblige the followers under obedience, especially the sisters, to answer the questions posed to them with all honesty, and at the same time to forbid them to speak with the Rev. Father Kentenich or their other superiors about what they have discussed with the visitator."

March 23, 1951. The apostolic visitation began in Schoenstatt. Father Sebastian Tromp, Dutch Jesuit and professor of dogmatics, arrived as the visitator appointed by the Holy Office. After a week, however, he formed a very positive opinion about Schoenstatt. During the visitation, the so-called "four-member coalition" of Sisters of Mary, including Sister Anna, continued to bring their grievances to the auxiliary bishop in Trier and evidently found a more attentive ear than the other members. In his closing talk, Father Tromp praised the talent and sacrificial spirit of the former general superior but also confirmed that she was incapable of governing because "her fantasy, her feelings, and her dreams controlled her reason." Full of joy, Father Menningen immediately sat down and reported to Father Kentenich—who as the general delegate of his community was on his third trip to Latin America—about the positive results of the visitation. "He—Father Tromp—would like to come to an agreement with you on the questions that still remain open so as to be able to endorse these results before the Holy Office. ... In our last conversation, the visitator expressly explained to me once more that he has no reason to doubt your personal integrity ... He said a nightmare came to an end once he had come to certainty in this matter." At the end of the month, the visitator traveled to Trier.

Banished from Schoenstatt

October 22, 1951. Both of them looked sadly at the spot where he had gotten into the car that was to take him to the Koblenz train station. The visitator, Father Tromp, no longer wanted to see him in Schoenstatt. He was only still allowed to give the scheduled October Convention, but then he was supposed to disappear again. Dreary fall weather reigned not only in the forests but also in their hearts. Father Menningen struggled to find words to say; Sister Edelgart, a member of the general council, wasn't faring much better. They stood motionless in the hallway of the Bundesheim, still unable to fathom it: the founder, divested of all offices and exiled from Schoenstatt. "Rumor has it that he has to leave Europe." Silence again. For several minutes no one said a word. They both thought back on the events of the past months that had unfolded at lightning speed. "At the beginning Father Tromp had actually gone to Trier with such a positive disposition," said Father Menningen, the first to break the silence.

"Yes, but there, during the follow-up discussions about the visitation, he was met with just one single objective: 'Father Kentenich must go!'"

And so it happened. The follow-up conversation in Trier at the end of March was reflected in a letter from general vicar Father Meurers to Father Tromp dated April 10, 1951. In it, Father Meurers cited the alleged comment of a German bishop: "The bishop thinks it might be necessary to replace Father Kentenich with a different person ... It is very questionable to me personally whether we will be able to come to any solution at all regarding the person of Father Kentenich." At the end of his third trip to South America, Father Kentenich left from Brazil and arrived in Rome on April 19, 1951. He was invited to the Holy Office. A total of four conversations with Father Tromp took place there, consisting mainly of efforts to persuade him to withdraw from everything and leave Schoenstatt.

Father Menningen turned away from the window and said to Sister Edelgart, "In the HO (Holy Office), all conversations pursued one single goal: Father should resign from all offices and disappear from Schoenstatt! These dark days have been unforgettable for me. He was so serious, like I have rarely experienced him. He was not allowed to speak with anyone about their conversations, but I guessed rightly that they must have advised him to resign voluntarily. They did in fact issue an ultimatum: If he voluntarily renounced all offices and left Schoenstatt, there was a chance he could be allowed to return to Schoenstatt again. Otherwise he would 'only return in his coffin'! He asked for time to think. It was a situation much like the time before January 20, 1942. He asked me, '*Alex, do you go with me?*' I can still hear the tone of his voice, soft and peaceful. I knew exactly what he meant. He wanted to know if I would interiorly go along on this incomprehensible way that God was now demanding of us! He wanted to know if I would say yes to the whole superhuman burden now falling on Schoenstatt and to the things being done to his person! But that was impossible for me! Do you understand, Sister Edelgart, how the whole thing simply left me stunned? I freely said to him, 'Father, I can't do that!' He looked at me. I will never forget that look. He asked me three times, and three times I replied straight to his face, 'I can't do that!' Then he said no more; instead, he went to get a pile of letters from Sisters of Mary, the leaders of the individual 'courses.' I was supposed to read them. I read them all night long. I was overwhelmed by the trust in God they expressed and the readiness for his will. I was so touched by this that I could no longer do anything else but give Father my yes the following morning. 'Yes, I will go with you!' He wrote to me in April, *'The current situation represents a repetition of January 20, 1942 and might later stand beside it as its equal in its effects. Right now I don't want to write more.'"*

"He himself answered the HO, *'Voluntarily, never! If I am sent, immediately.'* It's a superhuman test of faith for all of us! And also a test of love for the Church: To take nothing back of one's love for the Church despite disappointments in its representatives, and at the same time to remain faithfully united to him and his mission."

"Many who had been enthused and stood by him in the past are now turning their backs on him. People to whom he gave so much are turning away, just like that!" There was something bitter in the sound of his voice.

"The weight of Church authorities makes them doubt. One decree follows another. He's severely criticized everywhere! It's quite a demand to remain steadfast and faithful and not to lose faith in him!"

"Yes, I know. That's not easy, for the priests above all. They are still their bishops!"

Sister Edelgart nodded. "The fateful disaster was that one authority unquestioningly believed the other. The auxiliary bishop believed the former general superior without thinking twice about it, the archbishop believed his auxiliary bishop, and the German bishops believed their colleagues in Trier."

Father Menningen struggled with the emotions that now arose within him. "And Father is the target they've zeroed in on! No one cares about the factual issues anymore!"

"They think the founder is the crucial disruptive element. If he's out, everything will settle down by itself. And then it will show whether Schoenstatt is truly a work of God, not merely to be traced back to a genius leader personality. They surely think it can also develop prosperously without him."

Father Menningen raised his eyebrows. "What I can't understand is: Aren't they aware of the contradiction? Scripture itself says that a good tree doesn't produce rotten fruits, and a bad tree doesn't produce good fruits. On the one hand, they esteem Schoenstatt and the sisters; they praise their work, the image they present, and their radiance ..."

"And on the other hand they blindly believe those who claim that the vast majority of the Sisters of Mary, especially those in government, are not personalities capable of an independent opinion and let him control them like a dictator. In reality I have never experienced a man who places so much confidence in us as women with regard to autonomy, independent opinion formation, and governing capacity as he does."

"King Arthur's Round Table pulled out all the stops on that point. That's absolute nonsense to say he's a dictator and that he cultivates dependency."

"In Trier they think—as does Father Tromp—that the only independent ones among the Sisters of Mary are the poor general superior who was removed from office and the few who have distanced themselves from Father Kentenich," said Sister Edelgart.

"Yes, it's a tragedy that the pedagogical practice that has developed and been tested over the course of three decades is so contested!"

"It seems to me that Father Tromp is simply not the right man to understand Father and Schoenstatt at all! He's too 'old-school.'"

Father Menningen nodded and sat up straight. "They say the whole thing is an administrative measure. That means that actually there is nothing solid against him. It's all still an open question."

"Yes, the visitator can mandate everything, how long the exile lasts, and he doesn't even need to give reasons for why Father is being sent away at all ... And no one can defend themselves."

"Father General Turowski asked the HO for reasons for the measures against Father Kentenich and has received no answer to date."

"Whoever is accused there has no chance to make a defense. There's no provision for that there. Father General told me that Father had written to him in February of this year, '*Should we give up the fight and postpone it for some time in the future?*' And then he himself declared: No, this generation has to go through the struggle."

"If a person is capable of leading others to God like he does, of opening them interiorly for God, he must either have his own intimate relationship to God or there is no God at all! What makes them so upset about him?" Father Menningen's fist finally hit the windowsill, as it had been poised to do for quite a while already, and he didn't even notice that the hard marble wasn't actually meant for that.

"I don't know how we're going to get out of this," added Sister Edelgart with a concerned expression on her face, "but Father places all his hope in the Blessed Mother."

"Yes, that's why he's also stayed so calm. He always says that she will do it, she'll take care that everything gets clarified."

Just a few days later, Father Menningen found this view confirmed in a letter from the founder dated November 7, 1951: "*We certainly want to continue to use all human means. But ultimately only divine omnipotence can work the miracle of my liberation.*"

9. The Years of Exile

On October 22, 1951, Father Kentenich traveled to Switzerland, and then from there to Rome at the end of November. After his removal from office as general director of the Sisters of Mary and as movement director, further measures and decrees were issued against Schoenstatt, the community of the Sisters of Mary, and him personally. Petitions to the Holy Father from leading co-workers in the movement remained unsuccessful.

On December 1, the decision was made that the North American province of the Pallottines would be his future place of residence. By instruction of the visitator, he was supposed to leave Europe by all means as soon as possible and not stay in Rome any longer than necessary. After all, he might contact or even mobilize other Church officials. Father Tromp's fear seems not to have been entirely unfounded because Father Kentenich was indeed able to have a few conversations with Father Augustin Bea, a Jesuit and consultor of the Holy Office. The future cardinal was evidently a man who had an open ear for the critical situation regarding Schoenstatt and its founder. Some time after these conversations, Father Turowksi wrote to Father Kentenich, "Furthermore, I found out from Father Bea that you made a very good impression on him. Yes, you did cling rigidly to your point of view, but he believes this comes from the mission consciousness every founder must have if he wants to achieve something." But Father Bea was not the commissioned visitator, and so his possibilities to influence the situation remained limited. The visitator decided that Father Kentenich should not wait in Rome for his permit of entry into the USA but in South America.

During his stay in Rome, he took the opportunity to make a pilgrimage with a few confreres to Pompei, right next to Mount Vesuvius, at the beginning of January. He had read about this place almost forty years earlier and it had inspired him. Back then, what he read had seemed like a discreet signal on the horizon of the time. He had followed his inner inspiration—a seed of God for the beginning of Schoenstatt which had already grown for so many years now and produced so many fruits. Mary, he firmly believed, had accomplished all this. She, *"the faithful, permanent associate of the Lord,"* the *"Mother and model of faith,"* and the three times admirable "undoer of knots"! Shouldn't she be able to help in this entangled situation and keep Schoenstatt from falling into the dangerous abyss that had opened up before it? Father Kentenich spent a long time there before her picture of grace in the large pilgrimage basilica ...

January 15, 1952. He got on the plane in Zürich and flew to Argentina to stay with his confreres there. A few days later, he celebrated the dedication of the Schoenstatt Shrine in Florencio Varela, Buenos Aires, built as an exact replica of the original. He had promised the sisters the last time he was there, *"I will come back by all means, no matter where I am!"* Now, in spite of everything, he had really been able to keep his promise and come—even if there was great suffering on both sides because no further contact was permitted ... He accepted requests to give talks to the German-speaking community of women and mothers, other movement members in Buenos Aires, and his confreres. Then he traveled to Chile, where he held days of recollection for youth, men, and women. It was here that he began another extensive study letter called *Das Lebensgeheimnis Schönstatts [Schoenstatt's Secret of Life]* for the leader of the Priests' Institute, Prelate Joseph Schmitz, to answer questions that had come from the ranks of the priests. It focused on the so-called *"principle of construction"* of his new type of communities and their form of government, expressed in the dictum, *"Freedom as far as possible, (juridical) restrictions only as far as necessary, and spiritual formation*—referring to the cultivation of love—*as much as possible."* Upon the request of his superiors, he gave a training course of several weeks to his confreres in Brazil. It was only on June 20, 1952, that he was able to travel from Chile to the USA, where he arrived on June 21.

An almost endless expanse. Father Kentenich sat back in the wide American sedan, which with its three spring-loaded front seats was as soft as a leather sofa. He looked out the window at the broad fields, the sprawling farms and estates that passed by as the car drove toward its destination on the multi-lane highway. What a vast land, this America! It wasn't foreign to him. He had traveled through the states for three months in 1948 and had taken in the mentality, *"way of being, and piety of the inhabitants."* Cardinal Samuel Stritch, archbishop of Chicago, had once expressed that the American people might seem to have a materialistic disposition, but they are made of the type of "wood from which saints can be carved." He had appreciated that. So this "land of opportunity" was now to become the place of his exile. For how long? Who could tell ... But he hoped that it wouldn't last all too long.

Father John Haas and Father Herbert Schaak had picked him up at the airport in Chicago. What a joyful reunion it was to see former students from the House of Studies! Father Otto Boenki, who as the former provincial superior had invited him in 1948, Father Nicholas Wilwers, and Father William Brell had been in the country since the 1930s to do apostolic work in the spirit of Schoenstatt. Many memories of past times came alive in him: the beginnings of Schoenstatt, its growth in the midst of World War I, the fruitful 1930s, the years of persecution by the Nazis, his imprisonment, and his time in the concentration camp. Then—two years after his release—his appointment as the "general delegate of his community" for building up the Schoenstatt Work at his confreres' establishments in South America and Africa. They were years of upward growth and success amid times marked by difficulties and destruction—years full of light, but always years of battle, too, from the very beginning. Schoenstatt was and remained a *"child of war."* But Mary had consistently shown what she could do. She had *"done things in style,"* as he so gladly remarked with a sense of humor. And now the hard conflicts with Church authorities that had led all the way to his exile to Milwaukee—the large city on Lake Michigan in the state of Wisconsin. They had explained to him that it got its name from the Indians. But they had been forced back onto reservations, the only place they still lived today. In their stead, many Germans had immigrated in the nineteenth and twentieth centuries and marked the image of the city. Ten German breweries alone had been established here and supplied Americans with good German beer, which had become immensely popular.

As he looked out at the quickly passing landscape, the latest events passed through his mind once more. He was not permitted to set foot in Schoenstatt anymore, nor "to have any kind of connection, neither with the Institute of the Sisters of Mary as a whole nor with the individual sisters, neither orally nor in writing." The wording of the decrees still rang in his ears. However, he had realized already in Argentina that it was not feasible to keep it like this in public. Who of those present, knowing he was the founder of this community, would understand such altered behavior and such a demand on the part of the Holy Office? He would present this difficulty and explain how he envisioned going about it so that the Church would remain protected in public.

Removed from all offices. He now had to relinquish everything. In the name of the Holy Office, other forces from outside the movement now regulated the whole organization and tried their hand at modifying the general statute of the Work, which they hardly knew and had hardly understood. The father principle in the constitutions of the Sisters of Mary was supposed to be completely eliminated. But the general government and other leading sisters had protested and threatened to leave the community under such circumstances. They also resolutely raised objections against the demand that they take vows. And as a matter of fact, the visitator did give in. Yes, founder and foundation were being dramatically put to the test. Father Kentenich recalled what he had written to Father Menningen about all these measures against him, "*Whoever has an extraordinary mission must also endure extraordinary tests. The world and Church have a right to demand them and even to impose them. We may not become indignant about the means they use, even if it means dishonor, deprivation of rights, and homelessness. They need proof of the genuineness and divine origin of such a mission.*" No, he was not *indignant;* he had seen many things coming and remained firmly convinced that God stood behind everything—even behind all human weaknesses.

The Holy Office, as the highest Church authority, was not obligated to give reasons. There was likewise no provision there for a defense on his part. He remembered the moment he had received the banishment decrees. As the second consultant in the Holy Office, Father Bea had then asked him against all expectations whether he had anything more to say about the measures. He had replied, "*Ascetically, I have no objections. From a juridical standpoint, however, I cannot say yes to this.*" The document from the Holy Office addressed to Father Turowski in July of the previous year had stated *sub secreto* (under obligation to maintain confidentiality), "In umbra maneat"—"He must remain in the shadow." His name was to disappear from the lips of those entrusted to him, and as far as possible, also from their memory. It was not permissible to pray for him in community nor to act on his behalf. *In umbra maneat*—yes, now he had really gone into the shadow and disappeared, but not from the hearts of those who were united with him. Not everyone had been misled when Church authorities spoke out against him. Juridically, he remained subordinate to his general superior, Father Turowski, who had to forward all decrees of the Holy Office to him. In all affairs of everyday life, he was subordinate to his direct superior, the provincial Father Joseph Haas.

It all passed through his mind—the events in Rome and in Schoenstatt. It wasn't his sense of justice and truth that now caused him trouble. Yes, it had hit him hard, but what now occupied him much more—as was the case in January 1942 during his imprisonment by the Gestapo—was the question: How will those back home handle this time of testing? Now everything would depend on not letting their love for the Church diminish and not withdrawing any of that love in the face of disappointments. But at the same time, it was important not to compromise one's own convictions. "In the face of this tension—a great test of strength! Hopefully they make it through! Hopefully their faith is strong and their patience can hold out!" How often had he already brought this petition to God! God would ultimately be victorious. *"Those who have God on their side will not fear the powers of this world."* How often had he brought this home to his own. This trust would now be harshly tested. "If only they can manage not to stop believing that God stands behind everything!" He silently pulled out his rosary. Sometimes he simply held the little cross warmly in his hands, gripping it tightly. *"Whoever has a mission must fulfill it, even if it leads into the darkest darkness ..."* He closed his eyes for a moment. The car had accelerated. He tended to get light-headed. But flying was far worse. Before his first flight he had trained himself to overcome the fear of heights on the roof of Villa Montecucco in Castel Gandolfo. It was a success—he had gotten used to heights.

They were accusing him of so many things! If at the beginning it was only objections against Schoenstatt and his views about it, now the accusations were increasingly directed at his person. This was painful, but it didn't profoundly disconcert him. Many in Church circles thought he was being "stubborn and headstrong," that he considered himself "something special." He had put up with all these attacks or insinuations, even malicious suspicions and moral slander, no matter where they came from. With one exception. There was one thing he didn't let stand, something that really disturbed him and concerned his person. Via his general superior, he had sent the Holy Office a declaration on oath that he had never uttered the words of Martin Luther: "Here I stand and cannot do otherwise, so help me God. Amen!" He would drink the chalice of faith-filled obedience to this Church to the dregs and not allow his "theses" to be made public, no matter how he was publicly branded a heretic in seminaries and elsewhere ...

He was shaken from his thoughts. Someone had said something—oh, Father Haas had just announced that they were just crossing Bluemound Road. So they had almost reached their destination—the Pallottine provincial house, which stood on a very busy street right next to Holy Cross Church, where the Pallottines were in charge of the parish. The four-sided building with an inner courtyard was a former Capuchin monastery which they had acquired.

Hardly had the car reached the driveway when he was warmly greeted by Father Brell, who grabbed his suitcase with determination. Father Haas led the new arrival immediately into one of the guest rooms after his long journey because his little bedroom on the second floor was not yet completely furnished. His office, which he would soon get a look at, was likewise located on the second floor. It was spacious—a former classroom. The broad window right next to an outside door leading to a typically American iron fire escape provided a view of the grounds with its green spaces and flower gardens and the main street on the opposite side.

A few days after his arrival, the provincial superior invited him to visit a second establishment in Madison, where twenty-five Fathers were meeting for a retreat. Among other things, the topic was the question regarding the relationship between the Pallottines and Schoenstatt. When they heard that Father Kentenich had arrived in the USA, they unanimously asked the provincial superior if the founder himself couldn't speak to them about it. So both of them got into the car and drove to Madison, about 120 kilometers (seventy-five miles) from Milwaukee, where a small community of Sisters of Mary was responsible for the housekeeping of the Pallottine seminary. Shortly after they had arrived in Madison, Father Haas accompanied him to the dining room. When he walked in, all the Fathers spontaneously stood up and greeted him with applause. That same afternoon he gave them two retreat talks. On the way, Father Haas had asked him to give his confreres here the tertianship training course he had given a year earlier in Chile and last February in Brazil. Father Haas entertained the hope that this

Photo 14: At the beginning of his exile, Madison, USA

retreat would motivate the Fathers to a deepened surrender to God. Father Kentenich agreed. In the end he gave a total of forty-nine highly appreciated talks.

After extensive discussions at their province chapter, in which Father Kentenich did not participate, the Pallottine province decided as early as November 1952 to take up Schoenstatt as its apostolic "external work." So it happened that already the following year an exact replica of the Schoenstatt Shrine was built in Madison. Bishop William O'Connor celebrated its dedication. This was followed one year later by the construction of a second shrine, in Milwaukee, on the initiative of the Holy Cross parish youth. A Schoenstatt Shrine, the "Exile Shrine," as it was later called, rose up in the immediate vicinity of Father Kentenich's office in 1954, the "Marian Year" proclaimed by the Holy Father. On the evening of the dedication day, Father Kentenich expressed to the Pallottines, who themselves had helped build it, *"She has followed me into exile."*

He had already left Schoenstatt more than a year ago, and they still had no news about how he was doing. Sister Toni-Maria, like the other sisters, waited longingly for any information and made use of every opportunity to find out something whenever anyone came "from over there," from the other side of the big ocean. When she encountered Frieda Eicher on the street in Schoenstatt, the cook for the Pallottines in Milwaukee, she only found out that "Father Kentenich reads a lot and writes a lot." She said he ate little and that at breakfast he never had any special wishes, even though every priest could order something: "a fried, boiled, or scrambled egg; pancakes and syrup; fried bacon or sausage; cold cuts; cheese; jam; oatmeal—anything the heart desired. But he doesn't seem to desire anything." She said he just took buttered bread, and that for supper he asked for a glass of milk around 5:00 p.m., nothing else. "You can't live on that! Once he didn't come to a meal—I guess he didn't hear the bell. He came to me in the kitchen. But then I really made him something good. When he has visitors, he always comes personally to the kitchen to get something. He provides for them generously. He had me make four German-style shirts. He sure paid me well for that—Father Kentenich said four holy Masses for me," she proclaimed, smiling and full of pride.

Sister Toni-Maria was overcome by the thought, "If only this woman knew!"

She found out more when Father Provincial Haas arrived in Schoenstatt from Milwaukee in May 1953 for his home vacation. She eagerly took a seat across from him. "How is he doing—healthwise, I mean?" She started out cautiously. That much was harmless.

"He had the flu like all of us, but only for a couple of hours. I don't think you'd say he's aged. He has an incredible vitality. He's not sad, either. He walks down the hallway with a bounce in his step."

She was grateful to hear something about him and recalled how Father Meyer had shared with her from there: "Father Kentenich is always in good spirits. He likes to joke with us, although I do think he's homesick. Well, that's only human!"

Father Haas noticed that her thoughts had wandered away for a moment, and he waited. She nodded. He continued his report. "He did have to have all his upper and lower teeth pulled, though. That was a horrible operation. He lost a lot of blood that oozed out. He went to lie down afterwards, but only for ten minutes. When I went to him and asked him if he had pain, he only said, 'It's bearable!' But the priest who had taken him was very ill because of the experience. Usually people take anesthesia when they get their teeth pulled, but he didn't."

"What? He did it without anesthesia?"

"Our confrere said he didn't want any. The dentist had asked him, and afterwards he whispered to the priest who had accompanied him that he had never experienced such a thing before. When he showed his horror, Father Kentenich had simply answered in English, '*It is a holy pain.*'" Father Haas shook his head.

But Sister Toni-Maria was moved and thought, "He offered that as a sacrifice!" She turned once more to Father Haas with great interest and said, "And how does he spend his day?"

"We get up at 5:30 a.m.—but Father usually gets up earlier. He's usually the first one in the chapel and prays the stations of the cross privately already before morning prayer. After meditation comes holy Mass, and after Mass it usually happens that we eat breakfast together. ... After breakfast, Father wants to know what's in the newspaper. Then we get to work. The mail comes around 9:00 a.m. Father usually gets the lion's share. Around noon we meet for a short prayer in the house chapel and then go to lunch: cold cuts, vegetables, potatoes! After that, Father usually takes a little nap—for about half an hour. ... After the short rest, he usually goes to the neighboring cemetery."

"Yes, I've heard about that!" She already knew that it was on the other side of the main street, directly across from the provincial house and Holy Cross parish church. So he only needed to cross the street. It was a large, park-like cemetery with lots of pale gravestones and open grassy areas, no demarcation of the graves, no flower beds, only a flower bouquet or flower pot here and there in front of a gravestone on the grass, and scattered benches for sitting.

"He prays his breviary there, or the rosary, and meditates. The walk lasts for about an hour. Dinner, our main meal, is around

4:00 p.m. After supper we watch TV to see what has happened that day. We were able to watch Adenauer on his visit to America. At 6:45 p.m. we pray our visit to the Blessed Sacrament and our evening prayer because afterwards all the Fathers are busy with their apostolic work. We spend our times of recreation without Father because we speak English. We usually play cards. There are eleven Fathers, including two Germans, four younger Fathers, and two brothers in the house. After 11:00 p.m. we go to bed. Father Kentenich usually works until midnight; only then does the light in his office go out." He described how Father Kentenich liked to visit the older Fathers on the way to his office, and when they had common times of recreation, he would quickly peek in and joke with his confreres—but since he didn't smoke and had no interest in watching TV, he soon left again. He said Father Kentenich was very well liked among his confreres; many had chosen him as their confessor, and he was always very friendly toward everyone.

It was consoling at least to hear how he was doing. She was happy.

The Struggles Continue

Meanwhile, the pressure from without and the burden of not being understood continued to increase. At the beginning of August 1952, he unexpectedly received a further decree via his general superior: He was no longer allowed to leave Milwaukee, nor to "interfere in any way in matters of the apostolic visitation," nor to "discuss the question of Schoenstatt in any way or for any reason, neither verbally nor in writing, neither directly nor indirectly." He submitted his questions regarding the decreed stipulations to the Holy Office through Father General. Did the prohibition against working for Schoenstatt and its spirituality also refer to correspondence and pastoral conversations? He received no answer. Every effort Schoenstatters made for the person of the founder was seen "as disobedience to the Church" and blamed on Father

Kentenich. A statement about the founder was thus found in a letter and used as an opportunity to blame Father Kentenich for its content: "According to Father Schneider, Father Kentenich is said to be the most learned theologian, philosopher, and psychologist." He himself promptly took a stand on this: *"Those who keep in mind that such expressions inspired by personal admiration are found in a private letter easily know how to interpret them. ... It holds true for all times: Whoever martyrizes someone compels others, albeit unintentionally, to a far-reaching loyalty."* He also defended himself against the accusation that he had interfered in the ongoing apostolic visitation through his talks in South America and had "muddled everything up" there. *"If that means that I prompted the Fathers to take a stand on Schoenstatt and that a division of spirits was the result, then the situation has been portrayed correctly. I hope the case continues to advance to the general chapter. ... But it is incomprehensible to me how an accusation can be made out of that. To begin with, it doesn't affect the jurisdiction of the visitator in any way. ... Moreover, up to now I have never been prohibited from speaking about Schoenstatt. That just started now."*

No matter where the accusations came from, they accumulated and were followed by new directives and orders, prohibitions and constraints. His frankly honest efforts to set things straight and many of his attempts at clarification went unheard or remained unanswered. He was forced to interpret the silence as consent. Regarding contact with the Sisters of Mary working in Madison, he offered the suggestion that he would greet them and speak normally with them in order to avoid confusion. He asked to be informed by the Holy Office if they preferred it otherwise. When no objections came, he assumed that Rome was in agreement.

In the meantime, the Holy Office, represented by Father Tromp, and the German Bishops' Conference sought to redesign the whole Work. Father Kentenich wrote to Father Turowski *"that Trier, and Rome, too, in dependence on them ... is aiming at leveling Schoenstatt in a threefold vein: juridically, dogmatically, and ascetically." Juridically,* in the sense that the head was removed from the whole. Year by year, the same thing happened to more and more Schoenstatt leaders who saw themselves personally united with the founder or who stood up for him and the Schoenstatt Work. It happened already in 1952 to Sister Edelgart, who was a general council sister, the leader of the sisters working in the movement, and the leader of the women's federation. Despite many well-founded objections by the institute's leadership, Father Tromp removed her from office on a flimsy pretext. Sister Annette—who was a provincial superior—and other sisters in leadership roles met a similar fate. The only thing that could be prevented was the request made by the Holy Office and the Ordinariate in Trier to bring Sister Anna back to Schoenstatt and appoint her the general assistant. The bishop of Trier remarked about his own refusal, "We cannot appoint her. The sisters will suffer too much." The drama of the removals from office without an objective justification then continued among the priests. In 1954, it involved two close co-workers in the core leadership circle in Schoenstatt: Father Alexander Menningen and Father Franz Bezler. In addition, Father Joseph Fischer, leader of the pilgrims' movement and companion of Father Kentenich in the concentration camp of Dachau, had to leave Schoenstatt. Father Johannes Tick, Father Joseph Vermeegen, and Father Joseph Klein followed them at the beginning of the 1960s. After Prelate Heinrich Roth had assumed his office as general assistant of the Sisters of Mary with the explicit authorization of the Holy Office, he, too, was removed from office again three years later. That same year, Prelate Joseph Schmitz, long-time leader of the Priests' Institute, was likewise removed. This whole process reached its dramatic climax when in November 1962, Cardinal Frings, on behalf of the Holy Office, suggested that all leadership bodies of the Schoenstatt secular institutes should be completely removed from office and replaced by more—in their opinion—suitable persons. In this way a "radical transformation of the Work" was "to be initiated." At this point, Father Bea, who in all those years had benevolently sought possibilities for Schoenstatt and its founder, admitted that now he, too, no longer knew what he should do or advise.

Father Kentenich foresaw these efforts toward a complete *juridical leveling of Schoenstatt* already in the first year of his exile. It went together with the attempt to alter essential parts of statutes and constitutions. The *dogmatic* leveling he referred to involved the devotion to Mary. She was to be reduced to what was generally known and customary, without considering the concrete experiences of faith that people had had with Mary in Schoenstatt over the decades. *Ascetically,* members were asked to renounce everything original in Schoenstatt's spirituality. It was a *leveling attempt* that meant nothing would be left of what made Schoenstatt new and original. As its founder and witness of the whole history of its development, it was impossible for him to silently accept this. Father Kentenich decided to pick up the work he had begun on his extensive study *Das Lebensgeheimnis Schönstatts [The Secret of Schoenstatt's Life],* which he had already started in Chile. He hoped in this way to contribute to clarification for Roman or diocesan authorities. But he was disappointed every time. When a series of talks from the year 1933 about the *"Schoenstatt Secret"* fell into Father Tromp's hands, even just the title was reprehensible enough for him to forbid the text immediately—a text identical in content to a booklet published in 1934 with Trier's approval. While Father Kentenich still hoped that Father Tromp might take up the matter with interest and a new understanding, instead he took care with an almost panic-fueled meticulousness—despite all references to the already approved booklet—to have this text retracted and destroyed everywhere. And still, Father Kentenich didn't give up his long, written attempts to explain things, ultimately borne by the hope that future generations would know how to use the material and that future times would be able to muster a better understanding. Sixty-six years old at the beginning of his exile, he didn't even consider a well-deserved retirement. Now he had the time and opportunity to say something in great detail about the issues regarding his Work, the Church, society, and the world. Of course, his writing style took some getting used to. It was clearly noticeable that he was accustomed to formulating the facts of the case in Latin.

He used long, nested sentences with condensed trains of thought, choosing philosophical and theological words that presupposed various areas of knowledge. He wrote hundreds of pages of "*marginal notes*" and "*chronicle notes*" in this way. Over the years, it became thousands of pages of study material, sometimes in the form of a letter to Bishop Matthias Wehr of Trier, who had succeeded Bishop Bornewasser since 1951, or to Father Menningen, or to Father Turowski or Father Moehler accordingly, and sometimes on certain topics. When Pallottine Father Ray Piskula followed a confrere's suggestion and asked Father Kentenich whether he would be willing to draft the Lenten sermons for him during the Marian Year 1954, he happily agreed right away. The series of sermons later became a book of more than 400 pages published under the title *Mary, Our Mother and Educator*. In 1957, Joseph Kentenich devoted himself to a topic centered on a theological argument (Karl Rahner) that was far ahead of its time but that currently concerned him quite directly: "*On the Relationship of Tension between Office and Charism.*" Before the council, this topic was a hot potato in the Church; the word "charism" itself was considered suspicious in the Church. What he reflected on and expressed on paper didn't only involve his own fate or that of Schoenstatt, but also that of many spiritual movements of the twentieth century. The relationship of tension between office and charism and their fruitful interplay met with special interest only at and especially after the Second Vatican Council. Those who read the text attentively were able to get behind the weighty backgrounds of the way he thought and acted toward the Church. "*Actually, it is God who is active in a tangible way in Schoenstatt and through Schoenstatt. The fact that he uses human instruments as collaborators absolutely corresponds to his plans of world government and laws of world government. They culminate in the sentence: God works in history through freely active secondary causes. ... The secondary cause, exteriorly visible to the dull human eye, might step more strongly into the foreground, thus giving the whole process a humanly tangible character. But in the background—towering above and ruling everything—stands the First Cause: God.*" And concerning his own role, he brought a quote from Father Robert Grosche (1888-1967) into the discussion. In an article from 1955-56 titled "The Prophetic Element in the Church," Grosche, a "trailblazer of the council," wrote, "The 'prophet' steps into conflict with the status quo; therein lies the actual reason for his appearance ... Naturally, this 'emergence,' in whatever way it happened and happens, has an ambivalence not to be overlooked: He can renew the Church, but he can also divide her ... The conflict becomes opposition when he disengages and isolates himself from the context in which the conflicts persist. To be sure, the prophet is the man of truth, which he is called to represent, and as such, he stands in contrast with the status quo. But the challenge now consists in that he does not absolutize this one truth. By disconnecting a truth and making it absolute, the prophet becomes a heretic who does not renew the Church but divides her. The heretic is thus nothing but a failed prophet. But if the conflict does not become opposition, then he becomes fruitful: He is accepted into the Church. It is clear that this cannot happen immediately. The representatives of the institution guard the heritage entrusted to them. They advocate for the status quo, which has come under attack and which has history on its side, even if the present might be against it ... When something new makes itself felt in the Church, the institution initially 'smells' the 'heretic.' This is understandable if one thinks of the dangers the Church had to overcome in the course of her long history ... Precisely because he loves the Church, the prophet will not let himself be pushed out of her nor persuaded to deny his mandate."

In 1961, Sister Eileen, a student at Marquette University, asked him about his "philosophy of education" because she wanted to write her thesis about Schoenstatt's pedagogy. The topic appealed to him so much that it became a brief study, composed in German and titled in English: "What is my Philosophy of Education?" That same year, he drafted the paper, *"Krise um Regierungsformen [The Crisis Surrounding Forms of Government]."* It was precisely this study that dealt with the issue of authority and obedience in a way that would only emerge as a topic of discussion in the Church in the wake of Vatican Council II. In it, he especially illustrated a central theme that had moved him in a pedagogical sense already since 1912 and which he gave to the leadership forces of his communities for the future as a guideline for government: "*Authoritative in principle, democratic in application.*" According to this guideline, there is a hierarchical order in principle, but in the practical application, freedom, co-responsibility, and democracy should determine the cooperation of superiors and subordinates to the greatest possible extent.

Father Kentenich gave an account of his every step to his general superior. In May 1953, his provincial superior spent some time in Germany and stated that he was "a model of absolute obedience" and "of calm, serenity, and acquiescence." Indeed, even when Father Kentenich applied for a new passport and had to leave Milwaukee to pick it up in person at the German embassy in Chicago, he asked Father Turowski to request the permission of the Holy Office.

While the most extreme pressure of the visitation initially burdened Joseph Kentenich and the sisters' community, stringent measures were also taken in early fall 1952 against the Schoenstatt Movement and the priests involved in it. The visitator issued seventeen individual stipulations that forbade things that for the most part had never been done or claimed. Even the Schoenstatt priests, like the Sisters of Mary, were subjected to false suspicions, and substantial damage was done to the reputation of the movement for many years in Germany. Even the founder's closest co-workers fell into doubt and struggles of conscience on account of the ecclesial measures. After all, the strict measures were issued by the highest government body of the Church, considered before the Second Vatican Council to have an inviolable authority. After the council, its practices were reformed from the ground up, and the office was renamed.

No one knew exactly where the ever new accusations at the Holy Office were coming from. Father Kentenich wrote to his general superior about the "*murky springs*" forming the background of the false allegations. He had to be aware that every step he took and every word he spoke was observed, reframed, and passed on as an accusation. And still, he felt interiorly free. The "self-assuredness" with which he presented himself and the carefree peace he radiated were simply uncanny to many. But it was clear to him that these tests of fire had to come and had to be passed. In any case, his silent hope that the present battles were *"the God-willed way to bring the movement into close contact with the Holy Father"* and *"to obtain a positive statement from him"* was not fulfilled. In the years that followed, other forces were faster and interfered in adverse ways. For many years, he didn't respond to the increasingly defamatory attacks and slander against his person, which imputed psychological and intellectual defects as well as immoral behavior to him. Since he never went beyond a handshake or a priestly greeting of peace in the form of an embrace among confreres, it must have been hard for him on a human level when it was claimed that he had illegitimate children all over the world or that he had an "Oedipus complex" because of his illegitimate birth. The floodgates had opened wide to *"wild hallucinations."* He remained silent about it all, whereas his general superior's sense of justice did indeed speak up. Father Turowski had specialists provide their professional opinions regarding Joseph Kentenich's psychological and intellectual state and sent these to the Holy Office. It was only in 1960 that Father Kentenich himself, in the style of Cardinal Newman's "Apologia pro vita sua," wrote—but never sent—a detailed justification and defense of his person as well as his life history and the history of Schoenstatt bound up with it. In it, he underlined that he had never crossed the societal and moral boundaries of physical touch (*regula tactus*). His faith in the divine origin of the whole Work could not be shaken, even though he was harshly tested on a human level. *"The more helpless we feel, the greater our trust may be,"* he wrote in a letter. Misunderstandings and misinterpretations, once they have been spread, are hard to dispel. But he didn't give up. Regarding the insinuation that Schoenstatt was "mystical," he argued that a Work that has grown and developed so much according to the laws of a very simple faith in divine providence, without drawing on visions of any kind, mystical apparitions, or belief in miracles in the traditional sense, cannot possibly be called "mystical." Amid the whole surge of skepticism, doubt, and rejection toward Schoenstatt and himself, he wrote to Prelate Joseph Schmitz in Vallendar in September 1952, *"It's necessary above all to place the family scepter ... in the hands of the Blessed Mother, so that she herself ... will document the supernatural character of her Work. This must be the unambiguous response to Father Tromp's question: 'Is all that has developed in Schoenstatt enough to support this conviction of faith?' The answer is up to us in the first place. We must prove our great Educator's power of transformation through the blank check and inscriptio* (toward God) *practiced in life."*

He celebrated his anniversary of priestly ordination in Madison on July 8, 1952. Such Masses celebrated in a small circle provided the only opportunity now and then to say something immediately afterwards to those present through a freely spoken prayer from the heart. By means of this prayer he could encourage them and also surely himself: *"Today's anniversary makes me think back to forty-two years ago. ... If we assess what has developed, then we can say that the words have been confirmed, 'All things work for the best for those who love God.' Those who love God are the ones who no longer seek or want anything for themselves. ... All things work for the best for those who can really love, regardless of whether it's a matter of blows of fate or of some other thing. The deep reason for this faith is the fatherly wisdom, fatherly goodness, and fatherly omnipotence of God. ... Blessed Mother, give us today anew the spirit of childlikeness that does not wish to change anything at all, but only asks, 'What is in the Father's plan?' ... Allow me to ask of you—and this should be my thanks for the forty-two years—'Mother, do with me what you will.'"* What kinds of things were still to come?

At home in Germany, the battles continued to rage and the conflicts took on ever more dramatic forms. The Sisters of Mary literally fought for their existence. The visitator prohibited contact with the founder but also everything original that had unfolded under his leadership and inspiration over the decades. It was all supposed to disappear. The sisters obediently followed the decrees, even if it was very painful. But they couldn't follow the visitator's reasoning. His open dislike for the person of Father Kentenich allowed no trust to develop between them and Father Tromp. He was unable to understand many things because his approach was rather out of touch with everyday life and he lacked pedagogical experience. Instead, he merely insisted on his authority. On account of this, he saw only one single way to construe things: He interpreted the defenses and arguments of the sisters as a "lack of ecclesial spirit." Sister Bonifatia, whom he himself had appointed as general assistant, expressed in a letter of petition to the Holy Father what many sisters felt in their contact with the visitator: "I would have to violate my conscience if I were to share the Most Reverend Father Visitator's view of our founder. I was and am convinced that reverence, gratitude, and love for our founder are not contrary to an ecclesial spirit." She stated that meanwhile, despite all efforts, she felt incapable "of establishing a trustful cooperation between the visitator and the general council."

Father Tromp had little experience with community life and its internal laws, and even less experience with a women's community. That was the only possible explanation for why he continuously allowed a few individuals to lead him right past the community's official leadership—which enjoyed the trust of the whole institute—and why he intervened like a dictator in the community's concerns. Whether it was a matter of filling positions or making decisions regarding admission and dismissal, he took every autonomous right away from the community. As a gifted expert in dogmatics and a knowledgeable, typical representative of the pre-conciliar Church, the newness of this community of lay leaders, its type of community leadership, and its original spirituality simply remained foreign to him—and therefore suspicious. In addition, he had his sensitivities, particularly when he—a professor at the Pontifical Gregorian University and a consultor and delegate of the Holy Office in Rome—was frequently contradicted by women, even if they did it quite politely, as he admitted. Due to his somewhat arrogant self-image and his temperamental outbursts, every visit to Schoenstatt brought about ever new, intense conflicts. Both sides became so entrenched in their positions that he ultimately decided to close the novitiate. Petitions to the Holy Father and visits by Sisters of Mary to the Pro-Secretary of the Holy Office, Cardinal Ottaviani, were unsuccessful. The dissolution decree of the community was already lying on the desk of the Holy Father, Pope Pius XII, awaiting his signature, when the efforts yielded their first fruits. Father Bea, who had been sought for advice, gained increasing insights into the hardships and difficulties of the community and its founder. At the beginning of July 1953, he had the opportunity to speak personally with the Holy Father and explain a few problems. American-born Cardinal Aloysius J. Muench of the Roman Curia, first Apostolic Nuncio of the Federal Republic of Germany, reported via a Sister of Mary that the Holy Father appreciated Schoenstatt. He said that in an audience on July 30, the pope "spoke very benevolently about Schoenstatt." Pope Pius XII didn't sign the dissolution decree of the Schoenstatt Sisters of Mary; instead, he ended the papal visitation on his own initiative, backdated to July 11, 1953. The Holy Office pulled Father Tromp out of his assignment. But this didn't mean that the battles had already come to an end. On the contrary, the influence of the former visitator was by no means averted ...

A further trouble spot arose in the core leadership circle of the movement in Germany after the general chapter of the Pallottines in 1953. The strict measures of the visitation and the ecclesial accusations led to an entirely new conflict over the relationship between Schoenstatt and the Pallottines. Opinions on the matter increasingly diverged. For some, Schoenstatt clearly belonged to the Pallottines, while others felt that the movement was more of a "foreign substance." The pros and cons of Schoenstatt as an external apostolic work of the Pallottines were to be discussed at the general chapter of the Society in May 1953. For Father Kentenich, his Pallottine community was always the *"central and motivating part"* of the Schoenstatt Movement—but Schoenstatt itself was a new, independently developed foundation, a new initiative of God. The early death of Vincent Pallotti had left his foundation incomplete. Schoenstatt, so Father Kentenich believed, could enrich Pallotti's Work by way of a new source of recognition, life, and organization as well as by his new pedagogy. Naturally, this idea contained plenty of fuel for conflict. In any case, Joseph Kentenich considered the result of this tension and the starting point of the conflict to be a fateful matter. *"If I weren't so deeply convinced that the Society* [of the Pallottines] *is facing a question of destiny, I wouldn't put my whole person and life's strength into it. I could have it cheaper."* He wrote this in the spring to Father Karl Hoffmann, a member of the general council. He also stated that neither the one side nor the other would benefit from false compromises or trade-offs; such things would leave both Schoenstatt and the Pallottine community no prospects for a fruitful future. The clash quickly became evident: In contrast to Father Kentenich's view that the relationship of the Pallottines and Schoenstatt *"is a God-willed, bipolar entirety,"* Father Tromp, supported by Father General Moehler and Father Schulte, took the position that Schoenstatt was merely a timely offshoot of Pallotti's Work and not a new foundation. Therefore, in his view, it also didn't have its own founder, nor did it have a right to independent leadership. There was only one founder of the whole, so he claimed, and this was Vincent Pallotti. Father Kentenich knew that this view had far-reaching implications. These *"leveling attempts"* by Father Tromp and others aimed at assigning the leadership of the whole Schoenstatt Work and all its branch communities to the general government of the Pallottines in Rome. But this would have severely disrupted the sensitive balance of forces in the Schoenstatt Work, which was not led in a centralized way but had been structured around autonomous rights and cooperation. It would have torn the lay communities of the so-called "league" out of their diocesan legal framework, eventually divesting the bishops of every right of participation. But Father Kentenich wanted to maintain precisely this creative principle of tension and complementation for his Schoenstatt Work. On the one hand, he wanted to attach

Schoenstatt to Rome (through the "institutes"), while on the other hand, he wanted to integrate them into the local Church. However, if no one listened to him or read his writings, how should anyone expect to understand this way of thinking and the deeper reasons behind it? Individual German bishops gradually began to make these connections, and they spoke up in the years that followed. Voices spoke out against Father Tromp's goal to place the whole Work and its regulation under the control of the Pallottine general government. They pleaded for a separation.

The last plenary assemblies of the general chapter had just ended. Father Karl Hoffmann, who had served the community and Schoenstatt for many years as the vice general, former general superior (1937-1947), and general procurator, sat across from Father Turowski, who had held the office of general superior until just recently. The whole development of the past days was still unfathomable. One day before the opening of the general chapter, May 14, 1953, they had found out that the Holy Office had appointed a Father Ulrich Beste to preside at the chapter. He was a Benedictine Father who thereby took the leadership of their general chapter out of their own hands. Everything was supposed to proceed only via this Benedictine Father. And at the general chapter of such an internationally renowned and universally acknowledged community, for that matter! It was unfathomable and felt like a slap in the face since it expressed open mistrust on the part of the Church against their Society. The chapter had thus lost every bit of freedom. In his opening talk, Father Beste raised the gravest accusations against Father Kentenich—accusations originating from the pen of Father Tromp. He had quickly forbidden any further talk of a renewed recognition of Schoenstatt as the Society's external work and any questions regarding a bipolar overall concept. Thus, the discussion so desired by Father Kentenich hadn't even taken place. "Some of us had already made a plan that when it came time to start with the topic of Schoenstatt in the general chapter,

Photo 15: During the exile, 1954

we would immediately make a motion to summon Father to the chapter so that he could answer any questions about the movement."

"It would've been so good at least to listen to him!" Troubled, Father Turowski stared straight ahead. It had gotten even worse. Even though Father Turowski would have certainly received a clear majority of votes in a free election, he was not allowed to be re-elected. It was a serious intrusion into the Society and its future, but also into that of Schoenstatt. The Holy Office had reserved the final decision on all positions to be filled. In doing so, they had not only decisively controlled the "election" of Father Wilhelm Moehler as the new general superior but also conducted the appointments of the other six members of the council.

Father Hoffmann spoke up again, lowering his voice: "Now all the ones who are favorable toward Schoenstatt are out. After the 'election' of the general superior, one of the chapter participants whispered to me, 'That is the most unqualified person that could ever have been instated in this context!' He's a diplomat, but you never know where you stand with him."

"That all remains to be seen, of course!" Father Turowski replied. But the frank Pallottine Father would turn out to be right. In the years to come, Father General Moehler would follow the views of the Holy Office more and more, and to a great extent, Father Tromp would keep all the reins in his hands, even after the end of the visitation. He continued to maintain his influence on the Sisters of Mary through the bishop of Trier, on the general presidium of the Schoenstatt Work through the presiding general superior of the Pallottines, and on the Schoenstatt Diocesan Priests through the German Bishops' Conference and its president, Cardinal Frings of Cologne.

None of the previous council members who knew more about Schoenstatt's development remained in office, including Father Hoffmann. When the news about the "election" results reached Father Kentenich in Milwaukee, he became very serious and only said, *"Divine providence."* With that, he handed over all further developments to the heavenly powers. During these hard years of trial, he underlined time and again, *"God leaves everything in the dark. He needs children who take the Father's hand in the midst of the darkness—children of Providence!"* He immediately wrote to Father Turowski, *"God has ordained it differently. Contrary to all human expectations, you have become a victim of your courage, your conviction, and your faithfulness. I thank you—and the whole Schoenstatt Family joins me—for everything you have done in the past two years."* Shortly after that, he sent some lines to the former vice general, Father Hoffmann: *"Now your fate has been determined. I am sincerely happy about your transfer to Schoenstatt. ... Personally, I am fine. Please don't worry about my future; it rests in good hands. If you go to our shrine, don't forget me and our common life's work. Maintain a sincere inner benevolence, also toward our sisters."*

Such a federatively structured Work could not exist without the inner attachment to the founder as the author of its spirituality. But the measures against Father Kentenich and the movement took on such magnitude in the following years that there was no longer any explanation from a purely human perspective. According to the "Concluding Regulations of the Visitation," Bishop Wehr of Trier was appointed the final authority for the community of the Sisters of Mary. He was sent to Vallendar with clear instructions from the Holy Office regarding the community, the Schoenstatt Work, and the founder. The "Bishop's Statement," which he proclaimed there on September 12, 1953, "exceeded our worst fears," as expressed in the chronicle of the community. All accusations against Father Kentenich were repeated word for word as Father Beste had already presented them at the general chapter of the Pallottines. Moreover, all decrees concerning him were hammered down. "It is advisable to give up all hope that Father Kentenich might still return. ... By orders of the Holy Office, the election of a new general superior and a new general council is to be arranged. ... Only chapter participants who support the directives of the Church by their own inner conviction may be nominated for the election chapter." What did that mean? Were they planning to proceed with the general chapter of the Sisters of Mary in the very same way they had at the chapter of the Pallottines? Great concern overcame the government of the institute, but not only them. Since the bishop had spoken before superiors, leaders in the movement, and responsible educators and had asked them to notify all the sisters, his words caused inner distress in the community as a whole and in each individual member. They stormed heaven with constant prayer. More than a few of them offered their life to God for the resolution of this complicated and painful situation. Hardly had they overcome one plight when another took its place. It was "like being on a pirate ship ride," swinging back and forth between hope and despair, as the community chronicle of those years states. The assertion made in the bishop's statement shocked them to the core: "Pay heed that the Church has condemned not only the father principle as such but also the pedagogical principles on which it is based, which, to be sure, have been taken from modern depth psychology and psychoanalysis." The whole thing bore Father Tromp's tone, but now the insinuation against Father Kentenich had also come to light: depth psychology. They were accusing him of being a "Freudian." Everything he deemed valuable for religious growth within the framework of attachments, human relationships, and love was dragged into the dirt as the outgrowth of a dubious imagination. For several long minutes, the sisters spoke no word. Even the bishop kept an embarrassed silence. When Father Kentenich received the bishop's statement in his own hands, he wrote to Father Menningen, *"Just received the letter and the bishop's statement! New suffering! A new source of blessing! ... Ultimately it's all about our source of life—and thus about matters of vital importance."* And three days later, he added, *"Any expert who reads the bishop's statement in context ... will have to admit that the moral murder of my person is accomplished."* After all, it was perfectly obvious that the continuation of his exile, together with the accusations that became public, *"invite[d] the question of purity and of the invulnerability of faith"* and gave new nourishment to all the rumors about what he had allegedly perpetrated.

All decrees against him were to remain a secret. So Father Kentenich never spoke about them with anyone, neither with his confreres living there nor with the people around him, who increasingly sought him out as a priestly advisor. Only very few knew that he was in exile, and hardly anyone sensed the harsh battles he had to endure during the fourteen years of his banishment. During the whole conflict, it became increasingly clear that a one-sided understanding of office and obedience was evident here; it would only be seen from a different perspective in the wake of the Second Vatican Council. In 1959, Father Kentenich wrote a letter of explanation to Father Moehler, trying to make him aware of precisely these different understandings: *"In all situations and under all circumstances, my intention was always to model for my followers how to practice perfect obedience in a complicated and entangled situation—without slavish anxiety or various forms of a lack of inner freedom."*

When the Israeli secret police succeeded in tracking down the Nazi officer Otto Adolf Eichmann in Argentina in 1960 and bringing him to trial in 1961, Father Kentenich followed the reports from the courtroom in Tel Aviv with great interest. Eichmann was responsible for the death transports of the Jews across the entire European continent, but he continuously made the excuse that he was only following orders in obedience to his superiors and that he did what his duty obliged him to do. He argued that he bore no responsibility for the happenings in Auschwitz, and during the trial he asserted his innocence multiple times. Already in 1912, by emphasizing the education of the personality, Father Kentenich had referred to what Hannah Arendt, a German-American political scientist who herself had escaped the Holocaust, wrote about the trial in her shocking articles in "The New Yorker." She stated that Eichmann was not a "monster" but a "nobody," someone who refused to be a person and a personality and thus to accept any responsibility for his actions. Father Kentenich was particularly concerned with Eichmann's concept of obedience. There were so many different ways people could conceive of obedience and act according to it! In this case it was obviously a matter of a widespread misunderstanding of obedience—a militaristic form of obedience that blindly carries out what the authority demands without any trace of personal responsibility or autonomous reasoning. Many things in Church tradition, too, had been permeated with such a concept—things that for Joseph Kentenich didn't correspond to an obedience of faith as he saw it in Mary's life and sought to emulate. Didn't it say in the Bible that she thought about it, she asked about it, and then she let the Spirit of God guide her? Such obedience of faith was at once supratemporal and timely. Based on the Eichmann trial, he attempted to show how dangerous "blind obedience" and the deactivation of one's own conscience can become for Christians living in a totalitarian state. From the beginning, his understanding of obedience included the co-responsibility of the subordinates.

The new Church, "*the Church on the new shore*," had to be animated by this understanding of obedience. It corresponded to his

Photo 16: At Lake Michigan, USA, early 1960s

own view and attitude—to decide and act according to the spirit of the lawgiver and with personal responsibility for the whole, and to stand up for his convictions with frankness whenever and as long as he was permitted to do so. For him, this view of obedience contained the root of inner freedom and true character as well as an orientation towards God that allowed him to be calm. The Spirit of God would bring the matter to completion; when and how he would do it was up to him. In a private letter he acknowledged, *"I don't notice that I'm getting older. The momentary blows of fate make body and soul fresher and stronger ... I wish you the same gift also."*

Caring for Souls with Heart and Soul

Not long after Father Kentenich had arrived in Milwaukee, Father Provincial gave him work to do. He was asked to offer days of reflection, retreat talks, training courses, and the sacrament of confession in Madison; in addition, he was asked to celebrate holy Mass on Sundays at the orphanage in Wauwatosa for the Carmelites of the Divine Heart of Jesus and their one hundred orphaned children. He remained faithful to these duties until 1959. These activities were only interrupted during the time he was strictly forbidden to leave Milwaukee. But after Father Haas raised objections against this in Rome during his stay in Europe, Father Tromp gave in somewhat, at least verbally.

In the meantime, Father Kentenich resumed what he had always liked to do: He kept extensive correspondence in order to accompany people who sought contact with him and asked for his help. Ever since the beginning of World War I, this rather hidden activity had been tremendously important to him. He never seemed to get tired of the detailed work involved in caring for souls. For the most part, he picked up in his letters where he had left off in conversations, confession, or inspirations on days of reflection before his exile. Something radiated from him that simply attracted people, even if the image he presented and the way he spoke didn't intentionally aim at this. As much as the many decrees restricted him and the spiritual debate surrounding his Schoenstatt Work kept him busy and demanded strength, he did not allow himself to take a break when it came to devoting himself to concrete people. Mr. Louis Jost, an electrician who often worked in the house, soon figured that out. In his enthusiasm he told his wife, who was somewhat surprised by this new "pious" side of her husband, "Why are you looking at me so amazed? That priest made an impression on me! He's a man of God! He radiates such peace and joy. He gives me advice and he's"—he paused—"my confessor!" Mrs. Jost fixed her gaze on her husband as if she couldn't believe her ears. But he got even more excited. "You have to meet him! He's like a reflection of God the Father for me. Somehow when I'm with him I have a sense of what heaven is like. Whenever I knock at his door, he right away says, 'Ave!' ('Greetings!') in his friendly, joyful tone, and when I go in, he usually says, 'Oh, here's Louis,' making me feel like he had been waiting just for me!" Mrs. Jost listened thoughtfully. Later on she was able to understand her husband better ...

Through the Pallottines and the Sisters of Mary, who had been living in Madison already for a longer time, interested lay people had been coming together in Schoenstatt groups. They came for talks or to seek advice in personal conversations. One day, Mr. and Mrs. Laufenberg also appeared with the Brabender Family. They quickly gained trust in the priest who couldn't yet speak English so well and for whom Sister Winfriede, the secretary of Father Haas, had to interpret. Mrs. Dorothy Gmeinder and her husband Henry belonged to one of the first groups for couples in Madison. On October 18, 1952, they had sealed the covenant of love together with four other couples and considered this "a special type of Marian devotion centered around the shrine." The following year, they, too, sought closer contact with Father Kentenich whenever they came for their monthly meetings. "This gave our introduction into Schoenstatt's spirituality a new dimension. We found ourselves with a priest, a very kind, loving, fatherly gentleman, who now started to explain what we had not understood. He untangled what had confused us; he counseled those who needed advice; he consoled those who needed consolation—and he shocked us sinners by telling us that we all could become saints, '*everyday saints.*'" But she hadn't initially been so enthused ...

The couples were gathered in the little farmhouse in Waukesha, where the sisters had just purchased a large piece of property. With much effort and by their own hard work, the sisters had turned an old farmhouse and pig barn into a cozy little house for the budding movement. Father Kentenich wasn't able to make it, but the meeting was still supposed to take place. Today someone in the couples' group was celebrating a significant birthday. Father Kentenich stressed that they should come together precisely for such occasions, enjoying each other's company and cultivating community. Acquaintances arrived from Milwaukee and Madison. One of the couples hadn't been in the group very long. They wanted to know: "How did it happen that all of you have such close contact with Father Kentenich?"

Now individuals began to share stories, starting with Mrs. Gmeinder. "It must have been 1952 or 1953. I had been in a terrible mood for some time. Everything in the world, everything about me and with my husband seemed to go wrong. Yes, we lived together, but we seemed to be growing apart more and more. One particular day when I was especially dissatisfied, a few friends came to visit me. 'You absolutely have to talk to the priest we just met,' they advised me. But at that moment, there was nothing *less* I wanted to do than visit a priest. My friends strongly insisted, and Henry agreed. I finally let myself be talked into it, but I immediately made it clear: 'I'll go with you, but I'm not saying a single word! You have to do the talking.' But no sooner had we taken a seat and exchanged a few words with Father than I felt at home with him. His words opened me somehow. He began the conversation by showing interest in the normal things of daily life, my family, etc., and I felt like he was there just for me. I sensed that he could see deep inside me. At first, I didn't mention anything about my problem, but soon I was able to tell him everything. After this meeting, we went to his talks every Sunday for a whole year. When I think back on all this, I wonder what would have happened if I hadn't gone to see Father. Father really changed our lifestyle as a family. He explained a few fundamental principles to us, and we tried to orient our life on these."

They simply called him "Father," and not only because this is the customary address for a priest in English. Germans also called him "Father," something unusual in Germany. And everyone knew who was meant. It came spontaneously from within because he was simply like a father to them, and it soon became a treasured habit that didn't bother anyone.

"The topic of one of Father Kentenich's first talks was *'How to Learn to Love God More!'* And with that we knew what Schoenstatt was actually all about. In the following years, we couples became Father Kentenich's 'private students.' It was the time when he blessed our homes."

"More couples joined us. Every family and each family member was important to him from the very beginning."

Mrs. Horn, from Milwaukee, remembered, "Our youngest son, Peter, just two years old at the time, had severely burned himself

Photo 17: At a celebration with families, 1963 or 1964

with a cup of coffee and had to go to the hospital. I was inconsolable. Father called every day to ask how little Peter was doing. And when I was worried about my husband because he worked in a brewery and was drinking more beer there on the hot summer days than was probably good for him in the long run, I turned to Father."

"We didn't have anything else to quench our thirst. It was beastly hot inside—and it was free," Mr. Horn interjected with an embarrassed smile.

"Father said to me, 'We'll pray together for a solution so that your husband doesn't keep getting into danger.' But neither of us could have expected *the way* that prayer would be answered!"

"The company went bankrupt and I lost my job. We wanted to build a house, and now we couldn't pay the bills. I was unemployed for half a year. Father even wanted to lend us money and gave us a check. But we didn't want that, and finally the bank gave us a loan and I got a good job. An even better one than before, and well-paid."

"Our parents were far away in Europe. But he became father and mother in one for us and our family."

The others nodded with a smile. Yes, that's how he was. He had an open ear for everyone and everything. From the very beginning he was different in many ways from the priests they had known until then. When the Laufenberg Family wanted to celebrate their twenty-first wedding anniversary in Madison with a holy Mass and a "family blessing," they invited Father Kentenich to do it in the first shrine in Madison that had recently been dedicated. He gladly made the many trips from Milwaukee to Madison, sometimes also by bus. That same evening he offered a talk to all of them and "immediately began to speak about the significance of the shrine." Mrs. Laufenberg always kept her notes with her and now read out loud from them: "'*The first question: What does it mean that the Blessed Mother is active from this little shrine in a very special way? She is a wise, masterly educator.*' And here's where he talks about us as Americans: '*Are there stone blocks here, too, that can be carved into saints? I recall some words from Cardinal Stritch that I've already quoted a couple of times. He truly knows the American people. ... These brilliant words come from him, and I will never forget them: "Americans are made of the right wood for carving saints." I'm also ... personally convinced of this. The more I get to know the American people with their childlike hearts, their simplicity, and their openness, the more I am convinced that we have within us the stuff we need to become saints. But then the cardinal says that we're just lacking the ... carvers who can carve such figures. What does that mean? We're lacking the educators. And then the Blessed Mother says, "If you are lacking them, here I am, I will do it!" You see, the Blessed*

Mother is the great Educator. What does she want? To educate the educators who will form saints!'"

Mrs. Gmeinder now recalled many things again. The "newcomers" listened to her account with growing attentiveness. Both Gmeinders really did seem so happy, and the more they shared, the more their eyes radiated. "Father had a deep influence on our married life. We don't know what would've happened without his help! After every Sunday talk, he would chat with us for a little while. Our reaction would give him a reference point for more personal conversations. We usually didn't say what we needed at the moment. ... But after our conversations with him, we would ask each other, 'How did he know that? It was exactly what we needed right now!' He made us so interiorly free and relaxed. It was a tremendous feeling of happiness. Now we were able to have conversations with each other, we were able to talk to each other, we were able to listen to each other. We simply felt good. Father taught us the right way to understand each other and ourselves. He explained that we shouldn't expect to think in exactly the same way since we are two different people. Earlier, whenever we would go to a talk and discuss the content with each other afterwards, it would usually end in a fierce argument. With Father's help, we understood that different ways of thinking are justified. He also helped us to understand ourselves and to understand the other. ... He never told us specifically what we were supposed to do. He gave us certain principles and left their application up to us."

Mr. Gmeinder lovingly pressed her hand in affirmation and added, "The greatest gift I received from Father was my respect for my wife and my children. ... He stressed again and again how important it was for the parents not to have too many social engagements. It was more important for them to stay at home with their children. His advice was exactly the opposite of what everybody else had been suggesting to us. He said more often, *'Don't forget that your children are your greatest treasure. Your care for your children is more important than anything else.'"* Mr. Gmeinder reached for his big notebook and read out loud what he had jotted down

Photo 18: In the shrine (Milwaukee) during the exile

from the talk on their seventh wedding anniversary in June 1954: *"You are renewing your covenant of love. You are giving your hearts to one another anew. What can the husband give his wife? And what does his wife have to offer him?"*

"In December he picked up that train of thought in a freely spoken prayer for both of us in the shrine: *'The love we promised each other at the altar has become stronger, deeper, and more fruitful. We understand each other better. We love each other more. We accept ourselves better and bear each other's burdens. We have learned to leave each other freedom and to lead one another higher and higher toward our goal. Sunday after Sunday we were led more deeply into your (God's) wishes. We have lost our hearts in the shrine. Above all, we have given up everything that could have a negative influence on our covenant of love and our family life ...'"*

In the meantime, this had become second nature to them. American men of the 1950s and 1960s in particular were involved in many activities outside their families. To a large extent, they left the housekeeping and the raising of their children to their wives. They were successful in their professions and in social committees and sometimes even held high positions. But they knew too little about their own children. Father Kentenich encouraged them time and again to make their families their first priority. They should rethink their own position as father of the family after the *"example of the loving, kind, serving Father God."* He made them aware of how indispensable they were as fathers for the development of their children. He didn't only promote their family life in this way through conversations and talks but also showed his appreciation for the family by accepting their invitations to their homes to celebrate house blessings and, later, "dedications" of the so-called home shrines.

Now their conversation turned to a new topic—the birth and life of the "home shrines." Father Kentenich had led the couples to the covenant of love and had spoken about the Schoenstatt Shrine and how Mary works there as an Educator. Mrs. Kubicek shared how she got the idea to invite the Blessed Mother into her home to educate her children *there.* Would that be possible? They had brough this question to Father Kentenich. "He listened to everything and then simply said in English, *'Please do it!'*" Little by little, the crucifix and the MTA picture became the center of the house for them and their children, a center of living faith, a type of domestic church.

"The home shrine," another mother continued, "is much more than a place to pray. We bring our joys and difficulties there, our big and small sacrifices, our questions. If we have to talk about something, we meet there. It's become our conflict resolution center."

A veritable stream of life came about among the families under the keywords "home shrine" or "living shrine." Father Kentenich happily took it up. It would soon spread all over the world. The amazing thing about it was that many of their children, too, carried it in a lively way.

"Our children just love Father Kentenich's visits," Mary Fenelon shared. "One time, the highlight of his visit was a candlelight

Photo 19: Visiting a family, USA, early 1960s

procession. The rooms in our house are in the form of a circle, so you can start in the dining room, where the home shrine is, and go through three other rooms before you get back to the home shrine."

Richard, her husband, added, "I gave lit candles to Mary, the children, and Father, and then we went on a procession through all the rooms until we had sung all the verses of a song." He smiled as he recalled his children's enthusiasm.

And his wife added, "I sometimes wondered what would happen if the house were to go up in flames ... But everyone enjoyed it so much!"

Helen and Anthony Post vividly recalled many scenes. "Our children love Father. They are so happy when he comes to visit us. Back when we still lived in our apartment, our children showed

Father their rooms and their toys. They made so much noise that the people underneath us complained."

But what they still had to get used to was the way he dealt with gifts. Even if someone gave him something he urgently needed, it wasn't certain what he would do with it. Mrs. Wacker had a thing or two to say about that: "I often saw visitors come out of Father's office with gifts in their hands. He always had to give away the things he received immediately. At first, it was hard for us to understand Father's generosity and joy in giving. We often worked hard to prepare him a gift, but after a while he would give it away. Only later did we notice how happy he was to hand out gifts. Now it makes us happy to be able to make Father happy in that way."

Over the years, the families could have filled entire books—their own library consisting of marriage seminars, various talk series, and conversation notes, all with an original marriage and family pedagogy. "Father helped us with the education of our children. The masterstroke in education consists of motivating the children's free will. Father also helped us acquire an understanding for the originality of each child."

"He taught us to make good use of the TV and radio since we are living in our times. But we shouldn't become slaves of modern achievements."

"We wrote many things down right away because they seemed so important to us. '*If we aren't relaxed and can't play with our children, then we can't speak with God, either. If we can't take a walk with them in nature, then we can't speak with God, either. It's good for our family to spend as much time as possible on our farm. If we don't make use of the natural ways and means, then we also won't know how to use the supernatural means.*'"

Mrs. Gmeinder added to her husband's depiction, "When we spoke with Father, it wasn't really his rootedness in supernature that stood out to us. We felt good in his presence above all because he was so realistic, so genuine, and so natural. He didn't advise us to pray all the time. He guided us to be very natural and to master life in a healthy, natural and supernatural way."

Photo 20: In his office in Milwaukee

Another couple said in response, "He spoke to us about the Heavenly Father in a way we had never heard before."

Mrs. Schimmel confessed, "Once we started going to see Father more often, our children noticed a change in our life. One time, shortly before Father's birthday, we spoke about it with them. One of our daughters said, 'Ever since you've been going there, you are both really different. You don't scold as much anymore."

Father Kentenich didn't give exact recipes or behavioral instructions to the people who came to him. Instead, he helped them to find the solution themselves. That simply fit to his pedagogy. One of the mothers related how she often felt helpless because of her teenage son and would go to Father Kentenich to complain. Eventually she asked if she could just send the boy to him once. He agreed. And the first thing he asked the "young man" had nothing to do with his impossible behavior toward his parents or siblings. Instead: "*What do you want to be later on?*"

"An architect," he proudly proclaimed.

Father Kentenich gave him a friendly smile and said, *"One day you will become a great architect, but first you have to learn how to build the house of your soul."* That was it. From that day on, not only did his way of dealing with others change, but he also did indeed become a successful architect later on.

Not every couple was immediately enthused. It also happened that one or the other didn't really have anything against "Father Kentenich" but had no interest in him either, and so remained at a distance. Some only discovered later that there was something special about his personality. He didn't court the favor of others or intentionally gather people around himself—and yet more and more people came to him. He left freedom and adapted himself to the other person. Mr. Gilbert Schimmel—like many other family fathers—became a "son" of this father. One time as Mrs. Schimmel was looking at a photo of her husband with Father Kentenich, she spontaneously said, "Father and son!" It was amazing that these men in their fifties allowed "the child" in themselves to awaken.

"How can one acquire such a love for people?" one young doctor of physics wrote in her journal after her first conversations. She had come to the USA on a student flight. Interiorly, many of his visitors experienced a growth in their faith, a strengthening of their love of neighbor, and a certain transformation that made them happy.

Mr. Horn liked to go see Father Kentenich either alone or with his wife. One time, when asked what was so special about that man, he only said, "He makes you feel like you're the most important person in the world."

Many others had a similar experience. Someone who had experienced the effect of this respect put it in a nutshell one time when he openly asked him, "How can it be that someone departs from you a better person than when he came?"

Father Kentenich obviously had the extraordinary gift of being able to look deeply into the other person, to take hold of hidden longings, and to understand human nature in its specific originality. His love for people, as his visitors interpreted it, had supernatural roots. Many people who encountered him were eventually moved by the thought, "If a human person can be so good and so kind, full of personal interest in me and my concerns, what must God himself be like?!"

"It's as if he can see right through me and understand me perfectly!" someone said. "I can speak with him about everything that goes through my mind. I can tell him things I would never tell others."

The trust others gave him was precious to him, and he tried to model what he proclaimed. *"The lived example is what has the greatest effect on the modern person, who depends so much on life."* When the young physicist—who had heard some critical remarks about him in Germany—left the USA, she noted as a concluding thought from her encounters with him, "He is credible."

Even though the battles dramatically mounted and accusation after accusation, slander after slander, darkness after darkness followed, the burden that weighed upon him could only rarely be perceived. One time, he put down a letter with new bad accusations and said to his secretary in a sad tone of voice, "What more could there possibly be?" Erika Schnuerer, a German university student who had offered her secretarial services to him during her stay in Milwaukee, sensed how much he was being humanly tested in his faith and in his power of endurance. The many families had no idea about any of it. More than a decade into his banishment, when Mrs. Riedl—who maintained extensive contacts—found out that he was in exile and that only a fraction of the measures against him were perceptible to the outside, she was firmly resolved to take it to the press. How could the Church make "such a holy man" suffer just like that?! Father Kentenich was able to dissuade her from this plan with a humorous "trick." *"No, no! If the hen cackles too soon, her eggs will get taken away."*

During these years, many young German priests and seminarians also visited him to seek his advice and receive inspirations for their pastoral work and personality formation. The encounters often made such a deep impression on them that they

Photo 21: Conversation with young seminarian Guenther Boll

savored them their whole life long and gave witness to them in many ways.

It might have been the end of February 1959. Mrs. Schimmel closed the door of the new office he had moved into. It was now on the ground floor with a view to the garages and smaller than the former one. She had lost her husband Gilbert just a few days earlier. Despite the piercing pain, she headed home somehow relieved and consoled. Actually, he was far too young to depart from this life—he had been at the height of his years. She was so happy that Gilbert had still been able to say goodbye to Father Kentenich, who went to see him in the hospital. Then he had peacefully fallen asleep. "His visit gave Gilbert so much strength!" she pondered to herself. She recalled the beginnings in 1954—her "Monday evening talks" with Father Kentenich, and how after their first conversation with him back then, her husband was sitting next to her in the car, and at the stoplight they both said at the same time, "That's it!" They had been looking for such a priest with whom they could speak about everything. This priest was able to listen attentively for a long time without interrupting them even once, and he could seamlessly and *"organically"* connect everything they told him with God. In the process, his words never seemed feigned, overly pious, or artificial. Since that moment, they had gone regularly to him, and one day he had said, *"If you know anyone who would like to hear something about the Blessed Mother or talk to a priest about questions concerning their family, you can invite them to our meetings."* They knew someone, but when they proposed it to the two of them, the wife, Mrs. Horning, only said, "Oh my goodness, John already meets with priests, bishops, and archbishops from all corners of the globe. Now another one's supposed to join them?" The only difference was that this time she could go along.

What began back then had now become a treasured habit for years. Monday evening after Monday evening, Father Kentenich met with couples in his large office. He gave talks in a conversational tone in German; Sister Winfriede interpreted them. There were only a few couples at first, but by the beginning of 1956, the number had grown to fourteen. The meetings were meant not only to be a help for mastering life but also to enable them to help other couples. The Wacker, Graber, Augur, and Day families joined back then, and many years later it was still unanimous: "That was so beautiful!" Mr. Horning later confessed, "I never became as aware of my religion as I did back then when he (Gilbert Schimmel) introduced me to Father Kentenich. God spoke through him! I don't know how my life would've turned out, and my relationship to the Church, if I hadn't met him. ... He liked me and I liked him."

"So it can really be that simple to proclaim the faith," thought Mrs. Schimmel. At the last two meetings, Father Kentenich had taken the whole evening to speak about her husband. She was touched by this and sensed the big hole that had appeared in her life. How understanding Father was of each one! When Mrs. Johannsen asked him what she should do because she always went bowling on Monday evenings, he encouraged her to go ahead and go bowling. There she would meet people and establish contacts, and that was also important. But he would wait for her before he gave the closing blessing. And indeed, he always waited until Mrs. Johannsen came from bowling, gave a few more spiritual inspirations that she could take home with her, and imparted the evening blessing.

"Behind everything he passed on to the families," thought Mrs. Schimmel on her way home, "were his own experiences of faith." He never spoke purely theoretically or abstractly. He was simple and uncomplicated, and yet he also didn't shy away from speaking to them about the heights of holiness. Thinking of her husband, of Richard Fenelon, of the Yanks, of all of them, she could see the effect this had on the men. What was remarkable was that he never spoke about his own suffering. There surely must have been quite a bit ... But even one time when he told them about Dachau in answer to their wish, he didn't just focus on the atrocities, but also demonstrated how to prepare for trials and master difficult challenges through faith. He knew them all so well and led them gently to the heights without taking away their freedom. In conversations here and there, their husbands had highlighted more often that for him, it was a matter of a lay piety and holiness, a topic the official Church hadn't yet broached at all. Even though he was far away from Rome, Germany, and Europe and never left Milwaukee, he knew so much about what was going on in the Church and world that their husbands were always completely captivated. The Monday evening talks brought them closer together, creating community. In the midst of her current difficult situation, she gained a lot from this family-like community with the other couples. Mrs. Schimmel recalled how one of his "penitents" had spontaneously asked him if there was any way she could thank him. She said he had only replied, *"Pray for me, that I will be able to better lead those entrusted to me into supernature. Pray that I will become even more a father."*

One day—Father Kentenich had already been in exile for seven years—the young chaplain Father Edward Geiskopf, who had been responsible for the Germans in Milwaukee, approached him. He said that since he was going to be transferred, he was looking for a successor for the German emigrants who gathered for Sunday Mass once a month in the lower church of St. Michael's. This made it possible for them to sing German songs and hear a sermon in their native language. Father Kentenich agreed, but only under three conditions: The holy Mass should take place regularly every Sunday, and at a time when families with children who wanted to sleep a little later on Sundays would also be able to come. Moreover, he wanted to hear regular confessions every Saturday so that the German "parishioners" would have the chance to go to confession in their native language. Since then, Father Kentenich sat in the confessional of the lower church of St. Michael's Saturday after Saturday, and Sunday after Sunday he celebrated holy Mass at 10:00 a.m. Over the years, as it became apparent that a parish awareness had grown among the Mass attendees, Father Kentenich registered this "German parish" with the Department of Foreign Affairs of the German Bishops' Conference.

Hardly had he climbed out of the car at the side door that led to the sacristy of the lower church when he was already surrounded by children. He always had something to pull out of his pocket for them. The pockets of his cassock must have been huge because whole oranges, chocolates, and other tasty treats appeared. He preached every Sunday, usually much too long. And people still came. Inspired by the Church liturgical year, the sermons became a real compendium of the Catholic faith, an everyday catechism. Somehow he understood how to place the central truths of the faith into a context that was close to life. He knew how to keep the world of his parishioners in mind, having gotten to know them well in the meantime through lots of personal contact. In doing so, he addressed essential questions of modern-day evangelization. One of his young listeners insisted on being married only by him. When asked why, she said, "He made a deep impression on me. His

Photo 22: During a sermon at St. Michael's Church, USA

sermons were often too high for me. But one day, I will tell my children about the old priest with the white beard who preached about God Sunday after Sunday with such certainty and enthusiasm that people thought he had experienced him himself and had just come from him."

Because of his long, white beard, children would also ask him on the street, "Are you Santa Claus?" He let the little ones pull on his beard to test its authenticity.

One American woman took a long bus ride with multiple interchanges straight through Milwaukee to St. Michael's Church every Sunday just to sit in the front pew and look at him. "Why do you do that? You don't understand a single word of German!" people asked in astonishment.

"It gives me peace for the whole week!" was the only answer of this mother of many children.

When individual members of the church choir organized by Father Kentenich complained that his sermons were too long, three men were selected to "make him aware" of this. "But when we went to him," related Mr. Horn, "the other two said nothing. So I spoke with him and asked him to limit his sermons to twenty minutes. I myself had experienced that I wasn't able to take in anything more after twenty minutes. Father smiled about it. He admitted that it was a weakness of his to preach so long, and he said he wanted to try to fulfill our request. The next two Sundays he kept his resolution. But on the third Sunday he broke it. Then we went to him again and asked him for shorter sermons. He laughed and said, '*Well, well, a leopard can't change its spots.*' One other time, Father had spoken too long again. When he looked at his watch, he commented, '*Oh, you asked me not to speak too long, and now I've done it again!*'"

After every holy Mass, he greeted the attendees and spoke with them, and soon he knew all the families by name. He made every baptism, wedding, and family event into an event for the whole parish. They rented a small hall at the so-called Jacobus Park where they could happily celebrate. He liked to inspire them to organize dances, and he himself would appear at them, going from table to table, speaking with individuals and sharing their joy in dancing. Together with some parishioners, he started a parish newspaper called *Heimatklänge [Sounds of Home]*, which helped create a family-like parish atmosphere.

Turning Point: the Council

Far away in Europe, the waves of debate surrounding Schoenstatt and its founder had already been surging back and forth for more than ten years. And none of it had remained hidden from him, while his surroundings knew basically nothing of it all, except his secretary. Erika had often observed him, including the moments when he received the harshest decrees and dictated difficult letters. He reacted calmly and peacefully, without bitterness or animosity, simply calm. She liked his play on words: *"Gelassenheit in der Verlassenheit ist höchste Vollkommenheit. [Calmness in abandonment is greatest perfection.]"* Hadn't he been abandoned and misjudged by the Church? One time, when she was filled with intense indignation, he smiled and said that if she said something like that again, he would write to Father Tromp about it. No, he stood by the Church and its authority. His love for freedom never meant wanting to accuse or do away with the hierarchy. It was obvious that no human weaknesses found within the "ground crew of the Lord" ever robbed him of his faith in the divine commission of the Church. Well-informed circles knew that bishops and bishops' conferences, Roman congregations, and ultimately also council participants, and in the meantime three popes, had studied and were studying Schoenstatt and its founder. But as always, everything remained dark. How could he be so cheerful and express a sense of humor that so often made people laugh? He walked through the house with a bounce in his step as though there were nothing amiss.

1962. The dramatic battles over Schoenstatt had reached their climax. The plan to steer the 1954 general chapter of the Sisters of Mary in such a way that a general government opposed to the founder would take the helm did not succeed. The community had elected a general superior, Sister Heriberta Ross, who knew how to exercise her office in a motherly way, was loyally united to the founder, and wouldn't let herself be pulled onto Father Tromp's side. But in the early 1960s, the matter was on thin ice once again.

Every last person responsible for leadership in the Schoenstatt Secular Institutes was to be removed from office. And just at the moment of greatest distress, a decisive turn came. Through the engagement of the Schoenstatt Diocesan Priests, the Sisters of Mary, and the Ladies of Schoenstatt, the ears of the German bishops had perked up. The life of a lay movement working fruitfully in their dioceses was being suppressed by the Society of the Pallottines, who from the past had the right to offer it pastoral care. In practice, they saw none of the Schoenstatt members exhibiting the "lack of ecclesial spirit" Schoenstatt was being accused of. Cardinal Joseph Frings, President of the German Bishops' Conference, supported by three other cardinals from overseas, turned to the Holy Father, Pope John XXIII. They requested in writing to have the Kentenich and Schoenstatt case moved from the Holy Office back into the responsibility of the Congregation for Religious and to have the General Statute of the Schoenstatt Work reworked under its charge. He and the other German bishops had realized in the meantime that it was necessary to take the whole thing out of the state of paralysis it was in due to the ever-new restrictions by the Holy Office. They had to find a way to make it possible for this movement to unfold its life more freely and powerfully. It just could not go on like this. The Holy Father agreed. At the beginning of 1963, Cardinal Alfredo Ottaviani, Secretary of the Holy Office, handed over the whole "Schoenstatt" case to Cardinal Ildebrando Antoniutti, Prefect of the Congregation for Religious. A few bishops went one step further and urged the pope, who had become seriously ill in the meantime, to rehabilitate the exiled founder. But it no longer came to pass because John XXIII died before the matter had been properly concluded. In the Curia, a climate of goodwill toward Schoenstatt slowly began to spread, not least of all due to the new image of the Church that had gained increasing acceptance in the debates of the council auditorium and through many individual conversations that had taken place in the columned halls of the council.

Father Kentenich had followed the happenings and official statements of Vatican Council II from its opening on October 11,

1962, with great attentiveness. Weren't the topics precisely the ones in which he had been so little understood until now? The focus on the laity; the opening of the Church to the world and society; a new type of pastoral care, catechesis, and asceticism corresponding to the modern person; and finally a freer style of leadership with a changed understanding of obedience and a new pedagogy. Many Schoenstatters hoped, prayed, and sacrificed for a new vision of these things and a freer, more autonomous life for the movement.

It was actually the document of the Holy Office from June 1956—which had been meant to level this autonomy and place the Schoenstatt Work entirely under the leadership of the Pallottines—that initiated a process that ultimately opened the way for the idea of separating Schoenstatt from the Pallottines. This idea had already been in consideration the previous year. Basically, the Holy Office, by its one-sided "Proposal for the Solution of all Questions," had brought the protests of a few German bishops onto the scene. Since then, they had become more aware of the significance of all this for the future of Schoenstatt and the Schoenstatt priests in their dioceses. Already at that time, Bishop Keller of Muenster had turned to the Holy Office and expressed his reservations about attaching the Work exclusively to the Pallottines. But instead of bearing this objection in mind, Father Tromp sought to firmly establish his own view of things through a further document. But by doing so, he permanently obstructed the way to a peaceful cooperation and coexistence between the two communities and mobilized leading members of the Schoenstatt communities to plead for a separation from the Pallottines. For Father Kentenich, who was convinced that the Pallottines were meant to have a special task and role in Schoenstatt according to God's plans, the separation process looming on the horizon was extraordinarily painful. But under the given circumstances, he, too, saw no other possibility in the long run. After the election of Pope Paul VI in 1963, the "Schoenstatt" case got moving again. The Congregation for Religious, now responsible for the movement, demanded a reopening and a new examination, and it seemed a matter of course that they were not satisfied with the older judgments. Once Joseph Hoeffner, meanwhile bishop of Muenster, had made himself available as the protector of the Schoenstatt Work, and Prelate Wilhelm Wissing, Director of the Catholic Office in Bonn, was ready as its assistant, things moved ahead. The Congregation of Religious put Father Hilarius Albers, provincial superior of the Dominicans in Ecuador, in charge of a new visitation of Schoenstatt. This led to a first breakthrough in the time that followed. At their plenary assembly from February 17-19, 1964, the German bishops unanimously spoke out for granting autonomy to the Schoenstatt Work. In the spring of that same year, the advisory opinion of the visitator, Father Albers, arrived at the Congregation for Religious in Rome. It was clearly more reasonable about the whole case. Moreover, the new visitator made a series of recommendations in his concluding report on how to do justice to the Schoenstatt Work and newly resolve things. Bishop Hoeffner complemented the advisory opinion with a report on his observations and his positive evaluation. In the end, right before October 18, 1964, the fiftieth anniversary of Schoenstatt's founding, the Holy See issued a directive that declared the Schoenstatt Work autonomous. The Work was thereby officially confirmed by the Church as an autonomous entity. The joy in Schoenstatt was indescribable; Father Kentenich, who had spent the day in the newly built Schoenstatt Shrine in Waukesha, rejoiced quietly and deeply. The separation from the Pallottines made it necessary to found a new community of priests that would be fully available for the formation and education of the movement. Pallottine priests and seminarians who had sided with Schoenstatt waited with deep longing for the Church's permission for this founding. The Institute of the Schoenstatt Fathers could in fact be constituted as the newest of the secular institutes on July 18, 1965, by Bishop Adolf Bolte.

But what about the founder of this great Work and his rehabilitation? He was still subordinate to the Holy Office and still in exile ...

10. The Return Home

Mrs. Horn held the receiver in her hand, her tears silently running down her cheeks. She still couldn't fathom it. She had just received the news from Father Kentenich that he had been called to Rome. He had gotten a telegram, transmitted telephonically by the post office: "Immediately come to Rome!" He was told that the sender was the secretary of the Pallottine general superior. Mrs. Horn had promised him not to tell anyone yet, but when her husband came home, he immediately sensed that something serious had happened.

Shortly after that, Father Kentenich's secretary called to ask him to bring boxes to "Father" at his office. Now he knew why his wife was so sad. "But we wanted this so badly for him!" he said, trying to console himself and his wife.

"I know," she sobbed, "but we might never see him again."

"We'll visit him when he's in Schoenstatt! For sure!" promised Mr. Horn. And he headed out, for now there was a lot of work to be done ...

Already the next day, the news spread like wildfire. It was unfathomable to everyone. As much as they were happy about it, they were also filled with inexpressible pain at having to say goodbye. They simply could no longer imagine life without "Father." While Father Kentenich still made all his already- promised visits to families even up to the last evening, everything in his office got sorted and packed. Mr. Horn had driven off right away and helped as often as he could, until Father Kentenich's departure on September 16, to pack piles of books and other important things into the boxes he had brought along. Something was actually moving now after all these years of waiting and hoping ...

Already in the summer of 1963, leading members of the movement had drafted a petition to the German bishops, bringing up the question of Father Kentenich's return to Schoenstatt. The document illustrated once more the whole severity of the measures against the founder and ended with the request to newly examine the matter. However, the questions concerning the Schoenstatt Work and its autonomy had absorbed all their strength in the time that followed. But in the long run, the solution to these questions benefitted the Kentenich case. In June 1965, before Rome's summer break, Father Menningen had surprisingly received an invitation from Cardinal Ottaviani. This audience resulted in the idea of possibly bringing Father Kentenich to Rome in October of that same year for conversations.

As a result, the Apostolic Administrator of the Schoenstatt Work, Prelate Wissing, had traveled to Milwaukee to have a "lengthy exchange of ideas" with Father Kentenich. For the first time, the Holy Office had also taken up direct contact with the founder. The telegram of September 13 seemed to be entirely in keeping with these considerations. After a short stopover in New York, he landed in Rome on September 17. But what a bitter surprise: No one at the Pallottine generalate had any knowledge of a telegram that was supposed to have been sent to him. Even though he made a declaration on oath that he had received such a telegram by telephone, as was customary in the USA, his unexpected appearance in Rome awakened the suspicion that the "old man" had gotten tired of his exile and departed without authorization.

The application to be subordinate to Prelate Wissing and not Father General Moehler in the still ongoing proceedings had previously been prepared and was initially granted. Father Kentenich was allowed to take up residence at the generalate of the Steyler Fathers in Rome. But then another page turned. On that "black Friday," September 24, 1965, all hopes were dashed once more. A plenary assembly of the cardinals of the Holy Office took place on that day. They decided to send the almost eighty-year-old priest back to his place of exile for the time being and thus to restore the state of affairs as it was before the mysterious telegram story. All official inquiries had failed to gain new insights as to the sender of the telegram. Father Kentenich's arrival was construed as an unlawful, unauthorized action. He had to move into the Pallottine generalate around 9:00 p.m. that same evening.

There was still a weak ray of light: The cardinals commissioned Cardinal Bea to hold a conversation with Father Kentenich. After all, he knew the founder and had been familiar with the whole Schoenstatt affair since 1951. The cardinal looked for a way out. Could one even expect the aged founder to make such a hard trip back overseas? Father Kentenich was accompanied and advised by Heinrich Tenhumberg, member of the community of Schoenstatt Priests and auxiliary bishop of Muenster. On Monday afternoon, September 27, they drove to the Brazilian College on Via Aurelia to meet Cardinal Bea. The two faced each other again after fourteen long years. "You've become a cardinal in the meantime, and I spent fourteen years in exile," noted Joseph Kentenich in a calm voice soon after they had greeted one another. Like an observation without bitterness.

The cardinal approached him about the decision of the Holy Office to send him back to the USA and tried to build him a bridge. "Did you survive the long trip? How is your health?"

"Superb."

"But a return trip would be quite a strain, right?"

"I am personally in agreement if I'm supposed to return to the USA, but one has to keep in mind that then the whole story could be interpreted against the Holy Office. It would shed a negative light on the authorities."

The conversation turned to other topics. When Cardinal Bea met Cardinal Ottaviani, he couldn't keep his judgment about Father Kentenich's attitude to himself. "Father Kentenich is ready for everything in obedience as a matter of course, even to return to Milwaukee immediately if he is asked to do so. He also says there are no hesitations on account of his health. He says he's pretty healthy. And he raised absolutely no accusations about the past."

Cardinal Ottaviani was visibly impressed by this reaction. "That gives witness to the genuine ecclesial spirit of Father Kentenich." His misgivings that a bitter injustice might have been done to this man became stronger.

On October 11, Prelate Wissing finally succeeded in getting a private audience with the pope to clarify the matter. But the result troubled him. He said Father Kentenich had to go back to the USA right away and that the new Schoenstatt Fathers' community was to be dissolved again. He affirmed that Prelate Wissing had his complete confidence and had done good work as the Apostolic Administrator of the Schoenstatt Work but said that he was no longer needed. Had he dared to go too far in this delicate situation? What had influenced many of these reactions? Did they have to give up entirely now? As he was still occupied with these thoughts, the Holy Father's question suddenly surprised him: "What do you personally think of Father Kentenich?"

"He is absolutely a man of the Church, a person of integrity!"

"Advisors of the Holy Office are of a different opinion! But I want to have the Kentenich case re-examined, and I will inform them. The Schoenstatt Work is definitely a great and significant work and should be able to fully unfold."

Torn back and forth between hope and resignation, Prelate Wissing withdrew. As he left the Vatican, he found out through Monsignor Wuestenberg about the "non-stop activity" of the other side "against Father Kentenich." Prelate Wissing flew back to Germany with sadness, without having been able to reach Father Kentenich anymore. The latter had waited expectantly for a report about the audience. Once again—so it seemed—everything was being called into question and had dramatically come to a head.

In the end, no one knew exactly how it went from these happenings to an event of far-reaching significance only a few days later, on October 20. Unexpectedly for many, another plenary assembly of the cardinals of the Holy Office resulted in a positive decision regarding the Causa Kentenich: The founder of the

Schoenstatt Work, Father Joseph Kentenich, did not have to return to his place of exile. And what's more, the Kentenich case was handed over to the Congregation for Religious. With that the measures and decrees of the Holy Office against him were null and void. Two days later, Pope Paul VI officially confirmed the decision of the Holy Office, making it legally valid. Soon afterwards, Father Kentenich also received the official permission for his incardination into the diocesan clergy of the Muenster diocese. Bishop Hoeffner gladly accepted him as his "youngest diocesan priest." Although in German-speaking areas the title "Pater" only referred to a priest belonging to an order or a religious community, Bishop Hoeffner jokingly said that the familiar address "Herr Pater," [a title unique to Father Kentenich], should continue to be used in the future.

The mood at the Vatican offices had meanwhile become favorable to Schoenstatt and Father Kentenich. And yet, when Auxiliary Bishop Tenhumberg made another visit to the Congregation for Religious at the end of October, Cardinal Antoniutti handed him a document from the Holy Office that bore the memo, "Father Kentenich may go anywhere, just not back to Germany."

Auxiliary Bishop Tenhumberg wondered, "Why shouldn't he go back to Germany? He's a free man again now! For sure they want to be considerate of the mood among the German bishops and in the Society of the Pallottines, which is suffering from the separation and fears losing many members to the new Institute of the Schoenstatt Fathers. There may be no celebration, above all no 'victory celebration'!"

But all assurances that they would rejoice as discreetly as possible didn't help. It was said that Father Kentenich had to be patient, that maybe in a year ... And yet, hope is the last thing to die; it continued to determine the atmosphere. On November 13, Father Kentenich was able to leave the Pallottine generalate and move into the large new house of the Sisters of Divine Providence in Mainz to celebrate his 80th birthday with the representatives of the Schoenstatt Family who were present. A special joy, deep and full of gratitude, reigned on that day. They still couldn't believe all that had happened in these few weeks since the mysterious telegram had arrived in Milwaukee. Father Kentenich was personally convinced that this telegram was a sign from Mary. She had obtained his freedom just as he had quietly asked her to, *"that all honor may be given to her alone"* ... On his birthday he was also accepted into the diocesan clergy of Muenster. Early in the morning, Father Kentenich presented himself to the Blessed Mother in the house chapel, wearing his new habit. The first congratulatory telegram came—astonishingly—from Cardinal Ottaviani. The Schoenstatt Family gave him the model of a small shrine as a symbol for the planned construction of a Schoenstatt Shrine in Rome, in Belmonte. As a response, he developed his vision of a new Church on the closing day of the Council (December 8). During this time, he met with the leadership circles and gave them fundamental talks on important topics in the movement.

Accompanied by Auxiliary Bishop Tenhumberg, he met with Cardinal Antoniutti for the first time at the end of November. When the latter benevolently said, "Let's forget about the past!" Father Kentenich replied, *"Yes, we want to forget the cross and suffering, injustice and the like, but we cannot and may not forget the wondrous deeds of the dear Blessed Mother!"*

Efforts to obtain a papal audience for Father Kentenich were in the making. But that was no easy affair. A papal audience, according to a statement from the prefecture, would amount to a publicly demonstrated rehabilitation. Therefore, Father Kentenich needed a recommendation from Cardinal Antoniutti as the one responsible for him if he was to be added to the list of audience participants. Shortly before Christmas, the cardinal did indeed give this recommendation, and one day before the audience, Father Kentenich received a notification from the Vatican and the ticket to the audience. On December 22, 1965, Father Kentenich was received by Pope Paul VI within the framework of a group audience of about seventy people. As he entered the audience hall, a security guard approached him and motioned with his hand that he should

Photo 23: During the audience with Pope Paul VI

stand at the end of the row of participants. "The Holy Father wants to dedicate more time to you," he whispered to him. Finally the founder stood before the Holy Father, holding a small, black case in his hand. Inside this case, which he now opened, was a simple, golden chalice. He handed it to the pope as a gift for the planned "Mater Ecclesiae" Church to be built in Rome as a memorial of the Council. In a short, prepared address, the pope expressed his gratitude to the founder. On his part, Father Kentenich thanked the Holy Father for all his benevolence and for his rehabilitation. He promised him that Schoenstatt would cooperate in the postconciliar mission of the Church to the best of its strength. Then the pope added some personal words to his written address. He shared that Bishop Carlo Manziana, a friend from his youth and a fellow prisoner with Father Kentenich in Dachau, had told the pope with great gratitude that Father Kentenich had saved his life by sharing his food packages during the terrible time of hunger.

Surrounded by representatives of his Schoenstatt Family once again, the founder happily shared about this event and offered an interpretation: *"By and large, it's much more than one could have expected from the outset. ... Seen in context, it is doubtlessly an extraordinary seal upon Schoenstatt as a work, Schoenstatt in its structure, Schoenstatt in its mission ..."*

There was just one more big wish on the Christmas wish list of the whole Schoenstatt Family—that Father Kentenich could be in Schoenstatt for Christmas. It didn't look like this wish would be fulfilled. Everyone started planning to celebrate Christmas in Rome ...

Cardinal Antoniutti had promised to ask the Holy Father during the Curia's Christmas congratulations on December 23 whether Father Kentenich could travel to Schoenstatt for Christmas. Up to the last minute, everything remained uncertain. Everyone was on edge, both in Rome and in Germany. One day before Christmas Eve, Cardinal Antoniutti called him personally. He could travel to Muenster, Germany, for Christmas. Father Kentenich thanked him very sincerely for all his efforts. But then he hesitated. Wouldn't it be too hard for the Schoenstatt Family if he didn't first go to Schoenstatt? And how would the public interpret this? In that case,

Photo 24: Return home to Schoenstatt, Original Shrine, December 24, 1965

it would be better to spend Christmas in Rome after all. Cardinal Antoniutti understood and accepted these considerations.

And finally, what had been hopeless up to that point did indeed occur. On the morning of December 24, the message came from Muenster that Father Kentenich could travel to Schoenstatt for Christmas and only needed to report in Muenster after that. Amid joyful excitement, the packing began. In an act of great confidence, one of the sisters had simply not canceled his plane ticket ... So at 12:15 p.m. they could start the trip to the airport. Extremely eventful, dramatic weeks lay behind all who boarded the Alitalia plane.

After more than fourteen years of exile, the founder arrived in Schoenstatt on Christmas Eve 1965. To more than a few, it seemed like a "Miracle of the Holy Night," which Sister Mariengard had described in her letter to the Christ Child already back in 1941 at the time of his imprisonment: "Father's" return home to the little shrine. His first steps took him, of course, to the Original Shrine, where he very silently knelt down in front. God alone knows the things he placed at the feet of his Mother, the "Mother Thrice Admirable," during those minutes of prayer ...

The auditorium of the Marian School in Vallendar was filled to overflowing. The young generation crowded the balcony to get a good view of everything, especially of "him." As he stepped into the large room, accompanied by Auxiliary Bishop Tenhumberg and Father Menningen, the applause knew no end. Handel's Hallelujah Chorus resounded. Somehow everything seemed incomprehensible. What everyone had hoped for with great longing for fourteen years was now a reality. A few speakers took to the podium and spoke words of welcome and greeting. People heard them but didn't really hear them ... Finally Father Kentenich stepped on the stage and began his short address: *"My dear Schoenstatt Family, I can imagine you are eager to hear the first words I intend to say to you at this solemn reunion after fourteen years. They could be twofold. I could remain on earth with you, but I could also climb upward with you, upward to the stars, upward to heaven."* No word of complaint or accusation, no "reckoning" with those who had made his life difficult. For him, climbing *"upward to heaven"* meant *"looking into the heart of God, trying to determine God's plans, and applying them to our own life, in order ... to be able to look into the future with greater clarity."* That wasn't only true of that evening. It determined his program in the years that

Photo 25: In the auditorium of the Marian School before his first address after exile

followed. He celebrated Christmas Mass at midnight in the Original Shrine.

Father Kentenich took up residence on Mount Schoenstatt, in a tiny apartment in the "Schulungsheim," the retreat house of the Sisters of Mary. It had a bedroom, a small bathroom, and a space that served as a living room, workroom, and dining room all in one. That was it. During the following three years, this little apartment became the "hub of the world" for the Schoenstatt Movement. There was a constant coming and going, there were phone calls during the day and often also at night, and there were visitors of all ages with various expectations and hopes. From then on, resting was out of the question.

Father Kentenich dedicated himself entirely to his communities, who had had to renounce the founder for so long. In the years that followed, he gave all the retreat courses of the Schoenstatt Priests, the Sisters of Mary, and the Ladies of Schoenstatt, so that each member could personally encounter him. He visited the women's federation, the family branch, the branch of the women and mothers, the branches of the men and the youth, the Brothers of Mary, and the newly founded community of the Schoenstatt Fathers. There was no Schoenstatt community to which the founder didn't speak. In between he traveled across Germany to visit some of the Schoenstatt centers that had come into existence. Father Kentenich also sought conversations with a number of German bishops. Well-known dignitaries of the Church and world came to Schoenstatt from home and abroad. They wanted to meet the man who had borne so much out of love for the Church, calling such a Work into existence and yet not being understood for so long.

In February 1966, Father Kentenich met with an extended leadership circle of the Schoenstatt Sisters of Mary at the provincial house in Borken, Westphalia, to prepare the general chapter for the following year with them. This first and only chapter in the founder's presence took place in Schoenstatt from September 8 to November 21, 1967. He worked out fundamental principles with the participants present from home and abroad, wishing to enable them to derive concrete applications from these principles always in keeping with the current times.

As he did after Dachau, he now had the opportunity to take a fundamental stand on questions of the time, of society, and especially of the postconciliar Church. At the large October conferences and Christmas conventions in the following years, Father Kentenich spoke to delegates of the Schoenstatt Family about important trends of the time and their response as a spiritual movement, their service to the Church of the future. He continued to make himself available nearly day and night for many individual and group conversations.

How great was his surprise one day when among the visitors from all over the world two familiar faces appeared: Mr. and Mrs. Horn from Milwaukee. The joy was indescribable, and of course both of them were given the best care and lodgings. They were flabbergasted at the immensity of Schoenstatt—the many central houses of the individual communities and so many sisters and priests in one place! Not least of all, they could admire the

Photo 26: At the celebration of the founding jubilee of two communities, Schoenstatt Family Work and Brothers of Mary, Dachau Memorial Site, 1967

construction of the Adoration Church of the Most Holy Trinity on Mount Schoenstatt. Full of pride, Father Kentenich led them around the extensive grounds. Yes, God had blessed his Work, but also his sacrifices. There was no question.

The bishops' visits during the years from 1965-1968 represented a particular highlight. They came from all over the world: Africa, the Philippines, Pakistan, India, Syria, and North and South America. In 1965, still during the Council, Auxiliary Bishop Tenhumberg had accompanied a larger group from Rome to Schoenstatt. After they had seen the Original Shrine and the various community houses and were full of praises, including about the "very good food," they listened to Father Menningen's explanations of Schoenstatt's spirituality and history in Latin. Then they asked their questions, for example, "How does Schoenstatt contribute to the dioceses and parishes?" They marveled at the wealth of symbols and were impressed by the institution of the course communities that had grown in an original way in the institutes and federations. They had been introduced more closely to the courses at the house of the Ladies of Schoenstatt. During these days they were struck above all by the realization that the covenant of love was obviously the central point in Schoenstatt! They came to speak about the suitability of Schoenstatt's spirituality for daily life, *"everyday sanctity,"* and many other topics. How strange—what had been the object of so many attacks and heated disputes suddenly found open ears. At the Marian School, the delegation listened to Sister Isabell Nei's presentations about Schoenstatt's pedagogy with great interest. They reported that it was Schoenstatt's family character as a whole, the "family spirit," as they called it, that had especially impressed them. They noticed that the priests, sisters, and brothers, the women of the federation, the Ladies of Schoenstatt, and even the children and young people were marked by it. At one meeting, German folk songs were sung and such a relaxed, joyful atmosphere was created that the bishops hardly wanted to leave. The farewell at the Original Shrine was visibly hard for many of them. There was something special about that place. They all sensed it. If Auxiliary Bishop Tenhumberg hadn't intoned the "Salve Regina" with his powerful voice to signal the end of the visit, they might not have gotten to the airport on time. When Father Kentenich told the Schoenstatters gathered in Rome about this first visit, he said, *"That was a very great event. It wasn't just something incidental, one act among others; it was a splendid conclusion of our past history, a bridge from yesterday to tomorrow and the day after tomorrow."*

And that wouldn't be the only visit of its kind in Schoenstatt. In October 1966, a further delegation of bishops from all continents arrived, and yet another one in 1967. They all wanted to meet the founder and get to know Schoenstatt. He not only gave a talk in Latin but was also happy to answer any questions. They got to know the different institutes. The founder and his Work were met with open admiration. How times could change! What he had promised the Holy Father at the audience of December 22, 1965—to help the Church fulfill her postconciliar mission—was beginning to take shape. Above all, the new spirit that Schoenstatt had long since internalized, and which had manifested itself in the Council, came to the fore. Father Kentenich pointed to these connections time and again: Schoenstatt and the postconciliar Church. The Church had acquired a new self-concept, moving from the image of a rather static, immovable rock of Peter to the image of a "pilgrim Church," a "pilgrim people of God." This made it possible for the Church to develop a new dynamic. Instead of maintaining a concept that basically turned away from the world, the Church had embraced a new openness to the world. It was a Church that increasingly moved out of narrow, purely hierarchical structures and into a more fraternal community. This new self-concept also allowed the Church to be open to a new understanding of obedience—a "*family-like, co-responsible obedience*" that required "*mature and well-formed Christian personalities.*" In his many talks, it was Father Kentenich's great joy to highlight this changed self-concept, promoted through the Council, of a Church that saw itself more as the "family of God." Now Schoenstatt could hope to be far better understood than before. He could still recall the words of Cardinal Bea in Rome very well: "Without the Council, you would never have been understood!"

Sunday, September 15, 1968, Feast of the Seven Sorrows of Mary. Just like every morning, he got up earlier in the *Schulungsheim,* long before the alarm clock sounded, even though it had been a late night as was so often the case. He took a shower, put on his best habit and shoes, opened the window wide, and took a deep breath in and out. The car that was supposed to take him to the church was already waiting at the entrance. It would be his first holy Mass in the newly built church. It had just been consecrated in June, on Trinity Sunday; it was dedicated to the Most Holy Trinity. The three mighty towers were meant to be a reminder. The peal of bells also rang in harmony—the deep God-the-Father bell, the somewhat higher-pitched Christ bell, and the clear, high Holy Spirit bell. The small and even higher-pitched Marian bell joined in. Every morning and evening, when the Angelus was rung, the mighty Father bell began first, and the Marian bell "responded" almost tenderly to its powerful "call." But it wasn't only the peal of bells that resounded far beyond Mount Schoenstatt into the valley; the church, an *"Adoration Church,"* rose up like a mighty fortress made out of quarry stones, calling to mind the many medieval fortresses in the Rhine River valley that had been places of refuge in danger for the people of the area. This church was meant to be a modern place of refuge for the people of the *"newest time."* Through the windshield he contemplated the edifice with gratitude and pride. It had been a promise to the Triune God during the war time for having protected Schoenstatt in answer to their prayers. He hadn't been able to take part in the consecration celebration due to health reasons. But now he was feeling better. He had still spoken on the phone with Bishop Tenhumberg the evening before. It had been quite lively at the eighty-second German Catholic Day in Essen. Many critical voices had spoken out. Around 2,000 Schoenstatters had taken part in various events, and a few had constructively cooperated. Several had written to him, called him, told him about it. After the Council, many people in Germany publicly vented their criticism of the Church. Just a few days earlier, he had composed a greeting to the Schoenstatt Family gathered there under the heading, *"With hope and joy, confident in the victory, we go with Mary into the post-modern age."* This wasn't meant to be a declaration of war but a sign of his personal confidence. The Church was steering toward a new shore but just hadn't quite gotten there yet.

A mild September morning was perceptible. "How many sisters does the West Province have?" he asked.

The sister at the wheel answered, "About 500, and most of them are coming, but so are the sisters living here on the mountain."

So about 600 sisters would be gathered for his first holy Mass in the new church. Two additional priests were coming to the holy Mass to assist him: Father Joseph Weigand and a newly ordained priest, Drago Maric, a Yugoslavian Carmelite who was a guest in the Mission House. They would be able to help distribute Communion.

Sister Virginia Perne walked at his side, accompanying him up the steps, and pointed out the fountain with its seven water basins as a symbol for the seven sacraments. Father Kentenich stood there briefly and looked into the bubbling water. He entered the church through the side door and climbed the three steps into the sacristy, off the side of the sanctuary. Sister Anneluzia Heuberger had already arranged everything. She was nervous because she was still learning her new task, and she was happy when he gave her his hand and whispered something personal to her. One of the priests assisted him in vesting, and then they walked, actually earlier than planned, to the altar. When he had asked Sister Anneluzia for a clock, she had opened the closet and said, "Here's one!" Even though it wasn't time yet, he had said cheerfully, *"Then we can get started!"*

Father Kentenich celebrated in Latin, and this time still with his back to the people, as he was accustomed. He held the host up for an unusually long time at the consecration, even though that was normally quite difficult for him. "Now he's offering his church to the Triune God!" thought the sacristan. She was touched as he laboriously tried to genuflect, at first somewhat unsteadily, but then all the way down to the floor.

Many sisters still went to receive Communion from him. So he distributed Holy Communion for a correspondingly long period of time, even though he did so at a good pace. "Corpus Christi."

"Amen!"

The provincial superior of the West Province was celebrating her nameday today. They were happy they had succeeded in attending the founder's first holy Mass in the newly built church on this family feast day. When the Mass was over, the priests made their way back to the sacristy. Father Kentenich removed his vestments, and after a silent thanksgiving, began a short conversation with the newly ordained priest, asking him where he was from and letting him share a little. When Sister Anneluzia discreetly slipped him a bag of rosaries, he blessed them with devotion. He loved to bless. Afterwards he invited the two priests to lunch. They were visibly happy. But suddenly they were startled. Sister Anneluzia immediately turned around because she had heard a deep sigh, and she saw that Father Kentenich was bent forward, supporting himself with both hands on the vestment table. With great presence of mind, the priests quickly reached under his arms, left and right, and looked for a chair where they could seat him, but his body became too heavy. He collapsed, so they had to lay him down on the floor.

"Do you have a cushion?"

"A cushion! Where can I get a cushion?"

The sacristan quickly hurried to one of the adjoining confessionals and took one from there. On the way there she saw the sisters going down to the auditorium beneath the church because Father Kentenich was supposed to give them a talk there right away. Pale as a ghost, she called out to a sister, "Quickly, get Sister Emanuele!" She was the new general superior, a German who had worked for many years as a missionary in Brazil and who had been elected by the general chapter one year earlier. Then she gently placed the cushion under Father Kentenich's head. Father Weigand gave him general absolution. Sister Emanuele hurried into the sacristy. When she had grasped the situation, she immediately called the family doctor, Dr. Steinkamp. The doctor lived in Vallendar and was able to come right away. Father Weigand felt for a pulse and asked for the holy oil for the anointing of the sick. Father Kentenich suddenly reached for his heart with his left hand, took two deep breaths, and then—silence. Perfect peace covered his face.

When the doctor arrived and examined him, he could only ascertain, "His heart has stopped."

"A massive heart attack!" Now the sacristy space became filled with people praying. Father Menningen stood there stunned and finally knelt down next to the dead founder.

The burial was to take place five days later. During the days prior to it, Father Kentenich's open casket was surrounded day and night by innumerable spiritual sons and daughters of his. They didn't leave him alone for a single minute. They came from all over to bid farewell—praying, singing, keeping silence. It was as if the peace that covered his face passed over to them ...

Permission had been granted for him to be buried in the Adoration Church of the Most Holy Trinity, where he had celebrated his last holy Mass and taken his last breaths on this earth.

His final journey in his casket led to the Original Shrine, where he had begun his Work, and from there up the mountain to the Trinity Church. An endlessly long procession of people walked this journey with him. He found his last resting place in the former sacristy, in a simple basalt sarcophagus above ground. The stone bears the inscription he had once wished for on his gravestone during his exile: DILEXIT ECCLESIAM. He loved the Church. He had lived and suffered for this Church. On the front side of the stone is his name: PATER JOSEF KENTENICH. And the dates of his life: * 16.11.1885 † 15.9.1968.

A number of those who instinctively knelt down next to the sarcophagus wondered, “At the end of such a life, should one now pray for his ‘eternal rest’?” Would he simply rest now? Wasn’t he urging them once more to keep going?

“Go! Set the world on fire!... And don’t forget: Those who really abandon themselves to God have built their cities on the edge of Vesuvius.”

Photo 27: During the 1967 Christmas Convention

Appendix

Timeline

Nov 16, 1885	Born in Gymnich near Cologne
Nov 19, 1885	Baptism at St. Kunibert's parish church in Gymnich
1891-1892	Stay in Strasbourg
Apr 12, 1894	Admission into the Oberhausen orphanage and consecration to Mary
Sep 23, 1899	Admission into the private high school of the Pallottines at Ehrenbreitstein
Sep 24, 1904	Beginning of novitiate in Limburg
1905	Beginning of studies in theology and philosophy with the Pallottines in Limburg
Jul 8, 1910	Priestly ordination in Limburg by Missionary Bishop Vieter (SAC) from Cameroon
Oct 27, 1912	Assumption of office as spiritual director at the boarding school (House of Studies) in Schoenstatt
Apr 19, 1914	Founding of the Marian Sodality at the boarding school in Schoenstatt
Oct 18, 1914	Founding of Schoenstatt: Talk ("Founding Document") in the former St. Michael's chapel, today "Original Shrine," in Vallendar near Koblenz
Aug 20, 1919	Founding of the "Apostolic Federation"
Aug 20, 1920	Founding of the "Apostolic League"
Oct 1, 1926	Founding of the Institute of the Schoenstatt Sisters of Mary

Sep 20, 1941	Imprisonment by the Gestapo, four-week solitary confinement and prison in Koblenz
Mar 11, 1942	Transport to Dachau, arrival at the concentration camp on March 13, 1942
Jul 16, 1942	Founding of the Institute of the Schoenstatt Brothers of Mary and the Family Work in Dachau
Apr 6, 1945	Release from the concentration camp of Dachau
May 20, 1945	Return to Schoenstatt
Oct 18, 1945	Constitution of the Institute of Diocesan Priests
Feb 2, 1946	Constitution of the Institute of the Ladies of Schoenstatt
Mar 14, 1947	Private audience with Pope Pius XII
1947-1950	Longer travels to South Africa, Argentina, Brazil, Chile, USA
Feb 19, 1949	Beginning of the episcopal visitation of Schoenstatt
Mar 23, 1951	Beginning of the papal visitation of Schoenstatt
Oct 22, 1951	Banishment from Schoenstatt
Jun 21, 1952	Arrival at the place of his exile: Milwaukee, Wisconsin, USA
Jul 18, 1965	Constitution of the Institute of the Schoenstatt Fathers by Bishop Adolf Bolte, Fulda
Sep 17, 1965	Arrival in Rome
Oct 22, 1965	Rehabilitation by the Church
Dec 22, 1965	Special audience with Pope Paul VI
Dec 24, 1965	Return home to Schoenstatt
Sep 15, 1968	Death in the Trinity Church on Mount Schoenstatt
Sep 20, 1968	Burial in the former sacristy of the Trinity Church
Feb 10, 1975	Opening of the process of beatification by Bishop Bernhard Stein, Trier

Biographical Literature about Father Joseph Kentenich

Monnerjahn, Engelbert: *Joseph Kentenich: A Life for the Church.* Capetown: Schoenstatt Publications, 1985.

Neuenhofer, Josef M. (Ed.): *Only and Always Father.* Vallendar, Germany: Schoenstatt Verlag, 2014.

Niehaus, Jonathan (Ed.): *A Movement in Chains: Sketches of Schoenstatt and Father Kentenich in Dachau.* Waukesha: Schoenstatt Fathers, 1984.

Niehaus, Jonathan: *Brushstrokes of a Father, Volume 1: The Storms of Youth.* Waukesha: Schoenstatt Fathers, 2009.

Niehaus, Jonathan: *Brushstrokes of a Father, Volume 2: Marian Trailblazer.* Waukesha: Schoenstatt Fathers, 2010.

Niehaus, Jonathan: *Brushstrokes of a Father, Volume 3: Tested by Fire.* Vallendar, Germany: Schoenstatt Fathers, 2011.

Niehaus, Jonathan: *Brushstrokes of a Father, Volume 4: Prophet in Tumultuous Times.* Vallendar, Germany: Schoenstatt Fathers, 2013.

Niehaus, J., Niehaus, M., & Niehaus, D.: *Brushstrokes of a Father, Volume 5: Accompanied by a Father.* Waukesha: Schoenstatt Fathers, 2020.

Niehaus, Jonathan: *New Vision and Life: The Founding of Schoenstatt.* Waukesha: Schoenstatt Fathers, 2004.

Niehaus, Jonathan: *Visit to America: Father Kentenich's Travels in the United States.* Waukesha: Schoenstatt Fathers, 1999.

Savage, Barbara: *Mary's Prophet.* Cape Town: Schoenstatt Publications, Creda Press, 1993.

Schlickmann, Dorothea M.: *Autumn Storms 1912: A Revolution Within Begins, Sketches of the Pedagogy of Father Joseph Kentenich.* Waukesha: Schoenstatt Editions USA, 2013.

Schlickmann, Dorothea M.: *The Hidden Years: Father Joseph Kentenich, Childhood and Youth (1885-1910).* Waukesha: Schoenstatt Editions USA, 2009.

Uriburu, Esteban: *A Father to Many: The Life and Work of Father Kentenich.* Cape Town: Schoenstatt Sisters of Mary, 1983.

About the Author

Sister M. Doria (Dorothea) Schlickmann was born in 1956 in Neuss, Germany. In 1978, she entered the Secular Institute of the Schoenstatt Sisters of Mary. She studied German, history, and educational sciences and received her doctorate from the College of Philosophy at the University of Muenster with a dissertation on Father Joseph Kentenich's pedagogy (*Die Idee von der wahren Freiheit* [*The Idea of True Freedom*]). Today she works in the field of historical and biographical research and as an author and educational consultant within the Schoenstatt Movement as well as in broader societal and ecclesial spheres.

Additional publications of the author:

Dorothea M. Schlickmann, *The Hidden Years. Father Joseph Kentenich: Childhood and Youth (1885-1910)*, Waukesha 2009; *Autumn Storms 1912: A Revolution Within Begins, Sketches of the Pedagogy of Father Joseph Kentenich*, Waukesha 2013; *Entscheidende Jahre. Pater Josef Kentenich von der Priesterweihe bis zur Gründung Schönstatts*, Vallendar 2014.

Photo Credits

Cover: © Jaeger (ASBM = Archives, Schoenstatt Brothers of Mary)
Title page photo: © Hostrup-Zender, Stuttgart.

Photo 1 p. 13: age two-and-a-half, © ASSM.[1]
Photo 2 p. 27: first Communion, 1897, © ASSM.
Photo 3 p. 35: student at Ehrenbreitstein, 1902-03, © ASSM.
Photo 4 p. 39: entrance into novitiate and studies, 1904, © De Vos, Oberhausen.
Photo 5 p. 58: priestly ordination with Bishop Vieter, July 8, 1910, © ASSM.
Photo 6 p. 64: newly ordained priest, 1910, © Tonger, Cologne.
Photo 7 p. 68: students at the House of Studies 1912, © ASSM.
Photo 8 p. 88: founding of the Marian sodality, April 19, 1914, © ASSM.
Photo 9 p. 122: Father Joseph Kentenich, 1933, © ASSM.
Photo 10 p. 179: internment in Dachau concentration camp, March 13, 1942, © ASSM.
Photo 11 p. 216: with former prisoners after release, 1945, © ASSM.
Photo 12 p. 218: planned return home with carriage, 1945, © ASSM.
Photo 13 p. 229: at the airport in Chile, 1947, © ASSM.
Photo 14 p. 268: in Madison at the beginning of exile, © Tormey, USA.
Photo 15 p. 284: during exile, 1954, © Minten, USA.
Photo 16 p. 289: at Lake Michigan, USA, early 1960s, © Neuenhofer.
Photo 17 p. 293: at a celebration with families, 1963/64, © Neuenhofer.
Photo 18 p. 296: in the shrine during exile, © Neuenhofer.
Photo 19 p. 298: with a family, early 1960s, © Neuenhofer.
Photo 20 p. 300: in his office in Milwaukee, © Neuenhofer.
Photo 21 p. 303: conversing with Guenther Boll, © Neuenhofer.
Photo 22 p. 307: sermon at St. Michael's Church, © Neuenhofer.
Photo 23 p. 319: audience with Pope Paul VI, © Felici, Rome.
Photo 24 p. 321: return home to the Original Shrine on December 24, 1965, © Blank, ASBM.
Photo 25 p. 323: Marian School auditorium, December 24, 1965, © Neuenhofer.
Photo 26 p. 325: Dachau Memorial Site, 1967, © Jaeger, ASBM.
Photo 27 p. 332: Christmas Convention, 1967, © Jaeger, ASBM.

---

[1] "ASSM" refers mainly to original photos or reproductions found in the archives of the Schoenstatt Sisters of Mary. In many cases it is no longer possible to determine—after more than 100 years—when the photos were taken and by whom, or who owns the copyright.